Silver Screen Buddha

ALSO AVAILABLE FROM BLOOMSBURY

The Bloomsbury Companion to Religion and Film, William L. Blizek
Buddhism and Iconoclasm in East Asia, Fabio Rambelli and Eric Reindeers
The Sacred and the Cinema, Sheila J. Nayar

Silver Screen Buddha

Buddhism in Asian and Western Film

SHARON A. SUH

Bloomsbury Academic
An imprint of Bloomsbury Publishing Plc

B L O O M S B U R Y
LONDON • NEW DELHI • NEW YORK • SYDNEY

Bloomsbury Academic

An imprint of Bloomsbury Publishing Plc

50 Bedford Square	1385 Broadway
London	New York
WC1B 3DP	NY 10018
UK	USA

www.bloomsbury.com

BLOOMSBURY and the Diana logo are trademarks of Bloomsbury Publishing Plc

First published 2015

© Sharon A. Suh, 2015

Sharon A. Suh has asserted her rights under the Copyright, Designs and Patents Act, 1988, to be identified as the Author of this work.

British Library Cataloguing-in-Publication Data

A catalogue record for this book is available from the British Library.

ISBN: HB: 978-1-4411-8925-7
PB: 978-1-4411-0536-3
ePDF: 978-1-4742-1783-5
ePub: 978-1-4742-1784-2

Library of Congress Cataloging-in-Publication Data

Suh, Sharon A. Silver screen Buddha : Buddhism in Asian and western film / Sharon A. Suh. pages cm Includes bibliographical references and index. ISBN 978-1-4411-8925-7 (hardcover) -- ISBN 978-1-4411-0536-3 (pbk.) 1. Buddhism in motion pictures. 2. Motion pictures-- Religious aspects--Buddhism. I. Title. PN1995.9.B795S85 2015 791.43'682943–dc23
2014033260

Typeset by Fakenham Prepress Solutions, Fakenham, Norfolk NR21 8NN
Printed and bound in Great Britain

Contents

Acknowledgments

While writing this book has largely been a solitary activity taking place in my study at home with the requisite cup of coffee, it has certainly not been undertaken in isolation. Instead, the research and writing of this book has emerged in the context of multiple overlapping communities of fellow scholars, friends, Buddhist practitioners, and family members that have sustained and nourished me along the way. Perhaps one of the most enjoyable and humbling aspects of writing a book is the opportunity to pause at the end to reflect and express deep gratitude to all who have helped this work come to fruition. It is therefore fitting that such thanks come at the book's beginning. Much like the famous Jeweled Net of Indra from the *Flower Ornament Sutra*, my work is informed and improved by the countless other beings whose brilliance and intellect is reflected in and shines through this work. From cups of coffee and snippets of conversation during meetings, to meals and direct consultation via phone, email, text, and social media, I have benefitted immensely and immeasurably from a whole host of guides gently helping and, at times, pushing me to make this book more coherent, articulate, and meaningful.

I wish to express my continuing admiration and gratitude to Susanne Mrozik, whose *bodhisattva* wisdom, generosity, keen intellect, and selflessness has nourished me since my days as a master's student at Harvard Divinity School, through my PhD program in Buddhist Studies, my first book, and now this second book. I have always admired her ability to concurrently inhabit the spaces of deep and incisive intellect, authenticity, compassion, and humbleness. She is a wonderful model of brains and heart. I would also like to thank the wonderful crew of APARRI (Asian Pacific American Religions Research Initiative) scholars whose comments on my work have proven invaluable—especially Jane Iwamura and Joseph Cheah, whose own works you will find referenced in this book. Special thanks also goes to the following Buddhist scholars and practitioners par excellence—Mark Unno, who invited me to deliver a paper at the 2013 American Academy of Religion to test out my ideas to the Buddhist Studies community; Douglas Osto, who has shared with me his tremendous work on women in the *Gandavyuha*; and to Jason Wirth, my colleague at Seattle University who invited me to deliver earlier chapters to the Eco-Sangha, and who has been a wonderful support in the *dharma* at Seattle University. I have had the great fortune of working at Seattle University since 2000 and am grateful that the institution continues to offer generous support for my research—I have benefitted greatly from two Provost's Summer Faculty Research Fellowships and sabbatical leaves that allowed me the necessary and much desired time and resources to begin and complete this project. I am also so fortunate to work in a department of talented, encouraging, and truly enjoyable colleagues.

Special thanks also goes to Janice Harper, a writing coach extraordinaire whom I had the fortuitous occasion to meet at a memoir writing workshop. After learning of her work as an anthropologist and casually mentioning *Silver Screen Buddha* to her, she generously offered her time and expertise to help me contain my panic and redirect it towards the completion of this book. Janice prove invaluable for helping me embrace a more clear and simple way of writing and to let go of *some* of my beloved yet tedious academic phrases. I say *some* because you will perhaps find a few instances where I simply could not let go so let me apologize in advance to Janice by simply saying that you can lead a horse to water, but you cannot make her drink.

I would also like to express my gratitude to my editor at Bloomsbury, the wonderful Lalle Pursglove, whose ready interest, support, and patience have been invaluable to the publication of this book. I appreciate, in particular, her flexibility and encouragement in allowing me to embrace a more constructive and creative approach as the project unfolded. I would also like to thank Anna MacDiarmid for all of her assistance and Kim Storry, the publications manager for this book.

I offer my most heartfelt thanks to my dear friend David Kyuman Kim, an unsurpassed *kalyāṇamitra* or good spiritual friend/advisor and interlocutor beyond measure. His unwavering support and enthusiasm for this project led to many hours of reading and commenting on the manuscript over the past few years. His compassion, generosity, and sharp mind also helped me write my better self into being. I am so grateful for his encouragement, brilliance, humor, and kindness. He encouraged and inspired me to write the book I *really* wanted to write and not merely the one that I thought I *should* write. May we all be so lucky to always have such *kalyāṇamitras* in our lives.

Special thanks to Alex who has supported me for many years of my scholarly life and helped me find the time and resources to do the important work that I needed and wanted to complete. My daughters Emily and Olivia are the joys of my life and continue to remind me every day of the depths, rigors, and responsibilities of love and the importance of deep presence. What a gift it is to be your mother. And what a gift it is to be the daughter of my incredible father Dong S. Suh. I bet that if I let him edit this book as he once offered, he would have helped me create a much more compelling book! His unwavering support and love has carried me through the rough and tumble of everyday life and he has shown me again and again what it takes to nourish, provide for, and guide one's own child so that she may flourish with resilience. I hope that I may one day be able to offer even just a small measure of such love, courage, and support for my own daughters. And one day, Dad, I will get around to writing that popular textbook on Buddhism!

List of Illustrations

This book is dedicated to my lovely daughters Emily and Olivia,
and to my father, a wonder of a man.

1

Introduction: Buddhism and Film

Focus the mind on the following scene: In Bae Young-Kyun's Korean Buddhist film *Why Has Bodhidharma Left for the East?* (1989), an elderly Zen monk sits in meditative stillness in his mountain hermitage far from the bustle of the city below. So powerfully has he trained his mind that he remains erect in the lotus position even as life slips quietly from his body. Once his consciousness has left his form, the Zen master's body slowly falls to the ground and he is immediately cremated by his disciple who spreads the master's ashes to the elements of earth, air, fire, and water.

Settle your mind onto another scene of Buddhist life: In Kim Ki-Duk's *Spring, Summer, Fall, Winter... and Spring* (2003), an old Korean Buddhist master builds a funeral pyre on a small boat floating on a serene mountain lake and places his body in the lotus position atop the pyre. He places torn strips of rice paper with the Chinese characters for "shut" over his eyes, nose, and mouth; he sets the pyre ablaze, and meditates in silence as the flames consume his body. Uttering not a sound, the master's body is soon engulfed in fire as his consciousness slips from his body and passes into that of a water snake that slithers through the water back into his floating temple.

Visualize the following: In Pan Nalin's *Samsara* (2001), a young monk remains in a meditative trance in a mountain hermitage in Ladakh in complete isolation. For three years, three months, three weeks, and three days, the Buddhist monk controls his body and mind to transcend the needs of food, water, and human contact. He has attained one of the highest states of spiritual realization in the Tibetan Buddhist tradition. Upon his return to the monastery, he receives the greatest of reverence and praise from his fellow disciples and is awarded the title *khenpo*, which attests to his high spiritual attainments.

And finally bring your mind here: In Marc Rosenbush's independent film *Zen Noir* (2004), a Japanese Zen master and his detective-turned-disciple sit

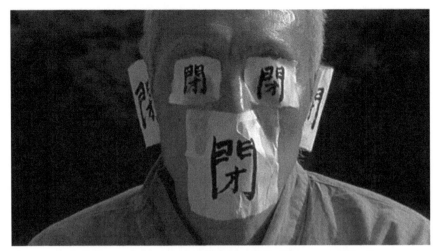

Figure 1.1 *Elderly monk from* Spring, Summer, Fall, Winter... and Spring

side by side in *zazen* meditation for hours, their bodies perfectly still as the dramatic score creates a palpable suspense that contrasts with the hush of the *zendo*. The Zen master meditates with his eyes half shut and without any prior notice, the monk's body suddenly teeters over in silence, falling dead onto the meditation mat. Following his death, his white disciple takes up the mantle of temple master.

We have here in these four scenes reflections of widely held beliefs that meditation is the central, if not the most important, ritual in Buddhist practice. They also focus on monks as the primary actors in the Buddhist world and their near magical ability to comport themselves peacefully even unto death. And yet, what sorts of visions of Buddhism are on offer through film? What forms of Buddhism are obscured? Are they forms of Buddhism that actual Buddhists would recognize as their own tradition? If not, how might we recuperate forms of Buddhism that are truer to lived practices from the oversaturated images of masterful meditating monks found in the widely influential medium of film? Are there other images of Buddhists to be found that have yet to capture the popular imagination? How are we to account for the plurality of Buddhism when what we mostly get in the movies is limited to monks in meditation? This book offers an answer to these questions.

There are several potentially troubling elements to the portrayals of Buddhism we get through film that warrant significant critical attention.

What and who. Meditation happens in Buddhist practice but it certainly is not as common among Buddhists as popular culture might lead us to believe. And monks are not the only Buddhists in the world. In fact, most Buddhists are lay Buddhists who practice little to no meditation at all.[1] By lay Buddhism, I mean nonmonastic Buddhists who may practice devotional worship and may or may not go to temple, yet still consider themselves Buddhists by way of birth, upbringing, or world view. In addition, I utilize the term lay Buddhism to refer more generally to the intersecting categories of nonmonastic women, a normalized spiritually-enabling sexuality, everyday practices, and nonmonastic Asian and Asian American Buddhists that have been rendered either excessively devotional or marginal to a more "proper" Buddhism. While the cinematic expression of Buddhism provides an alternative world view and set of values that are easily accessible in movie theaters, on laptops, and in our living rooms, we have not adequately explored the effects of what bell hooks refers to as our "looking relations"—that is, how we look, who looks, who is looked at, and who looks back.[2] As a result, the seemingly straightforward representation of Buddhism in film as mimetic of an authentic Buddhism easily belies the all too real entanglements of social identities, racism, and gender hierarchies. One of the central arguments of this book is that the reduction of Buddhist practice to meditation in Buddhist film alone obscures and limits the projections and receptions of Buddhism and our ability to see lay Buddhists in general and lay women in particular in mediated forms. This limited scope, I argue, informs what we deem "real" Buddhism and what we do not. Nonetheless, not all filmic representations of Buddhism are so limited in their range and scope of vision; instead, there are many films that offer the potential for a more expansive vision of Buddhism that highlights the plurality of the tradition. I provide an analysis of a number of Buddhist films from the popular to the art house that contain progressive *and* harmful images of gender, sex, and race to provide a more balanced view of the religion beyond the ubiquitous meditating monk.

The meditating monk, the all too common subject of many of these films, has chosen the ascetic life and the pursuit of enlightenment in the temple and devotes several hours a day to meditation. However, this practice is but one of a variety of different ways to practice Buddhism, yet it is the one that receives the most attention on screen. But why is this the case? And why is it a problem? In what follows I offer an explanation for the hypervisibility of the monk on screen, an answer rooted in the complex relationship between religion, race, and gender that I will tease out throughout this book. The film viewer's seemingly untrained eye might hone in on the ascetic monk as the most significant symbol of the ideal Buddhist life and in so doing may overlook the vibrant religious lives of the laity in general and lay Buddhist women in particular. Yet as I will be arguing, this untrained eye is blind to the complexity of Buddhist life that extends far beyond the monastic hero. Surely, one of the horizons that the untrained eye does not see is the vitality of lay Buddhist women to the tradition and one of the main factors that obscures their presence is the complex work of race and gender in the experience of Buddhism.

What and how. These filmic depictions exoticize Buddhists as fundamentally different from other humans in their sensibilities, desires, capacities, and spiritual states. This exoticizing of "the other" valorizes the ascetic monk over the laity in Buddhist films produced both in Asia and the West and yet, as I will argue, the transmission of this male monastic paragon from Asia is not a matter of simple translation into Western films and popular audiences. Instead, the reception of the image of meditating monks as the defining characteristic of Buddhism is one mired in a tangled web of racialized difference that simultaneously exoticizes and denigrates Asian and Buddhist difference. That is to say, sometimes the two are conflated where Asian Buddhism and Asian Buddhists are presented as a tantalizing but ultimately unwanted other. At other times, Asian and Buddhists are clearly distinguished in a racial hierarchy where the Asian practitioner is associated with a kind of backwardness and superstition that reflects an inauthentic version of a Buddhism best occupied by white Buddhists. Such racial stereotypes also present Asians and Asian Americans as passive yet potentially violent, subservient yet devious, and deeply contemplative yet child-like in their understanding of the world. If these racial types were true to form, why then are there still so many mysterious and mystical monks in Buddhist films? Mystery in practice and a defining separation between the master and the ordinary are the presiding images one *might* get from these Buddhist films. I say *might* because, as I will argue, Buddhist films show the range and power of lay Buddhisms if we have the eyes to see it. When we turn to Buddhist films, this is largely the image we tend to get if we constrain our understanding of Buddhism to the domain of masters alone.

Who and how again. Race pervades these films. So does gender. And yet if we focus in Buddhist films solely on our masters and the ascetic life, who and what are left out? The "true" Buddhists in many of the films I analyze are predominantly Asian and male.[3] When women are presented in these films, one might conclude that their only role is to support men seeking salvation, or as symbols of sensuality and corruption, their enticing bodies and mysterious ways tempting men from their own spiritual objectives. To associate Buddhism primarily with exotic Asian ascetic monks is to perpetuate a narrow band image of Buddhism that I am arguing we need to break from. Buddhism is a world religion. And its leaders are nuns as well as ordinary people. To think otherwise, which is to say, to be led to think otherwise, is a disservice to the plurality of the traditions we call Buddhist. Let us consider how we might break from such bad habits.

We don't need to abandon Buddhist films to undertake this endeavor. Indeed, the primary aim of this book is to provide a critical practice for analyzing Buddhist films such that these bad habits don't prevail but give way to an expansive vision of Buddhism that rings true to authentic Buddhist life, and by authentic I certainly do not mean that there is some essential core to Buddhism that I seek to retrieve in this study. Instead, authenticity is more about matters of representation and reception of the varieties of actors that make up the Buddhist world and not just the stock character of the monk.

A guiding concern of this book relates to the disconnect between what is projected in film as real Buddhism and what I see in real life when I visit Buddhist temples in Asia or America. In these settings, I see women chanting, prostrating, and burning incense while they socialize and the kids run about. This is not to say that women are more interested in socializing while the men are hard at work mastering their salvation. But just as they do in many churches, women remain the primary actors in daily and weekly devotion in Buddhist temples.

Nor am I saying that the roles of men or monks are neither salient nor worthy of having their stories told. The point I wish to emphasize is that the monastic, meditative tradition that has been the ubiquitous focal point of the reception of Buddhism is but one thread in this rich tapestry of worship. Yet it is this thread that such interpretations, especially in Buddhist films, endlessly weave to the exclusion of all others. And it is this thread that I set out to untangle.

In confronting these competing images of Buddhism—the meditative male Buddhism that is represented in film—and the diversity of Buddhisms that are reflected in Asian and Asian American Buddhist temples—one must ask: are those Buddhists who do not meditate or engage in the monastic tradition any less Buddhist for not doing so? And what happens when the majority of Buddhists who make up the tradition are absented from popularized images of Buddhism or at least when the dominant narrative of how we ought to view Buddhist films indicates that only masters and exotic monks are the true Buddhists? Do they view themselves as less authentic Buddhists? These questions raise another significant issue: if women are as conspicuously absent from Buddhist films as are lay Buddhists, what is the reason? Why are there so few positive images of nonmonastic Buddhist women from Asia and Asian America on screen? And finally, are there any other ways to be Buddhist? Such questions reveal the vexing intersections between religion, race, and gender that lie beneath the surface of the popular image of the meditating monk that serves to discipline and constrict our vision. In *Silver Screen Buddha*, I explore these questions to demonstrate that the Buddhism that is presented in film is in many ways a Buddhism of the imaged and imagined elite (male monastic and/or white), and as such, subordinates the Buddhism of the laity as less important. In so doing, I engage in a critical practice that analyzes both the constructed images of Buddhism reflected in film through the work of the filmmaker as well as the reception and consumption of Buddhism on the part of the viewer.

Which brings us back to the question I previously raised: is there another way to imagine Buddhism? In other words, is there another way to see

Buddhism? In taking up the subject of Buddhism and film, I seek to inter-rogate received images of Buddhism, gender, and race to illuminate the complexity and vitality of the religious tradition. Thus, in *Silver Screen Buddha*, I address the following constructive concerns: How can Buddhism be constructed, refashioned, and adapted through the medium of film? How are these images implicated in the mediated constructions of race and gender? What are the kinds of Buddhism that have predominated in filmic texts and why? How can film be deployed to reimagine and re-image the prevalent construction of Buddhism's historically-marginalized others (such as, women, lay Buddhists, Asians, and Asian Americans)? And finally, how can such a diversity of Buddhist images transform popular constructions of the religion as forever foreign and exotic into something more salient to those who actually practice it?

These concerns are directly related to the fraught history of Orientalism and the construction of the "East" as weak, effeminate, and backward, thus justifying the colonial presence and superiority of the "West," that marked Asians and their Buddhism as somehow less than.[4] The Buddhism popularized in the West in the late nineteenth century was mediated through an Orientalist lens that deemed the Buddhism of Asians as a backward, super-stitious, overly ritualized tradition and therefore not worthy of emulation. The cultural logic of white supremacy driving Orientalism that determined that the truest and most pure form of Buddhism was in fact the meditative tradition was later popularized in the West through academic scholarship and media that continues to wield its influences today.[5] While this study approaches film as a potentially generative Buddhist text that can reshape and re-vision dominant discourses by and about the tradition, we need to learn to look beyond the half-truths of the exotic Buddhist monk as *the* icon of Buddhism. In exploring these issues, I do not mean to suggest that most Buddhist films about monastic life are not suitable subjects of a gender and race analysis. To the contrary, in what follows, I offer nuanced ways to reimagine what Buddhism might look like on screen and in the world when the constricting veneer of the meditating monk is removed or at least takes its place as one of many competing images of Buddhist life, while a close look at the underlying subtexts of these films illuminates the hidden transcripts of race and gender that demand critical attention before film can be used to rethink the religion.[6]

Visualizing Buddhism on screen

In Buddhist tradition, the concept of the gaze is a powerful metaphor for spiritual development. What is perceived is dependent on who is doing the perceiving. This relationship between perception and spiritual maturation is inextricably linked in Buddhist visual culture. The production of the many splendid bodies of Buddhas through art and meditative recollection (*Buddha anusmriti*) highlights the power of religious modes of seeing in the Buddhist imagination and their function in the transmission and reception of the *Buddha dharma*.[7] The visionary quest for the Buddha began over 2,500 years ago as devotees first captured the Buddha's footprint and the eight-spoked dharma wheel in sculptural relief to commemorate his first sermon. Following these abstract images, artists began to create more anthropomorphic paintings and statues of the Buddha. He was depicted as the royally garbed Prince Siddhartha, an enlightened being in flowing robes, and as a celestial form floating in a resplendent Buddha Land. Such images were commissioned and installed in large temples and home shrines and became a central focus for rituals of remembrance and veneration to incite deeper levels of spiritual insight.

In *Silver Screen Buddha*, I am extending the scope of Buddhist visualization to more contemporary modes of seeing by focusing on film as a potent spiritual interlocutor that compels new ways of seeing and new ways of being seen.[8] Recent technological changes have fundamentally transformed the viewing experience, as viewers now select among a range of viewing media. From instantaneous downloads onto the tiny screens of smart phones to interactive websites where the viewer can manipulate the story and its characters, or to the shared public viewing experience of a 3-D action movie, audiences can now pick and choose where, when, and even what they will view. How, then, does this ever-changing viewing experience shape how Buddhism is imagined and experienced in film? To answer these questions, I utilize the classic silver screen and contemporary films to consider how alternative images of Buddhism might be gleaned from mainstream representations.[9]

In *Silver Screen Buddha*, I am examining the effects that such mediated images have on the Buddhist tradition and its practitioners, and how we might selectively use such approximations of Buddhism as a way to reimagine the religion itself. In this book, I show how mediated images of Buddhism have largely neglected the active and self-enhancing presence of women's religious lives and have perpetuated images of Asian and Asian American lay Buddhist practices as less valuable forms of the tradition. In so doing, I provide a more complex understanding of Buddhism beyond the popularized image of the meditating monk—an understanding that emerges from my examination of the overlapping categories of race and gender that shape the popularized image and suppress the diversity within the tradition. While I engage in a critique of the gendered implications and racialized images of the religion found in Buddhist films, I also endeavor to provide a more balanced understanding of Buddhism that takes into account the multiple ways of being Buddhist. As such, *Silver Screen Buddha* is an inherently constructive study that argues that films can function as visual Buddhist texts of world-making that do more than merely reflect Buddhist teachings. Like the medieval Chinese Buddhist paintings of scenes in the *Lotus Sutra* studied by Eugene Wong, the book also approaches film as the "building blocks out of which a different architecture" of the religion might be construed.[10]

This study fits squarely within a mode of critique and re-visioning of Buddhist films that have been shaped by the legacies of Orientalism and Protestant constructions of Asian Buddhism in the late nineteenth century that posited a true Buddhism to be found only in Buddhist texts and practiced unchanged by meditating Buddhist monks. Such an ideology of unadulterated truth to be found only in the written text and the inadequacy of Asian Buddhism and lay practices continues to prevail in global film industries that reinforce rather than critique Orientalist, patriarchal views, and the workings of white supremacy. Simply put, Buddhism cannot be adequately understood and appreciated without laying bare its troubled historical intersection with race, white supremacy, and patriarchy.

These constructions of Buddhism have devalued the laity and in particular, Buddhist women by continually highlighting an idealized, abstract, and stylized Buddhism based on the archetype of the male monk as the truest and most pure representative of the religion. Such a narrowly conceived focus on what accounts for true Buddhism is itself based on an uncritical absorption of the canonical valorization of monastics over laity, and men over women that gets reproduced in film. Such a limited scope projects Buddhism as a kind of abstract religion that has been neutralized with regard to the politics of race and gender. In an effort to balance such an egregious lack of full vision, I intentionally mine those films that enable an informed method of looking to find and foreground the kinds of Buddhism I commend—namely, the lay Buddhist practices of women and men in a complex world where gender and race must be accounted for in order to fully understand Buddhist life.

Why "Buddhist films?"

The cinematic encounter with Buddhism has flourished globally in Asia and in the West over the past century. From Frank Capra's 1937 *Lost Horizon* to Kim Ki-Duk's 2003 international box office success *Spring, Summer, Fall, Winter… and Spring*, and Yōjirō Takita's 2008 *Departures*, audiences have had access to modern methods of visualizing the Buddha and Buddhism. As our own experiences prove, movies offer an entrée into a fictional world made temporarily real; therefore, their significance should not be overlooked in addressing the perennial ethical dilemma of, as Margaret Miles puts it, "how human beings shall live."[11] Throughout this book, I make explicit use of the term "Buddhist films" to refer to an emerging genre that can conventionally be defined by one or more of the following criteria:

- Contemplation and inquiry about the eradication of thirst or desire;

- The virtues and limitations of monastic life;

- Inclusion of elements of a prototypical Buddhist *mise-en-scène* such as a monastery, hermitage, or lay community;

- Exploration and application of Buddhist doctrines and philosophical concerns;

- Offer Buddhist interpretations of reality or a uniquely Buddhist solution to a social problem.

Whether by questioning the ultimate state of reality as ontologically real or evaluating the merits of monastic life versus lay life, Buddhist films have the ability to transform how we see and who we see so long as we look skillfully. Andrew Greeley underscores the power of film to invoke and renew religious sensibilities and induce the ephiphanic. As he puts it:

> The pure, raw power of the film to capture the person who watches it, both by its vividness and by the tremendous power of the camera to concentrate and change perspectives is a sacramental potential that is hard for other art forms to match.[12]

The power of film to re-vision reality moves it from the realm of popular culture alone and into the realm of meaning-making and re-making that we often associate with religion. In a similar vein, Hyangsoon Yi's study of the use of realism in Buddhist films demonstrates the medium's mimetic ability to reflect complex forms of religiosity and takes for granted a genre of Buddhist film that she puts forth as a uniquely Korean phenomenon.[13] Building on these themes, I explore how film engages in mimetic activity and how it can reimagine tradition by bringing creative attention to those areas heretofore overlooked.[14]

In her essay "Imagining Nothing and Imaging Otherness in Buddhist Film," Francisca Cho notes that film and art function as a kind of religious practice that entails serious reflection upon the nature of reality.[15] Because Buddhist metaphysics holds that reality itself is empty of inherent existence, film provides a most fortuitous medium that re-presents reality and imparts new modes of religious interpretation and experience.[16] As modern day religious texts, Buddhist films therefore have the potential to allow audiences to reimagine self and other(s) through the lens of a kind of visual scripture that gestures toward a new way of living in and through the world.[17] Cho's work is thus instructive for rethinking the role and representation of Buddhism in film such that it can effect a more expansive understanding of the tradition that rings true for its various practitioners. My approach to Buddhist film also resonates with the work of director and incarnate lama Khyenste Norbu, best known for his films *The Cup* (1999) and *Travellers and Magicians* (2003). Conceptualizing film as a *tanka* (visual meditational device) most often utilized in Tibetan Buddhism, Norbu explains,

> Buddhism has the tradition of using all kinds of mediums: statues, paintings, monasteries. And although it's difficult for people to accept, I see film as a modern-day *tanka*. Film has so much power because we're conditioned primarily by what we see and hear.[18]

In his approach, Norbu uses film as *tanka* to reimagine Buddhism for a contemporary Bhutanese audience; thus, our approaches are of a kind in placing film solidly in the Buddhist world of ritual implements creating new visionary experiences and insight that retrieves and highlights other ways of being Buddhist. While many of the films referenced in this book fit the conventional criteria for a Buddhist film, I suggest another set of criteria that account for the presence of women and lay Buddhists as key players in the Buddhist social world. Such criteria rest upon the belief that most of the Buddhist films available to us are in fact limited at best precisely because they do not reflect the multiple possibilities of what Buddhism is and who Buddhists are. The criteria for a more laudable account of Buddhist films are those that attend to Buddhism's inherent diversity, which is to say, Buddhist films that:

- Address the ordinary lives of the laity;
- Affirm everyday life as a potential ground for enlightenment;
- Represent women as agents in their own spiritual lives;
- Include Asian and Asian American Buddhists in the larger picture of Buddhism as it exists today.

These criteria thus expand the characteristics of the emerging genre of Buddhist films that I outline above.

Film as *sutra*

While the exoticized monk fits solidly in the classic Orientalist logic of Edward Said, I am interested in what lies *beyond* the popular reception of the ascetic monk's image in American culture and the male virtuoso found in Buddhist films from Asia and the West. Therefore this book entails not only a rethinking of Orientalism and Asian religions, but also the possibility of asking what exists beyond Orientalism. Does something remain that it is redeemable from such mediated images? If so, what might that something be? As such, I am positing a way to think through how this otherness might effect a new kind of religious identity formation in and through film. Such a rereading is inspired by a desire for a more inclusive range of vision through a retrieval of positive archetypes of a lay Buddhism historically excluded from monastic models *and* a future oriented construction of an ordinary embodied Buddhism that is recognized as [and recognizably] raced and gendered. If the exotic monk reflects a collective desire for otherness, perhaps there is a way to tease out what might be deemed the religious impulse that is encapsulated within such fascination where *a desire for otherness constitutes a form of religious experience*. I am arguing that it does, and by doing so I am drawing attention to the possibility of approaching media, and film in particular, as a kind of spiritual technology and discipline, namely, understanding *film as sutra*.[19] The spiritual technology of reading film as *sutra* holds out the possibility that the spiritual is not hopelessly irredeemable but is rather limited by the tight hold of Orientalism's legacies. While critiques of Orientalism still have a particular purchase in Asian American religious studies, I would argue that there is something of value that remains to be discovered, theorized, and perhaps retrieved and redeemed from such images. In other words, despite their Orientalist influences, there remain opportunities to reread and retrieve a progressive standpoint from a backward one that can be utilized to reimagine the tradition.

While revealing the hierarchies of monastic, male, and white privilege that implicate Buddhist films in a larger critique of gender, race, and religion, *Silver Screen Buddha* engages in the equally important process of reimagining Buddhism through a retrieval of otherwise suppressed and obscured images of Buddhist plurality. Such a method utilizes Buddhist films as a means of re-vision. I do so in order to restore a measure of balance to an otherwise imbalanced rendering of the religion. Such a reimagining highlights the virtues of an ordinary lay Buddhism that takes for granted the messiness and material nature of everyday life. It also de-pathologizes or makes ordinary the very sexuality that has been problematized by the undue attention given to male monasticism. Finally, it acknowledges the active presence of lay women in the Buddhist tradition. In so doing, this book both critiques the under-interro-gated consequences of a Buddhist religious, gendered, and racial orthodoxy as male monastic centered, and restores a diverse vision of Buddhism which is flourishing through a heterodox reading of Buddhist religious texts and films.

Although many of the popular Buddhist films I have watched over the past 25 years continue to perpetuate the male-monastic virtuoso as normative and lay Asian and Asian American Buddhists as inarticulate and/or somehow lacking in authenticity, it was not until I watched the less globally recognized 1989 *Aje Aje Bara Aje* (*Come, Come, Come Upward*) by Im Kwon-Taek, that I began to feel hopeful about the possibility of an alternative to the disciplining of gendered and raced bodies through film. *Aje Aje Bara Aje* features a young female nun expelled from the nunnery for inciting the passions of a crazed man. The young nun defrocks, and through her intimate relationships with men becomes an earthly *bodhisattva* administering to the needs of the suffering. What strikes me as unique and exciting about this film is that the young woman became enlightened *because of* rather than *in spite of* her sexuality. What this film offers, although perhaps not the intention of Im himself, is an opportunity to reimagine a Buddhism that no longer pathologizes sexual intimacy as somehow inimical to the religious life. Instead, after viewing Im's film, I began to wonder if there might be a way to cultivate a Buddhism on screen and in popular discourse that is more fully engaged with life as raced, gendered, and sexual beings that could acknowledge the richness and multiplicity of the lived practice of Buddhism. In an effort to *imagine otherwise* as Kandice Chuh suggests, I aim to construct a Buddhism that gives space to race, sex, and gender as appropriately and forth-rightly Buddhist rather than excessive to a proper orthodoxy.[20]

Films such as Im Kwon Taek's 1989 *Aje Aje Bara Aje* and Chang Sun-Woo's 1993 *Hwa-Om-Kyung* (*Passage to Buddha*)—all produced in South Korea—proffer visions of what I refer to as an *embodied female lay Buddhism* where the female body can materialize virtue and a healthy sexuality that is productive to enlightenment. I utilize such films to read over and against the grain of metanarratives of meditation and male monas-ticism that have shaped Buddhism's global reception. Such films support a Buddhist vision of social integration where monks and nuns are encouraged to seek enlightenment in the midst of lay society by descending from their isolated mountaintop temples. These films can be referenced and deployed to create new forms of Buddhism that counterbalance the meditational practices that have been interpreted as ones that transcend the body. My reading of these films is shaped by my desire to employ what bell hooks calls "the oppositional gaze" with regard to elements of the films that may rightfully be critiqued as androcentric even while highlighting female religi-osity.[21] I make the case, however, that an oppositional gaze includes more than healthy critique; it also includes robust reconstruction and re-visioning beyond what is reflected on screen.

What would happen if we were to imagine film as a visual entry point that opens up new vistas for imagining not the other or otherness but other*wise* in the religious sense of the world? We know, as bell hooks reminds us, that film creates culture. But how does it also create the way we view religion and its actors? How in turn does this reconstructed religion relate to racial and gendered identities? I am arguing that engaging in a robust critique *and* exploring film and other forms of media as spiritual technology can allow us to work beyond the Orientalized difference that has rendered Asian religions practiced by Asians and Asian Americans impotent in relation to a perceived pure form of Buddhism of the male monastic meditator. This approach opens up a possibility to explore how identities can be reimagined and recast along religious, racial, and gendered lines.

One way I imagine otherwise is to approach Buddhist films as *sutras* or Buddhist texts that shape new ways of looking and viewing reality. Approaching film and mediated images as *sutra* advances the notion that Buddhist films are themselves texts that are not only informed by *sutras*, but that can also reimagine the world that *sutras* themselves construct and convey. Films are visual and auditory texts that enable a rethinking and re-visioning of tradition, rendering a unique opportunity to imagine what a *sutra* often points to but does not necessarily fulfill. A rethinking and re-visioning of Buddhism through film is therefore an uncovering and application of a *sutra's* potency to reimagine and re-image the religion and its expressions in order to centralize the historically marginalized actors and challenge and remake the popular face of Buddhism.

If film can re-present reality, it has profound implications and potential for re-presenting race, religion, and gender. If film as art is indeed an inherently performative project, then it can create and reconstruct "presence."[22] It is with this notion in mind that I approach films as visual texts that make and remake religious, raced, and gendered meaning in order to re-vision popularized images of Buddhism itself. The notion of film as *sutra* is of course a gloss on Mahayana Buddhism that rests rhetorically upon an open canon, in which new teachings and *sutras* have been added and justified as examples of the Buddha's expedient means. As such, films as revelatory visionary experiences seem to fit rather smoothly into the Mahayana Buddhist textual tradition where extraordinary visions of the cosmos can be found in the single pore of an enlightened being and multiple Buddha lands are practically *de rigueur*. In this regard, film can surely serve as a performative medium that can re-present reality and impart new modes of religious interpretation.

Methodologically, I read and interpret many Buddhist scriptures in a rather heterodox manner akin to the counter-readings suggested by George Aichele and Richard Walsh in their edited volume, *Those Outside: Non-Canonical Readings of the Canonical Gospels*.[23] In their counter-readings of the Gospels, Aichele and Walsh encourage the individual to read as a "counter-reader" who is a "thief, one who steals the text from its proper owner."[24] The "proper owner" refers to the institution or those on the "inside" whose interpretations have been selected as "the truth." This study takes up this suggestion and imagines what Buddhism would look like if read with Hermes, the Patron Saint of the counter-reader, as guide. In this way it engages in the world of institutional readings and counter-readings to re-vision Buddhism and expand its institutionalized boundaries of what constitutes truth, center, and the margins. Taking the wing-footed god as guide signifies a move between the received institutionalized truth or "latent" meaning, and those outside the fray (counter, outside or "manifest" truths). It also challenges the institutionalized view that can only happen by crossing beyond the boundaries of the acceptable and the accepted. My reading of Mahayana Buddhist texts such as the *Avatamsaka Sutra* and the *Heart Sutra* that figure prominently in Buddhist films, both informs my reading of films and is re-formed by my reading of films. Those "inside" the "institutional guild" or orthodox view of the texts' interpretation constitute the imagined and actual *Sangha* of male monastics who are bound by the "parameters of accepted reading for those who wish to maintain acceptable status in the guild."[25] To engage in counter-readings and interpretive thievery does not occur outside of commonly held scripture but rather reinvigorates meaning and pushes the boundaries of what is considered an "acceptable" and latent interpretation.

Exclusionary looking relations: A gendered and raced Buddhist orthodoxy

The impetus for this study of Buddhism in film emerges from the tension I have continued to experience between my attraction to the captivating beauty of Buddhist landscapes and their inhabitants struggling for enlightenment and my inevitable disappointment when I encounter yet another stereotyped image of Buddhism. That is to say that I have encountered one too many baldheaded men speaking in broken English and espousing an illogical wisdom akin to the character of Mr Miyagi in the *Karate Kid* (1984). Mr Miyagi's unusual teaching included the infamous "wax on, wax off" method where his student learns the ins and outs of the spirit of karate by waxing the master's car with both hands. Mr. Miyagi's pithiness still elicits responses of humorous recognition some 30 years later. Yet for me, frustration and irritation arise over the lack of more varied visions of Buddhism in the popular imagination beyond that of Mr Miyagi's magical ability to capture a fly between his chopsticks, or of Chow Yun-Fat's character in *Bullet Proof Monk* (2003), a Tibetan Buddhist monk with magical powers who must protect an ancient scroll and comes to America looking for the next guardian. The male-centered focus of these films and representations fails to provide any positive images of ordinary Asian and Asian American Buddhists who are *not* magical and mysterious founts of kung fu power. Such films also rarely present Buddhist women; it is as if Buddhist women simply do not exist. Similarly, the prevailing beauty of utopic mountain hermitages found in *Why Has Bodhidharma Left for the East* (1989), *Samsara* (2001), and *Spring, Summer, Fall, Winter... and Spring* (2003) seems accessible only to men on the quest for their own spiritual salvation while female lay Buddhists are inevitably presented as practicing a less than authentic or less valued Buddhism.

In what follows, I present a carefully selected but by no means exhaustive collection of globally produced Buddhist films that are either complicit in shaping these dominant discourses about Buddhism and/or also present critically important accounts of lay Buddhism. These discourses privilege and create a hierarchy of ascetic male monks and meditation over and against a racialized and gendered Buddhism that has yet to receive appropriate scholarly and popular attention. Such an exclusion is rather curious and troubling considering that the majority of Buddhists worldwide do not meditate, but rather, engage in other forms of practice including chanting *sutras*, merit-making, observance of the holy days marking the Buddhist calendrical cycle, bowing, adhering to the five precepts of the laity and living according to the Noble Eight-fold path.[26] This exclusion is ever more troubling because such lay practices are often associated by scholars and popular audiences alike with a popular Asian Buddhism that does not warrant significant attention because it is perceived as less authentic. As I argue later in this book, Asian Buddhist lay practices are often negatively associated with women's devotional practices that are rendered superstitious. The exclusion of lay Buddhist practices is also influenced by a racial logic that holds that Asian Buddhism is somehow a weaker version than Buddhism in the West because it is too devotional and not as sophisticated as those who prize and practice meditation alone. It is these devotional practices that comprise the majority of the religious lives of lay Buddhists yet they receive scant attention. I am not suggesting that Buddhist films that feature only meditating monks are necessarily "bad" films, but rather that the reception and perception of such films as indicators of the most authentic form of religion is simply misguided and inaccurate. Thus, this book is an effort to raise up the virtues of lay Buddhism that have yet to receive adequate attention in either traditional texts and in popular constructions of Buddhism. It is also an effort to underscore the misrepresentations of Buddhism in film that have visualized a narrowly conceived image of the tradition. Film can both curtail or enhance our visions of religion and our lives through the interplay between the film, the filmmaker, and the film viewer. One of the guiding ambitions of this book then is to remake the image of Buddhism on screen and in real life such that those historically obscured from the historical center of the tradition both in Asia and in the West (that is, lay Buddhist women and Asian and Asian American Buddhists) can begin to see themselves in and through the screen as full participants in the Buddhist economy of meaning making. Such an endeavor seeks to redress the marginalization of women within the tradition and to lay bare the politics of race in the transmission of what gets misinterpreted as "real" or "true" Buddhism.

While taking seriously the power of visualization to offer religious insight and asking what we can learn about visionary experiences and visualized images of Buddhism through the film, I am also keenly aware that such an encounter might very well serve as a viewer's first entrée into the world of Buddhism—an entrée that shapes and informs the reception of Buddhism on a global scale. But if, as bell hooks notes, we go to the movies to encounter the unfamiliar and border cross into a terrain of difference, then Buddhist films can function as "fictive ethnographies" that reinforce the otherness of Buddhism that has captured the popular imagination.[27] As a result, there may be a resistance to viewing the ordinary as somehow worthy of classification as "real" Buddhism and therefore serious popular and scholarly attention.

Similarly, there may be hesitancy in drawing attention to the ordinary forms and practices of Buddhism that do not fit the category of the sensational and the exotic. As I argue throughout this book, the hesitancy to rethink what constitutes "authentic" or "real" Buddhism renders the ordinary of lesser value which in turn has serious implications for attitudes toward lay Buddhists whose practices do not include asceticism or meditation.

It's a man's world—or so texts and films proclaim

This book draws a connection between the historical prioritization of male monastics over lay Buddhist (and primarily women's) practices in the Buddhist tradition by exposing the pride of place given to male ascetic disciplines and meditative practices in popular constructions of Buddhism both in religious texts and in film. In so doing, this book also lays bare unquestioned presuppositions about women and lay practices as constituting less authentic forms of the religion in Buddhist texts that are absorbed into popular renderings of Buddhism that remain unchallenged in Buddhist films even today. Popular Buddhist films such as *Lost Horizon* (1937), *Spring,*

Summer, Fall, Winter...and Spring (2003), *The Cup* (1999), and *Travellers and Magicians* (2003) contribute to the perpetuation of a narrowly-conceived Buddhism characterized by the male monastic virtuoso as primary religious specialist, and meditation as the primary practice at the expense of other vibrant forms. As a result, popular perceptions of Buddhism give undue primacy to ascetic forms of Buddhism that come to be identified with a "proper" Buddhism. Yet, what might be the costs of this privileging of the monastic? The aforementioned Buddhist films are therefore limited in their vision of an expansive Buddhism that includes positive imagery of women, yet there are better ways to look for and see this vibrant Buddhism, and different films from the ones previously mentioned with which to do so. Furthermore, this approach helps us to retrain our gaze to focus on those characters who may appear marginal, yet are in fact central to the flourishing of this religious tradition.

To address this issue, I show how the undue weight given to male monastics and meditation in filmic accounts of Buddhism forecloses the possibility of a more diverse understanding of Buddhism that can expose the political claims of orthodoxy. In drawing attention to lay Buddhist women I certainly don't wish to argue that Asian Buddhist lay women are somehow the exemplars of what makes for "good" Buddhism/Buddhist practice, or that their inclusion in a film automatically makes for a better film. Rather, throughout this book I highlight and analyze the archetypes of women found in texts and in film who exemplify the kind of Buddhisms that I wish to retrieve and envision on screen and real life.

Sex in the texts

The Indian Buddhist monastic disciplines found in the *Vinaya* (monastic codes) of the Buddhist canon focus primarily on sex as the most difficult of desires to quell; if unchecked sexual desire can leave a monk trapped in the cycle of rebirth known as *samsara*. As Janet Gyatso observes in her chapter on sex within Buddhist canonical sources in *Critical Terms for the Study of Buddhism*, "at least we can say that it shares with the specialized rule for monastic virtuosi the sense that sex epitomizes the central problematic of Buddhism."[28] Sexual desire binds us to the world of rebirth and the desire for it is relentless. Hence, much of the Buddhist literature aimed at uprooting sexual desire in men hold up women and their physical bodies as embodiments of sexual desire who tempt them off the path of purity. Often referred to as Mara's (The Lord of Desire) daughters and "snares of *samsara*," women appear in Buddhist texts in varying forms of enticement and entrapment as:

prostitutes selling their bodies like vendors in a market peddling their wares; as beautiful lay women whose alms-giving brings anxious contact with the opposite sex; and as betrayed wives and mothers despondent over the loss of their spouses and sons.[29] Because the Buddha established a relationship of mutual dependence between monks and the laity, the monks were required to go on daily alms rounds to receive food from the villagers. Each morning brought contact with women who served the food; each morning therefore brought monks into close proximity with the bodies of women. Therefore, the monks were constantly advised to avoid the deceptive allure of women. As the monk Sabbakama wrote in the *Theragatha* ("Verses of the Elders") of the Theravada Buddhist Canon:

> Enticing sights, sounds, smells,
> Tastes, and things to touch—
> These five strands of sensual desire
> Are seen in a woman's form.
> They trap the average man,
> Like snares net shy dear
> Like hooks snag fish,
> And like pitch catches monkeys.[30]

Cast as snares with deceptive and impure bodies, women in early Indian Buddhist texts were excoriated for their beauty. As a result, male monastic Buddhism has pathologized the ordinary sexual lives of laywomen and construed their material bodies and desires as antithetical to the pursuit of enlightenment.

This monastic inheritance and aversion to sex finds its way into many contemporary narrative films of Buddhism such as *Spring, Summer, Fall, Winter... and Spring* (2003), *Travellers and Magicians* (2003), and *Samsara* (2001) that reinforce traditional views by envisioning the monk's journey to enlightenment as one first hindered and later compelled by aversion to the very being that so befuddled him. Each film's snare of *samsara* uses her gaze to lure the unsuspecting monk into her sensual clutches as she prepares for his downfall.[31] What I find striking about these filmic projections of women as embodiments of lust and desire is that such sexual encounters are usually redemptive for the monk—that is, the monk who falls prey to the mantrap experiences sex and its destructive powers and, in so doing, is then able to return to the monastic life with that much more understanding of the nature of suffering. The women unfortunately do not fare as well. For example, in *Spring, Summer, Fall, Winter...and Spring* and *Travellers and Magicians* both snares of *samsara* are killed off rather abruptly and the monks emerge spiritually triumphant.

In addition to envisioning women as temptresses with little possibility of liberation who are but the mere catalysts for male religious progress, images of women in Buddhist texts and film remain vexing precisely because they disavow the possibility of imagining and imaging an ordinary lay Buddhism that flourishes not just despite but *because of* the embrace of sexuality. In other words, if we were to rely solely on these films as primary sources for understanding Buddhism, we might think that most Buddhists seek the negation of sex rather than live sexual lives. While I certainly do not wish to claim that women in Buddhism can only be identified in terms of their sexuality, and only as lay Buddhists, it remains the case that both Buddhist texts and Asian and Western Buddhist films continue to breathe life into the stock characterization of women as snares of *samsara* tempting men in the marketplace of ordinary life and of nonmonastic Buddhism as less authentic and worthy of serious attention. Therefore, I am also theorizing a lay Buddhist practice that accounts for and renders spiritually potent the lives of ordinary women as religious virtuosos. Such a reading highlights lay Buddhism as an authentic, vibrant form of practice and not a degeneration of some pure form. As I contend throughout the book, films and texts continue to offer a limited scope of Buddhism not only with regard to women and lay practices, but also with regard to images of Asian Buddhists constructed and received in the Western imaginary. Such images simply cannot account for the variety and vitality of Buddhism as lived experience when narrowly represented as a male monastic tradition espoused in canonical texts and reproduced in popular culture.

My critique of the lack of positive female imagery in Buddhist film situates itself in dialogue with recent studies of bodily discourses in Buddhism such as Susanne Mrozik's examination of the effects of inscribing ethical virtue on human bodies in *Virtuous Bodies: The Physical Dimensions of Morality in Buddhist Ethics*.[32] Building on Mrozik's work, I argue that the representation of bodies and sexuality in Buddhist films are images invested in, and shaped by, earlier Buddhist discourses.[33] I am also indebted to the many extraordinary studies of women in Buddhism that reveal the profoundly negative view that monks have had of women and their bodies. These works include Diana Paul's foundational *Women in Buddhism: Images of the Feminine in the Mahayana Tradition*, Rita Gross's *Buddhism after Patriarchy*, and Liz Wilson's *Charming Cadavers: Horrific Figurations of the Feminine in Indian Buddhist Hagiographic Literature*.[34] Drawing from these pivotal texts I reimagine a Buddhism that includes ordinary women's religious lives—women whose sexuality is not seen as a snare to be avoided at all costs, but rather an expression of a healthy rather than pathological sexuality.

Admittedly the resources in Buddhist Studies have proven somewhat limited for such a Buddhist re-vision. Toward that end, I have found bell hooks's theoretical insights on black women's sexuality in film to be particularly illuminating. In *Reel to Real: Race, Sex, and Class at the Movies*, hooks interrogates films that received wide acclaim as "progressive texts of race, sex, and class" to see if they might in fact "promot[e] a counterhegemonic narrative challenging the conventional structures of domination that uphold and maintain white supremacist capitalist patriarchy."[35] Her reading of Spike Lee's *She's Gotta Have It* (1986) goes against the grain of many African American women who found the film progressive in its representation of female sexuality. Instead, hooks offers an incisive critique of protagonist Nola Darling not as a sexually-desiring "liberated black woman," as popular audiences believed, but rather an objectified woman whose sexuality is derivative of male pleasure because it lacks any autonomous gesture or agency.[36] hooks suggests that "[h]er assertive sexuality is most often portrayed as though her body, her sexually aroused being, is a reward or gift she bestows on the deserving male."[37] While critiquing films that uphold structures of domination, hooks's approach to racist and sexist imagery offers much to this study, for her work includes the ability to disentangle "revolutionary standpoints merged with conservative ones." Such a method is invaluable for a reading of film as cultural (and religious) texts that caution against both an uncritical acceptance of a liberatory female sexuality in film and an unwillingness to find the revolutionary embedded in the conservative.[38]

As I argue throughout this book, the over-emphasis of male monasticism and meditation as the *sine qua non* of authentic Buddhism has constructed a Buddhist orthodoxy whose effects are still seen in filmic accounts of the religion. *Silver Screen Buddha* is therefore an attempt to restore to the public eye the complexity of the Buddhist tradition that attends to the flourishing and validity of lay Buddhist practices. As such, this project is by no means a denigration of male monasticism and meditation but rather offers a pluralist account of Buddhism that is not saddled by claims to orthodoxy.

The racial life of Buddhism[39]

The casting of an exotic and peculiar Buddhism generates an emotional pull that entices, inspires, and intrigues spectators who yearn for such perceived difference, but such visual representations establish a disciplinary border to control who gains entry into such Buddhist paradises and who gets to leave. As I argue later in this book, Buddhist films such as *Broken Blossoms* (1919) and *Lost Horizon* (1937) engage in exclusionary practices that mimic U.S. immigration policies that regulated Asian immigration in the early 1900s.

As perceived threats to the "American National Family," Asians and Asian Americans were reduced to one or more of what Robert Lee coins "The Six Faces of the Oriental": the pollutant, the coolie, the deviant, the yellow peril, the model minority, and the gook.[40] The stereotypes of the Oriental cast Asian and Asian American bodies as indelibly different and therefore inherently unable to assimilate into mainstream American culture. Such faces appear in D. W. Griffith's *Broken Blossoms* whose Chinese Buddhist monk emigrates to London to bring Buddhist messages of peace—only to have his hopes of transforming the "barbarians" dashed when he turns into an opium addict pining away for an impoverished and abused white girl named Lucy. The monk, known as the Yellow Man or "Chinky" by Lucy, wears three of the six faces of the Oriental—the coolie, the deviant, and the yellow peril—stereotypes which mirror the social fears of Asian pollution and the intensification of the hostility toward Chinese immigrant laborers. As a shopkeeper, the Yellow Man lurks about Chinatown and oscillates between a sexual threat to Lucy and an effeminate Chinaman incapable of getting the girl. Similarly, Frank Capra's utopic construction of Shangri-La in *Lost Horizon* traps its inhabitants in a timeless captivity where they are sought after yet at the same time are incapable of leaving the borders of the Himalayas lest they revert to their real age and die.

When certain forms of asceticism (masculinist or not) predominate in what is held to be proper or orthodox Buddhism that is mediated for popular consumption, then surely there are costs that are borne largely by women, the laity, Asians, and Asian Americans that Orientalism and racialization historically constructed as the other. As this study shows, race became a factor in the Western world of Buddhism precisely because the largely lay Buddhist practices of Asians and Asian Americans have been and continue to be negated in the process of social and filmic adaptation of the tradition from Asia to the West. Such obliterations occur, on the one hand, because their ordinary and everyday practices of Buddhism fail to fit the images of Buddhist mysteriousness, exoticism, and alternative spiritual views that found expression in the earliest depictions of Buddhism through popular films such as D. W. Griffith's *Broken Blossoms* and Frank Capra's *Lost Horizon*. Although produced in the early half of the twentieth century, they nonetheless had a lasting impact on the imaging and imagining of Asians, Asian Americans, and Buddhism on screen and in popular culture. On the other hand, the devotional practices of Asian and Asian American Buddhists are often constructed as far too backward to produce any real positive benefit for a contemporary Western audience still imagining a far away and exotic Buddhism first encountered in Griffith's and Capra's films. In his introduction to *Money, Sex, War, Karma: Notes for a Buddhist Revolution*, David Loy notes that Buddhism has much to offer the modern West to combat the poisons of greed, ill will, and delusion that have been institutionalized economically and socially. Yet Loy's argument, while laudable, poses a particular dilemma for Asian Buddhists precisely because he endeavors to extract a true Buddhism and demythologize the tradition from its Asian frameworks in order to render it usable. Loy claims:

> The exotic names, robes, and rituals of Asian Buddhism are attractive to many of us, but sooner or later we must begin to distinguish the imported forms we appreciate from the essential Dharma that we need. Buddhism needs to take advantage of its encounter with modern/postmodern civilization—offering a greater challenge than Buddhism has ever faced before—to engage in a self-examination that attempts to distinguish what is *vital and still living* in its Asian versions from what is *unnecessary and perhaps outdated.*[41]

In a complicated series of representations and projections through film and other popular media, devotional Buddhism and Asianness have been conflated in Western culture such that the practices of Asian Buddhism have come to be regarded as backward, superstitious, and incompatible with the West. Such negative regard has of course serious consequences for how Asian American Buddhists are seen or, in this case, perhaps *not* seen but rather rendered invisible in the larger context of American Buddhism. According to this logic, meditational Buddhism is then treated as simultaneously authentic and modern. In his recent work, *Race and Religion in American Buddhism: White Supremacy and American Buddhism,* Joseph Cheah argues that the European colonial encounter with Theravada Buddhism in Southeast Asia during the mid-nineteenth and twentieth centuries through the Orientalist influences of scholars Henry Olcott and Thomas Rhys Davids undoubtedly shaped the development of Buddhism in the U.S.[42] According to Cheah, Victorian era Orientalist and colonial projects in Sri Lanka and Burma sought to purify Theravada Buddhism of its overly superstitious elements. In so doing, such efforts explicitly sought to elevate *vipassana* (insight meditation) as the most unadulterated form of practice that was authenticated through their discovery in Buddhist texts. Such claims to traditional veracity were tied to the Protestant emphasis on the textual sources of interpretation and translation, a practice that many believed to be most effectively and objectively carried out by the white European scholar.[43] Cheah thus reveals the white supremacy or "hegemony of whiteness" that served as the invisible yet all too powerful force in the construction of an American Buddhism. In such a Westernized Buddhism, Asian informant and lay Buddhists have been rendered less authentic and trustworthy translators of the tradition than the Western scholar. In much the same way that Orientalism functioned as a means of legitimating Western positional superiority over the East, Western

Buddhists advocated for a more "modernist Buddhism." This modernist Buddhism was contrasted with native Asian Buddhism, which was presented as a lesser, backward, corrupted, and watered down version of an orthodox Buddhism traced to the Pali Canon.[44] Thus the embrace of Buddhist meditation in the West emerged in the context of white hegemony that perpetuated the belief that the religion of Asian Buddhists was and continues to be weighed down by the excessiveness of their superstitions and popular rituals. Cheah's critique is thus instructive for revealing the modernist and Protestantizing influences behind such claims for a true Buddhism.

Buddhist films and Orientalist conceits

Any analysis of Buddhism, film, and race would be remiss if it did not take into account the rise of the Buddhist monk in American popular culture from the early 1900s to the present. Jane Iwamura's *Virtual Orientalism: Asian Religions in American Popular Culture* examines the American popular fascination with the cult of Asian personalities and Orientalized icons such as D. T. Suzuki, Maharishi Mahesh Yogi, and Kwai Chang Caine, and reveals the Orientalist underpinnings of what she calls the icon of the Oriental Monk.[45] The Oriental Monk is indeed a mediated being whose very presence serves as an embodiment of a collective yearning for otherness. However, this yearning is not for the sake of genuine engagement with otherness *per se*. Rather, it reaffirms images of U.S. geopolitical superiority *vis-à-vis* Asia. Such is the nature and project of Orientalism that constructs a seamless visual archaeology or genealogy of the mediated Asian male monk's body.[46] Like Iwamura, I pay attention to the negative effects of the mediated images of the Oriental monk and extend the analysis to Asian and Asian American male and female Buddhists that have been plagued by a vexing series of exaggerated readings as hypersexual to hyperdocile, hyperaggressive to hypersubmissive. Asian American religion scholars such as Cheah and Iwamura have of course devoted significant attention to these racist images and their Orientalist beginnings, yet few have taken on the role of the mediated discursive body that is marked religiously, racially, *and* sexually. Rather than treating religion, race, gender, and sexuality as separate frames of analysis, I argue that one cannot understand Buddhism without understanding their intersections. Iwamura argues that the Oriental Monk as a signifier of otherness, exoticism, nurturing, and femininity is also implicated in current American struggles to both contain and reframe Asian religions in ways that appease the desire for difference while rendering this difference tolerable for the viewer. In so doing, it is the viewer, and not the viewed, that remains in the position of power through the act of looking as the Oriental Monk soon comes to symbolize a virile white male Euro-American identity constructed over and against Asian and Asian American difference.

The field of Buddhist Studies has yet to adequately mine film as a powerful source of reflection and representation of the religion. While substantial work has been done on the relationship between film, religion, and cultural representations, little comparative analysis has been done that articulates the relationship between the constructions of Buddhism in Asian and Western film in both academic and popular contexts.[47] Such studies are prudent given the increasing commodification of all things Buddhist in contemporary culture. Scholars and journalists focusing on Buddhism such as Donald S. Lopez, Jr. and Orville Schell have brought their critical analyses to the Orientalist influences on the objectification of Tibetan Buddhism through Western teachers, music, film, and other media.[48] Yet there has been little comparative analysis of films that take up the category of Buddhist themes from a global perspective that reveal the complex raced and gendered life of Buddhism.[49] It is my hope that this book contributes to and expands that much needed discussion.

Overview of the chapters

Despite the challenges of finding race, gender, and sex-positive representations of Buddhism in film, my analysis holds that the genre is still worthy of serious consideration, particularly at a time when global constructions of Buddhism in film serve as the primary mode of reception for domestic and international audiences. Through an analysis of the mediated constructions of Buddhism through film, the following chapters offer both a constructive critique of such mediations and a reimagining of the tradition itself through the very same form of film. While I offer an analysis of the raced and gendered life of Buddhism in the popular imagination through film, my treatment of various archetypal films might not appear to give equal weight to both gender and race dynamics in each film. Yet, I approach individual films with an eye toward how each contributes to an unbalanced view of Buddhism that skews more heavily toward an undue valorization of a male and/or monastic model. The arguments I make include a critique of the cultural production and consumption of this monastic male difference in Asian and Western film and what this consumption means for Buddhism.

The following two chapters highlight the reception of Buddhism through film and utilize the transmission of Buddhism through film in the West as a starting point to foreground the ways that filmmakers and viewers engage in a process of cultural production and reception that is shaped heavily by the racialization of the religion.

Chapter 2, "Longing for Otherness through Buddhism," examines the earliest introduction of Buddhist films in the West through an analysis of D. W. Griffith's 1919 silent film, *Broken Blossoms* and Frank Capra's 1937 *Lost Horizon*. In this chapter, I reveal the Orientalist constructions of Buddhism as well as the context of anti-Asian sentiment and racialization that shaped the religion's entry in the American imaginary through the silver screen. Both films present Buddhism as a seemingly noble foil to Western capitalism and war, yet Buddhism and its practitioners are frozen into a timeless captivity of difference that makes it near impossible to imagine Buddhism, Asians, and Asian Americans beyond the stereotypes of otherness, foreignness, mysteriousness, and the Yellow Peril.

Chapter 3, "Zen Appetites: Consuming Religion and Otherness through Film," takes up the Western fascination with Zen Buddhism and its construction of Zen as an ideal example of cultural iconoclasm ripe for emulation. Through an analysis of the Coen brother's 1998 *The Big Lebowski*, Jim Jarmusch's 1999 *Ghost Dog: The Way of the Samurai*, and Marc Rosenbush's 2004 *Zen Noir*, I explore the exoticization and racialization of Buddhism as a spirit of heterodoxy easily adopted in the West that capitalizes on stereotypes of Asian and Asian American unintelligibility. I argue that the Western fascination with Zen essentializes its otherness as an easily adopted identity that exploits racialized constructions of Buddhist difference.

Chapter 4, "Plus ça change, plus c'est la même chose: Women as Snares of *Samsara*," introduces the age-old Buddhist textual view of women as impediments to the spiritual lives of monks absorbed rather uncritically by filmmakers that forecloses the possibility of envisioning women's flourishing in the Buddhist world. Exploring the textual image of women as snares of *samsara*, I show the continuing adoption of extremely negative attitudes toward women and sexuality in contemporary Buddhist films such as Kim Ki-Duk's 2003 *Spring, Summer, Fall, Winter... and Spring*. In so doing, I argue that many Buddhist films perpetuate the view that women are somehow antithetical to the ideal Buddhist life and that such a limited perspective delimits the possibility of lay women's spiritual potential. Often viewed as the downfall of men, women receive very little positive valuation in early Buddhist scriptures and contemporary films; as such, the widely held belief that ascetic monks have always been and will continue to be the virtuosos of the religious life is reinforced. While *Spring, Summer, Fall, Winter... and Spring* relies on early images of women as snares of *samsara* to be avoided at all costs, Kim's film also introduces the notion that engaging in sex with women can serve as the ultimate Buddhist lesson in the woes of desire and its fulfillment. Unfortunately, it is the women who are sacrificed in the man's quest for enlightenment.

It is rare to find positive instantiations of lay Buddhism (and especially lay women) in Buddhist film. Therefore, I argue, it is necessary to retrain the eye to see that which has always been a critical part of the tradition yet is often easily obscured by the working of patriarchy and sexism. Hence Chapters 5–8 highlight the potency of a lived and embodied Buddhism in the world that has been hard to find in the often racialized and gendered depictions of the religion seen on screen.

Chapter 5, "Coming Down from the Mountaintop: Engaged Buddhism in the World," rereads the negative view of women and women's sexuality presented in Chapter 4 with an in-depth analysis of Im Kwon-Taek's 1989 *Aje Aje Bara Aje* (*Come, Come, Come Upward*) to imagine what I call the radical acts of somatic compassion expressed through the work of a Korean nun who defrocks and returns to the lay life. While it might appear that women's transformation is negated by the fact that they engage their bodies sexually for the sake of male awakening, Buddhist films like *Aje Aje Bara Aje* also show us that their very sexuality is not only for male consumption and trans-formation. Instead, women themselves are able to attain higher levels of mental awareness and development with the very bodies that often got them into trouble in early Indian Buddhist literature. Thus, the female sexual body is re-approached as a potential source of spiritual insight. As a counterpart to this female-focused film, I conclude this chapter with an analysis of South Korean director Bae Young-Kyun's 1989 *Why Has Bodhidharma Left for the East?* to examine a similar dilemma of attachment to the individualized quest for enlightenment, this time by a man who has become a monk to escape his familial obligations to his widowed mother and his sister. Bae's film problema-tizes the dualistic view that holds the ordinary world and the world of the temple as wholly separate, and provides a vision of Buddhism that is far more integrated into daily life. While Bae's film focuses on the religious lives of monks at the expense of the active presence of women, it nonetheless provides a significant counter argument to the virtues of the monastic life for men as well. As such, it also proposes an alternative way of being Buddhist in the world.

Chapter 6, "The Ordinary as Extraordinary," also introduces a counter-balance to the over-determination of the male monastic in Buddhist scriptures and films by focusing on a completely different model of the ideal Buddhist life. Utilizing Yōjirō Takita's 2008 *Departures* as a meditation upon the signifi-cance of everyday life as the training ground for spiritual connection between all beings, I introduce another side of Buddhism that has yet to receive popular recognition in the West—the embrace and affirmation of the ordinary self as *karmically* limited yet spiritually potent. Rather than disciplining the self through asceticism and intensive meditation, the Buddhism of *Departures* is based on the Jodoshinshu form of Buddhism that originated in Japan and emphasizes the practice of compassion and gratitude in everyday life. Ascetic virtues are considered near impossible to master; instead, the most significant aspect of Buddhist life is the experiential understanding of one's indebtedness and interrelatedness to all other beings. *Departures* thus offers an opportunity to valorize the lay life over the monastic life and imagine how Buddhism can remain spiritually potent outside the temple walls.

Chapter 7, "Film as *Sutra*" specifically develops the concept of film as *sutra* by examining Chang Sun-Woo's 1993 *Hwa-Om-Kyung* (*Passage to Buddha*), which envisions the world through the lens of the famous Buddhist *sutra* known as the *Avatamsaka Sutra*. Chang's film offers an occasion to see film as a Buddhist text that envisions an integrated social world where the ordinary messiness of life is the most potent ground for enlightenment and spiritual transformation. In Chang's world, the character of the monk eats meat, drinks alcohol, and serves as the perfect foil to the over-emphasis on ascetic purity projected in many Buddhist films. I interpret *Hwa-Om-Kyung* as an opportune text that can revise how ordinary lay Buddhism is popularly perceived; rather than a diluted version of a pure form, the lay Buddhism of the young boy Sonje and his interactions with numerous social misfits cast as ideal spiritual friends overturns the idea that one must remain isolated in meditation to effect enlightenment. Here the margins of society (the poor, the disabled, the misfit, the female) are made center as its inhabitants become the salvific guides to the young pilgrim.

Chapter 8 takes an explicitly feminist hermeneutical approach to Pan Nalin's 2001 *Samsara* by rereading a classically male tale of the challenges of asceticism and foregrounding the story of the wife of the protagonist Tashi as an embodiment of a female lay Buddhism that embraces female sexuality and materiality as a virtue in the Buddhist social world. In this chapter, I depathologize women's sexuality and articulate a vision of lay Buddhism as a site for women's extraordinary insight. *Samsara* demonstrates that spiritual capacity is sometimes best honed outside the realms of asceticism. I argue that films like *Samsara* counteract the prevailing images of Asians and Asian religion as exotic and timeless, anchoring Buddhism in an embodied form that is engaged, informed by, and enmeshed in sexuality and desire—all those things that ideally should be avoided at all costs from both a scriptural and Orientalist perspective.

My concluding chapter "Recreating the Buddhist World Anew" closes this study with an analysis of what I call the other side of Buddhism. Taking Julia Kwan's Chinese Canadian film *Eve and the Fire Horse* (2005) as a point of departure from more exoticized portrayals of Buddhist difference, I lay down a framework to refocus our vision onto the everyday wonders of the tradition happening outside the temple and inside the home. In so doing, I approach this film with an eye towards its imaginative portrayal of Buddhism through the eyes of Eve, a nine-year-old Chinese Canadian girl. Kwan utilizes magical realism to bring the Buddha, Jesus, and Kuan Yin to life in the little girl's living room as they dance around the family's home that is populated with multi-religious statues. In so doing, she offers a playful yet provocative opportunity to examine the intersections of religion, race, and immigration in the lives of a Chinese Canadian family that situates the family's multi-faithed religiosity squarely in the realm of lived reality. No longer viewed as an exotic tradition of monks on mountains, Kwan's vision of Buddhism flourishes in the daily life of an immigrant family whose religious practices include Chinese folk traditions, Buddhist devotional worship, and baptism in a Catholic church. What makes the film's representation of Buddhism so compelling is its emphasis on the ordinariness of the family's multi-faith altar whose gods and goddesses are propitiated at different times depending on which one seems most appropriate to resolve a particular misfortune—family illness, miscarriage, and death. What is so valuable about Kwan's imaginative vision of Buddhism is its everyday integration to help the family come to terms with the vicissitudes of immigrant life in Canada in the 1970s. Such a film demythologizes the Orientalist fantasies that have preoccupied popular and scholarly interpretations of Buddhism that have made their way on screen and, in turn, contributed to the racialization of Buddhism and the perpetuation of negative attitudes toward women.

Lastly, I return to the concept of Buddhist film as a spiritual technology to create the world anew. I argue that film has the potential to serve as a corrective to the raced and gendered images of Buddhism that have foreclosed the opportunity to see the internal diversity of Buddhism and to remake religion, race, and gender so long as we cultivate the skillful means to do so. In so doing, I show the connection between film, spiritual technology and the Buddha's method of teaching known as *upaya* or skillful means, an expedient device to help incite a new of way of seeing. According to the *Lotus Sutra*, the Buddha offered multiple teachings in a variety of forms depending on the needs of the listener/reader. As an example of such skillful means, Buddhist films also have the power to teach in a form most effective in today's culture—through visions on screen. As a form of teaching that can inspire new ways of seeing the world, Buddhist films also function as *sutras* or texts that have the power to realign one's gaze so that one can see how Buddhism has been positively and negatively constructed and received by audiences globally.

2

Longing for Otherness
through Buddhism

It is perhaps the protean quality of Buddhism that lends itself to a multitude of meanings on the silver screen, some idealistic and some antagonistic. This chapter takes up the relationship among Buddhism, race, religious difference, and Orientalism with respect to D. W. Griffith's *Broken Blossoms* (1919) and Frank Capra's *Lost Horizon* (1937), two American-made films that foreground Buddhism as a marker of otherness and unassimilable difference. I begin with these two films to demonstrate how the idea of a pure meditative Asian Buddhism was and continues to be mediated through the lens of race, which I argue, has had a nearly indelible mark on popular expectations and receptions of Buddhism in the West. This is not to say that equally problematic portrayals are not to be found in Asian Buddhist films, but rather to note the origins of the racial life of Buddhism for American audiences. In addition, this chapter highlights the ways that racialization shapes the consumption of Asian Buddhism to offer a taste of difference both sweet and sour. As I show, the representation of the distinctiveness of Buddhism reflected a seeming appreciation of the religion's peacefulness as a tonic to American military aggression. However, because the image of the Buddhist monk and Asians were often conflated in the American popular imagination, the racial politics of anti-Asian sentiment balanced an otherwise affirming if not unrealistic image of the religion on screen.

When Griffith's silent classic opened on the silver screen, the film received wide acclaim as a progressive text about race despite continuing fears of Asian immigrants as embodiments of the "Yellow Peril." According to Robert Lee's study of racial stereotypes of Asian Americans from the Gold Rush through the 1990s, U.S. anxiety flared over the influx of Asian immigrants into manufacturing, laundering, and domestic services following the completion of the transcontinental railroad in 1869.[1] While U.S. immigration policies supported the recruitment of immigrants across its borders, it was not until the passing of the Chinese Exclusion Act of 1882 that a race- and class-based immigration policy was first instituted. Thus, the passing of this act prohibited Chinese laborers from entering U.S. borders and also marks the first time that illegal immigration was considered a criminal offense.[2] The Chinese Exclusion Act of 1882 legally marked the Chinese as indelibly different and alien and was followed by increased violence against Chinese immigrants who had moved from working the transcontinental railroad into alternative work such as coal mining. This transition often resulted in virulent attacks against the Chinese such as the 1884 Rock Springs Massacre of Chinese coal miners by 200 white miners in Wyoming that reflected increased anti-Asian sentiment and fear over the influx of Chinese workers into the labor force.[3] Angst over the potential threat of Asian violence and the potential moral corruption of the deviant Asian immigrant only increased after Japan's defeat of Russia in 1905. The Immigration Act of 1917 further legislated against all Asian immigrants as undesirables by establishing an "Asiatic Barred Zone" that curtailed immigration from most of Asia and the Pacific Islands.

It was in the historical context of highly charged anti-Asian sentiment that D. W. Griffith and later Frank Capra introduced the first seemingly positive if not innocuous images of Asian Buddhists as peaceful, almost childlike monks whose religion could serve as a foil against war. However, as I show in this chapter, the gentle Asian Buddhist monk was neither as innocent nor innocuous as he seemed. Instead, the Asian Buddhist monk's calm exterior belied a simultaneous weakness and deviance that still made him morally threatening to U.S. national interests and its investment in white dominance. The effects of such dualistic depictions found their way into the next major American film to highlight the Buddhist religion—*Lost Horizon*. Frank Capra's 1937 *Lost Horizon* painted a more idealized picture of Buddhism where Westerners are transformed by their sojourn in the mystical Shangri-La. *Lost Horizon* also introduces Buddhism through the Christian language of brotherly love as a way of rendering it compatible and understandable to its audiences. However, like *Broken Blossoms*, Capra's film offers little opportunity for the public to imagine a Buddhism that coexists peacefully in the West, for even in *Lost Horizon*, Buddhist inhabitants never leave this El Dorado-like locale lest they grow old, sick, and die. The unique introduction of Buddhism to the West through the moving image reflects an investment in Asian and Buddhist differences through dual processes of Orientalism and racialization that served to discipline and ornament Buddhism's entry into American culture. Buddhism became and continues to represent a noble foil to Western capitalism, greed, and war, and got its start on the silver screen in the character of the Yellow Man in Griffith's *Broken Blossoms*.

Broken Blossoms

Broken Blossoms introduced audiences to the first Buddhist priest to appear on the American silver screen in the character of Cheng Huan, a young Chinese monk who wishes to pacify the West by bringing as the film notes, "the message of peace to the warlike Anglo-Saxons." Although Cheng Huan is Chinese in origin, he is played by the actor Richard Barthelmess who dressed in yellow face by taping back his eyelids, hunching his shoulders, and adopting an effeminate gait in order to play the monk. By noting the phenomenon of yellow face here, I do not mean to suggest that the actor's race automatically makes this film racist or that an Asian actor would make the film more positive in its depiction of Buddhism. Rather, the phenomenon of yellow face serves to underscore the perceived exotic difference offered up by this heavily racialized image of the religion and its monks. Despite his desires to bring Buddhism to the West through his noble mission, the Buddhist monk unfortunately fails in his calling and he later appears as one of many Chinese immigrants stuck in the morally defiling Chinatown section of the lower-class Limehouse district. While *Broken Blossoms* was received as a progressive text of its time by introducing the possibility of interracial love between the failed priest and a young gutter-waif named Lucy, the fact that the Buddhism of the priest does not take hold in the West indicates both the religion's and the Asian immigrant's impotence and menace. Instead, the priest, later referred to only as the "Yellow Man," quickly abandons his Buddhism as soon as he arrives in the Limehouse district, where he ends up working in a curio shop and takes up the opium pipe. Wandering around in a foggy drug-induced haze, he merely tends to his job in the Asian enclave, and pines away for the young white girl at a distance.

The Yellow Man's missionizing efforts consequently fail, indicating that while Buddhism has the potential to transform the barbaric West, it can only do so within its Asian borders. Once Buddhism comes to Western shores, it is made impotent in its reach and effectiveness. That is, Buddhism cannot survive or assimilate into Western culture; in the form of the Yellow Man, the religion is rendered unassimilable, potentially dangerous, and an icon of racial difference. The Buddhism practiced by the Yellow Man has thus floundered in the West despite its popularity in Asia. Buddhism was used not only as a kind of curative and critique of the excesses of American culture, but also as a form of differentiation that imagined Buddhism an icon of a fraught Asian and Asian American identity in the 1920s.

As an icon of a morally questionable otherness grafted onto the image of Asian Americans, Buddhism was a marker of Asian difference that intrigued and repulsed in much the same way the interrelated yet visually opposed images of the good compliant Asian and the deviant Asian image functioned. Like Orientalism, the good pliant Asian and the dangerous polluting Asian were flip sides of a coin that showed the limited range of attitudes toward Asian immigrants that continued to dominate mediated images of Buddhism throughout the twentieth century.

In its prologue, *Broken Blossoms* asks viewers to consider the forth-coming tale of "temple bells, sounding at sunset before the image of the Buddha," and explains that, "it is a tale of love and lovers; it is a tale of tears." In so doing, Griffiths sets the tone of the film as a romantic tragedy affecting the former Chinese Buddhist priest, Lucy, and her brutally-abusive father, Battling Burrows, a famed welterweight fighter. The poor, abused body of Lucy becomes the one hope to bring the Yellow Man a glimmer of happiness in his otherwise forlorn and wasted life. Alas, true to the form of romantic tragedies, Lucy is later killed by her father in a brutal beating that brings the Yellow Man to the brink of insanity as he wields a gun and shoots Battling Burrows dead. After gathering the limp body of his beloved, the Yellow Man creates a makeshift Buddhist altar, prays before it, plunges a dagger deep into his belly, and dies as the temple bells ring once again.

Given the rather short-lived message and appearance of Buddhism in Griffith's film, one might ask whether or not this film even counts as a Buddhist film and, if so, what it might reflect about the tradition. As I note below, *Broken Blossoms* does not foreground Buddhism as a central component of the film but rather it provides the first visual introduction of Buddhism on the silver screen as an otherworldly religion whose difference is constructed as palatable for its peacefulness and, more importantly, incom-patible and alien to the West.

The tragedy of love lost begins in a port city of China where the Buddhist priest is seen in his ornate silken finery preparing for his forthcoming missionary trip. He is going west as an emissary of peace and receives wise counsel from an elder monk in his Chinese temple and "[a]dvice for a young man's conduct in the world—word for word such as a fond parent or guardian of our own land would give." The monk's Buddhism is thus considered intelligible and nonthreatening to its American audiences. Cheng Huan himself is depicted far more nobly than he is in the original story. The movie is based on a short story written by Thomas Burke entitled, "The Chink and the Child" in *Limehouse Nights* (1917) which has him arriving in London through devious means via Cardiff, Liverpool, and Glasgow. Cheng Huan settles in Limehouse not because of any pure-hearted missionary zeal, but simply because he is depicted as too lazy to find a way back to Shanghai.[4] What the Yellow Man of "The Chink and the Child" shares with Griffith's Buddhist priest is a poetic sensibility that renders both of them more sensitive than others. For Burke:

Cheng Huan was a poet. He did not realize it. He had never been able to understand why he was unpopular; and he died without knowing. But a poet he was, tinged with the materialism of his race, and in his poor listening heart strange echoes would awake of which he himself was barely conscious. He regarded things differently from other sailors; he felt things more passionately, and things which they felt not at all; so he lived alone instead of at one of the lodging-houses.[5]

Griffith's adaptation of Burke's story endows the lonely poet with a Buddhist nobility that makes him a romantic who longs for the girl Lucy, whilst at the same time a priest whose sensitivity urges him to go West "ever convinced that the great nations across the sea need the lessons of the gentle Buddha." *Broken Blossoms* thus introduced Buddhism to American audiences as a tonic to the brutality associated with the West through the character of the Yellow Man.

As he prepares to embark on his journey, the Buddhist priest readies himself by listening to the advice of the senior monks in the ornate temple adorned with Buddha statues, flowers, decorative panels, and incense wafting through the beautifully composed space. The Buddhist message of peace and gentleness expresses itself at the film's opening through the image of the young monk in an idyllic port city in China as he steps into harm's way to stop a fight brewing between raucous American sailors. He tries to offer them a message of peace: "[w]hat thou dost not want others to do to thee, do thou not to others." The message of Buddha, closely aligned with the Golden Rule of Christianity, is offered through the film's intertitles to imagine Buddhism as a gentle and, more importantly, safe and familiar religion whose main message parallels those of the Christian West. The Chinese port city is set up as an ideal place where beautiful Chinese girls walk together giggling as they shop, nuclear Chinese families spend their day in the market, and harmony prevails.

However, the pious monk's admonishments fall upon deaf ears when he himself is unceremoniously knocked to the ground as the brawl between the sailors continues; in other words, the Buddhist message of peace will not be enough to save the Anglo-Saxon barbarians. This scene of the monk's failure to pacify the drunken sailors portends the Yellow Man's unsuccessful journey from the Buddhist temple to London. It also foreshadows Griffith's not so subtle message that the religion and race of the Yellow Man are incompatible with prevailing notions of whiteness and Christian supremacy. The Yellow Man strikes out in his missionary endeavor and ultimately fails to get the girl. As a tale of "love, lovers, and tears," *Broken Blossoms* is also a story of the shortcomings of Buddhism beyond its Asian borders, the threat of interracial romance and what that signifies for U.S. race relations, and the conflation of religion and race through the image of the Asian Buddhist monk reduced to the stereotype of "The Yellow Man."

Griffith juxtaposes Buddhism's message of peace with the savage brutality of Lucy's father whose violence and excessive masculinity are found in equal measure in the boxing ring and domestic sphere as he metes out his frustrations on his boxing opponents— and on poor Lucy's little body made frail from his blows. *Broken Blossoms* thus carries a caution to its audiences in the prologue, namely: "We may believe there are no Battling Burrows, striking the helpless with brutal whip—but do we not ourselves use the whip of unkind words and deeds? So, perhaps, Battling may even carry a message of warning." The counterexample to this senseless brutality comes in the form of Cheng Huan whom audiences imagine as the hero to the villain of Battling Burrows—a foil to vanquish the evil savage brute. However, what were viewers to make of the image of the peaceful monk turned opium addict and suspicious Chinaman? Was his love of Lucy as pure as the film's intertitles suggest? If he was so noble a monk, why did this Asian immigrant seem most at home in the opium den among other Asian miscreants? How is it possible that a Chinaman could save a poor white girl and love her without ignoble intention? As Griffith's tale shows, it was not possible. The gentle Buddhist could remain in China and serve as an ideological deterrent to types like Battling Burrows, but he could not cross into the Western world and remain unsullied. Once on Western soil, the Buddhist monk is deemed impotent and engages in a morally suspect relationship with Lucy. The message received is one of a dubious respect for Buddhism, a distrust of Asian immigrants, and an equally strong message of anti-miscegenation.

The audience is not privy to the the details of Buddhist monk's subsequent voyage to the West or his transformation from Buddhist priest to lonely opium-smoking shopkeeper. When it does meet up with Cheng Huan after his arrival in London, the audience witnesses a former monk whose once-proud posture has now given way to a stooped and hunched man who lurks about Chinatown displaying all the characteristics of the racialized Asian man—sneaky, weak, effeminate, and suspicious. The Yellow Man no longer wears the ornate Chinese Buddhist robes; instead, he wears the loose shirt and pants associated with the "Chinaman." With his eyes taped back, Barthelmess is striking in his ability to represent what has come to be the stock character of the Asian man with his bird-like frailty, his mincing quick short steps, and the way he scurries about the Chinatown district. The Buddhist priest now inhabits the liminal space of the low-class neighborhood where he no longer preaches the word of Buddha, but rather spends his days in a drug-induced haze perhaps to forget his fall and his failed mission. In an ironic gesture to a pair of Christian missionaries who tell of their upcoming trip to convert the heathens of China, the Yellow Man merely replies, "Good luck."

Griffith's gentle spirit has been weakened by the Anglo-Saxon barbarians and his Buddhism was of little help to him once he crossed over to the West. His noble religion can no longer save him; it is only his tragic love for the abused Lucy that can offer any semblance of succor for his otherwise bruised spirit. But is his love so pure? Such is the question that audiences must grapple with, for the young girl (who is 12 years old in Burke's story) vacillates between a delicate child and eyelash-batting, flirtatious young woman. She is also white and the Yellow Man is, well, yellow.

The risky interracial romance between the Yellow Man and Lucy reads as a kind of experiment in cultural intercourse between Griffith and the audience about the limits of interaction and assimilation. The Yellow Man's body is displayed on screen for its exotic characteristics as we are privilege to a fictive ethnographic peek into his life in China. But the fascination with his difference brings about a collective anxiety when in the West precisely because he is both charming to, and charmed by, an innocent young white girl. Moreover, while Griffith poses the possibility of interracial romance, the very nature of the romantic tragedy offers his American audiences a sigh of relief that the threat of miscegenation won't be realized; the Yellow Man cannot have the white girl and this love story cannot end in any other way than a three-way death as it is in fact a tragedy and cautionary tale of the dangers of interracial romance.

The film juxtaposes the peacefulness of the Buddhist temple in China against the liminal spaces of the opium den where Asian immigrants while away the hours in their drug-induced reveries and loose lower-class white women puff away on the pipe while mingling with the exotic other. The opium den, and the larger Chinatown quarter that serves as the diverse ethnic locale of the Asian immigrants of questionable morals including as the film's intertitles note, "Chinese, Malays, Lascars, where the Orient squats at the portals of the West," reflect the cartography of racialized spaces drawn by dominant culture that marks off racial and ethnic difference as both exotic and dangerous. The Yellow Man also embodies the exotic and the dangerous as he attempts to control his sexual desire for Lucy. Just as Lucy oscillates between innocence and seduction, the Yellow Man oscillates between a sexually devious Chinaman and chaste hero who tries to save Lucy from the ravages of her father. These dual identities also reflect the ambivalence associated with Asians and Asian Americans in the early 1900s.

As noted above, it was during this period that anti-Chinese sentiments were at their peak, with large numbers of Chinese immigrants who had come to the U.S. to build the transcontinental railroad finding that with their work finished, so too was their desirability. Just two decades before Griffith's film, journalist Jacob Riis had published his influential book, *How the Other Half Lives*, in which he characterized Chinese immigrants as "a constant and terrible menace to society … who are in no sense a desirable element of society."[6] The Chinese, who had built the railroads, farmed wheat, operated fisheries, and even served in the Civil War, were suddenly characterized as gambling drug addicts engaged in prostitution and of no value to civil society at all. It was in this social milieu that the Yellow Man came to embody both the peculiar fascination and repulsion of Asians and all things "Oriental."

Griffith offers a few significant scenes that present the Yellow Man as both gentle caretaker and sexual deviant—these scenes take place, perhaps without surprise, in his bedroom atop the curio shop where he works. The Yellow Man observes Lucy as she wanders around the Limehouse district, for as the film proclaims, "The beauty which all Limehouse missed smote him to the heart." It isn't until Lucy wanders into the curio shop that the Yellow Man begins to reveal his duplicitous and sexually deviant nature. One afternoon Battling Burrows has been warned by his manager to lay off the booze and womanizing to prepare for a fight; the irate boxer then returns home and criticizes Lucy for serving his meal late. As he pounds the table, Lucy becomes more and more frightened and accidently spills a bit of food on him, which enrages the boxer as he jumps up from the table, throws back his chair, and grabs Lucy by the hand, taunting her with the whip that he regularly uses to beat her. Knowing her fate, Lucy begs for mercy, reminding Battling Burrows that "they'll hang yer" for beating her so often. As she pleads with her father to spare her, Lucy bends down and uses her torn dress to wipe the dust off his boots, hoping to divert his attention. But Battling Burrows offers no reprieve to his daughter. Instead of mercy, he drags Lucy across the tiny room that serves as the kitchen and her bedroom and proceeds to beat her nearly unconscious. Satisfied with the brutality he metes out, Battling Burrows tosses the whip and heads out the door. In a desperate act of escape, Lucy picks her battered body up off the floor, limps to Chinatown in a near delirious state, stumbles into the Yellow Man's shop, and immediately faints on the floor curled up in a fetal position.

At first the Yellow Man doesn't see her as he peers off into the distance, presumably in a drug inspired fantasy. Poor Lucy then stirs and the Yellow Man cannot believe his eyes—he rubs them numerous times to see if indeed this image of the young girl he later names "White Blossom" is real or just a figment of his imagination. But he quickly comes to and offers what Griffith describes as "the first gentleness she has ever known," nursing her wounds with the most delicate touch and care.

"Oh, lily flowers and plum blossoms! Oh silver streams and dim-starred skies!" the intertitles proclaim. His dream has come true; the object of his affections has appeared out of nowhere and is in desperate need of his care. The two gaze into each other's eyes and, as this moment of intimacy suggests, the Yellow Man bends down toward the frightened girl and is poised to lay a kiss upon her cheek. But his visage transforms from childish excitement and fatherly concern as his eyes darken and a sinister look washes over his face. Then just as quickly, he is chastened by her worried look and comports himself once again as the good Asian, carrying the fragile child up to his bedroom where he lays his White Blossom gently onto his bed.

In his simple apartment above the shop, the relationship between a poor white girl and a Chinaman blooms as he sets her up in bed in a "room set up for a princess." He dances about the room in joy as he lights incense, puts flowers in a vase, and adorns the girl in a "magical robe from an older day." Lucy rests in bed propped up like a true princess and receives all of the Yellow Man's gifts, which include a bejeweled hair comb and a mirror through which she can take in her new reflection. Dressed like a Chinese princess in silken robes and ornaments, Lucy changes from a gutter waif into an enticing woman.

As the intertitles tell us, "[s]he seems transformed—into the dark chambers of her incredulous, frightened little heart comes warmth, and light." As she prattles on in delight with each new gift from the Yellow Man, his love and attraction for her grows. "He dreams her prattle, her bird-like ways, her sweet self—are all his own." He has fashioned her into an exotically adorned object of fancy all for himself.

In the transgressive and intimate space of the bedroom, it is near impossible to overlook the affections that they have for one another. The young girl finally

Figure 2.1 Broken Blossoms. *Yellow Man about to kiss Lucy*

has a benefactor who treats her with kindness; she returns the favor by batting her eyelashes, stroking his face, and coyly asking, "[w]hat makes you so good to me Chinky?" Her question belies a suspicion of seemingly docile Asian men who may, in fact, have ulterior motives concealed behind their kindhearted actions. Such affections, shared in the closed quarters of the bedroom, send the Yellow Man into a near swoon as he gleefully mimics catching moonlight in his hands, so smitten is he with this alabaster-skinned young woman. Holding an overnight vigil by her bed as she sleeps through the night, the threat of the Asian man's sexual aggression once again emerges as the same sinister cast comes over his face and he reaches out to touch her robes and perhaps get his first taste of the young girl. Griffith even includes a reassuring note on the screen as the scene unfolds that states, "[h]is love remains a pure and holy thing—even his worst foe says this." Yet it is rather difficult to imagine the purity of his love, especially after he offers Lucy the baby doll that she has often admired in his shop window. He gifts the doll to Lucy and we watch her caress it and clasp it to her chest as she speaks to it as if her own child.

While Griffith may wish for the audience to imagine this scene as the gift of a maternal-like love to one so deprived as Lucy, the scene takes place on the Yellow Man's bed and his sexually threatening glances reveal a more troublesome scene where the young girl's transformation into a woman is complete. As Lucy caresses the baby doll and takes its hand to her own

Figure 2.2 *Yellow Man gives Lucy a doll*

cheek, she becomes the mother and imagined wife to the Yellow Man. Hence, the camera zooms in on his face which has again turned ominous as we see the look of a sexual predator angling toward his victim. Awakened from her own private reverie over having something beautiful of her own, Lucy quickly shrinks back and the Yellow Man retreats from his hovering and chastely kisses the sleeves of her garment. Thus, purity is restored. Audiences are brought to the brink of interracial romance, but morality holds sway and the two never consummate their love. Though dabbling in inter-racial romance, *Broken Blossoms* still maintains the prevailing sentiments of anti-miscegenation of the time. Even though the Yellow Man appears as both childlike and predatory, Griffith ensures that the failed monk does not consummate any physical relationship with Lucy; he can only imagine and play like she belongs to him.

Because of the perceived threat of Asians and Asian immigration, however, racialized spaces like the Limehouse Chinatown district require surveillance and disciplining of the Asian immigrant through characters such as the menacing fellow Chinese immigrant, "Evil Eye," who spies on the Yellow Man and his interactions with Lucy. Battling Burrows's underlings also serve as spies who work to regulate the Asian immigrant's behavior by informing Battling of his daughter's doings outside the home. The Yellow Man is thus presented as one of many immigrants whose behavior must remain proper by dominant standards of what is considered acceptable, lest they be punished. Once Burrows learns of his daughter's location, his "parental rights" take over as he sets out to teach the girl and the Yellow Man about the racial transgres-sions of, as Burrows proclaims, "[a] Chink after his kid!" After pummelling his opponent in the ring, Burrows rushes over to the shop, destroys the room, rips the robes off Lucy's body, and drags her back to his house where he gives her the worst beating of her life. In sheer terror, Lucy hides herself inside a closet and we watch her utter fear close up as she tears at her hair and spins madly about looking for a way out.

This harrowing scene, often recognized as a symbolic rape of the child, is infamous for its brutality, for audiences watch through Lucy's eyes as her father smashes through the closet door with an axe. He drags her out of the closet, throws her on the bed, and violently whips the girl to death and, as she dies, "... she gives her last little smile to the world that has been so unkind." Arriving too late to save her, the Yellow Man seeks vengeance on Battling Burrows. In a stand-off between the two, the Yellow Man shoots Burrows dead and escapes with Lucy's body. He flees to his apartment where he sets the body of his beloved atop the bed and worships in front of an image of the Buddha and burning incense. He then commits suicide by plunging a dagger into his body as audiences are brought back to the image of the temple, the final ringing of the temple bells sounding in the distance.

In her essay, "Artful Racism, Artful Rape," Julia Lesage offers an insightful feminist reading of Griffith's film to illuminate the two types of masculinities presented in the form of the Yellow Man and Battling Burrows, the peaceful gentle tragic hero and the violent aggressive "grotesque Other from the lower classes."[7] Lesage argues that such opposing roles reflect Griffith's "unconscious, artistic insights about the problems of the nuclear family under capitalism," where a man can be either "socially successful and conventionally masculine, or he can cultivate his sensitivity and imaginative capacity and live as an outsider."[8] Juxtaposing the effeminate clothing and mannerisms of the Yellow Man against the cocksure stance of Burrows who nearly bulges out of his clothing, Lesage acknowledges the racist constructions of Asian men as childlike, mysterious, and womanly. Yet at the same time she subsumes the reading of the racialization of the Yellow Man in favor of a social commentary and psychoanalysis of masculinity, its excesses, and its limitations.

In Lesage's reading, the Yellow Man functions as a kind of dreamy romantic and a stand in for the director himself perceived as artist and rebel. The Yellow Man as romantic hero is to be seen as a "poetic, peaceful Buddhist lover of beauty" whose portrait as an artist is painted in stark relief against the brutishness of Battling Burrows. Lesage reads the Yellow Man as "sensitive outsider" who "never lives out the fulfillment of his dream," and whose passive masculinity functions as an alternative to the hyperaggressive masculinity of Battling Burrows.[9] While Lesage's critical reading of the hyper- and hypo-masculinity functioning in Griffith's work provides a complex approach that draws together feminist, Marxist, and psychoanalytic theory, such a reading leaves underdeveloped the subject of race, the racialization of the Yellow Man, and their connection to Buddhism that figures so prominently in the film.

In as much as *Broken Blossoms* might be interpreted as an allegory of the ravages of capitalism and its troubling constructions of masculinity in Western culture, I suggest that it also be read as a cautionary tale that introduces Buddhism as an exotic other whose potency diminishes upon arrival in the West. As a metaphor of Asian immigration as one form of border crossing and anti-miscegenation as another, *Broken Blossoms* deploys Buddhism as a sign of difference that is incompatible with a white Christian nation, despite its initial introduction of Buddhism as a gentle, peaceful religion that can tame the savage West. According to this logic, *Broken Blossoms* reveals its placement in a larger national anti-Asian discourse where Buddhism and the Buddhist monk serves as a stand in for racial difference and threat to Euro-American investments in the white nation.

In the Yellow Man, audiences encounter a feminized Asian masculinity that is impotent outside of its Asian borders. The Yellow Man also plays into an American racial imaginary where the other comes in the form of a gentle, peaceful, and maternal surrogate father who may sexually desire the young Lucy but, in the end, is unable to seal the deal as it were and obtain the object of his fancy. Susan Koshy's analysis of *Broken Blossoms* reveals the troublesome racial politics of the film and ambivalent reception as either a racial apology or a reiteration of anti-miscegenation. While one might be inclined to imagine a more race-positive message in this romantic tragedy between an Asian man and a white girl, Koshy argues instead that, "*Broken Blossoms* needs to be read alongside Birth [of a Nation] as productive of an American racial imaginary that aestheticizes the injunction against miscegenation by paradoxically offering interracial romance as a solution to racial difference while demonstrating the impossibility of such romance."[10] Koshy thus claims that the categories of gender, race [and religion] cannot be so easily disentangled as separate categories of analysis which, when approached with an eye toward their intersections, reveal the ways that Buddhism is both gendered *and* raced in U.S. films like *Broken Blossoms*.

In her essay, "The Oriental Monk in American Popular Culture," Jane Iwamura argues that the racialized, feminized Yellow Man fits squarely in the tradition of Orientalism in that he represents all that the West is not.[11] In her study of the history of the representation of the icon of the Oriental Monk, the Yellow Man is the first in the filmic genealogy of the icon that Iwamura traces from the early 1900s through the present. Thus, the Yellow Man represents an alternate spirituality and sexuality (asexual), alternative gender traits (femininity and passivity), the "last of his kind," and later serves as a father figure for profligate sons who are then transformed through this surrogate relationship.[12] Iwamura's reading suggests that the Yellow Man reflects the superficially positive racialized characteristics that come from a Western preoccupation with itself more than anything putatively Asian which is of course a classic critique of Orientalism. Iwamura encourages us to see the development of the Oriental Monk and the Yellow Man in terms of the racialized characteristics of homogeneity. She argues:

> Racialization (more correctly, "orientalization") serves to blunt the distinctiveness of particular persons and figures. Indeed, recognition of any Eastern spiritual guide (real or fictional) is predicated on their conformity to general features paradigmatically encapsulated in the icon of the Oriental Monk: his spiritual commitment, his calm demeanor, his Asian face, and oftentimes his manner of dress.[13]

Iwamura argues persuasively that the Yellow Man is indeed a product of the Western fascination with the East for its own edification, but in many ways her reading of the Yellow Man as a precursor to the model minority myth surrounding Asian Americans rests on a more generous reading of the Yellow Man as a gentle weak figure that I am willing to give. She reads the Yellow Man as a gentle monk whose love of Lucy is pure and innocent. As such, the Yellow Man as good, gentle Asian functions as a foil to the brutish, lower-class men and a figure of disciplinary representation for the immigrant Chinese. Griffith's tale also holds up the vague threat that "If the Christianized West is unable to care for its children, the noble Buddhist East will."[14] The Yellow Man's Buddhism is thus seen as a kind of religious cultural salve in Iwamura's reading of *Broken Blossoms*, although it is worth noting that the Buddhism of the Yellow Man is rendered impotent once it reaches Western borders.

Griffith's Buddhism cannot solve the social ills that condemn the Limehouse denizens to their misery; despite his most noble efforts, the Buddhist priest's missionizing fails beyond its borders. The trope of the Buddhist monk as signifier of cultural and racial differences rather than an icon of an authentic Buddhist monastic is informed by the historical constructions of race and identity and has affected popular constructions of Buddhism and Asians as otherworldly, perpetually foreign, and at times transgressive. The Buddhism of the Yellow Man thus remains inextricable from his racialized difference.

Lost Horizon

In Frank Capra's 1937 *Lost Horizon* tale of a Himalayan utopia, an American swindler, a fussy paleontologist, a British diplomat, his younger brother, and a sickly American prostitute flee China via airplane when it comes under siege by natives. Midway through their flight, the group suddenly realizes that they have veered off-course and rather than heading toward Shanghai to safety, they are flying higher into the mountainous regions of Tibet. When the British diplomat, Robert Conway, knocks on the door to the pilot's deck, he is greeted by a suspicious Asian pilot wielding a gun. He returns to the group far calmer than his travel companions who have already started panicking and imagining their demise. When the plane suddenly lands in an arid plain at the foot of the mountains, a group of natives, "scantily attired, but wearing bayonets" rushes the plane to refuel it as the passengers are kept inside.[15] As quickly as the plane lands, it takes off once again with all its passengers intact for the long voyage as the altitude gauge reaches 10,000 feet.

Throughout the journey, audiences are introduced to the cast of characters—Robert Conway, a natural leader who continues to remain unusually calm during this perilous trip, and his younger brother George, who both admires and envies his brother's position but is far more prone to panic and suspicion. Paleontologist Alexander P. Lovett, American Henry Barnard, and the sickly prostitute Gloria Stone comprise the remaining passengers stuck in the cramped cabin of the prop plane. The plane crash-lands at its destination in the snowy peaks of Tibet, the pilot is killed upon impact, and a party of Tibetans miraculously saves the passengers.

Chang, a Chinese lama from Shangri-La who, unbeknownst to the passengers, has been dispatched to bring them to safety, leads the rescue party. Chang escorts the group as they make the perilous journey through the windy mountain passes until they reach a portal through the mountains that opens onto the beautiful lush and sunny Valley of the Blue Moon in Shangri-La. Amidst this stunning warm landscape, Conway soon learns that he has been sent for by the high lama of Shangri-La as the next heir and guide of this magical land. He quickly falls in love with a beautiful young European woman named Sondra and easily falls into the rhythms of this utopia with little interest in escape. Were it not for the dread and alarm of his younger brother George who only seeks escape from this magical land, Conway would have happily remained in Shangri-La and taken over the reigns from the high lama Father Perrault (a Belgian Catholic priest) who created Shangri-La some 200 years prior. However, succumbing to his brotherly responsibility, Conway accompanies his brother and his brother's new paramour Maria (a Russian inhabitant of Shangri-La) for home. Upon their escape, however, Maria suddenly transforms from a beautiful young woman into the elderly woman that she truly is and George plummets to his death. The magic of Shangri-La that keeps its inhabitants eternally youthful has worn off on the young woman who has left its borders; George dies in the Himalayas; and Conway spends months trying to return to Shangri-La, a paradise lost and found again.

Lost Horizon opened in 1937 to American audiences post World War I and the stock market crash with the following prologue appearing on the pages of a book on the silver screen:

> In these days of wars, and rumors of wars—haven't you ever dreamed of a place where there was peace and security, where living was not a struggle, but a lasting delight?

> Of course you have. So has every man since Time began. Always the same dream. Sometimes he calls it Utopia—sometimes the Fountain of Youth—sometimes merely "that little chicken farm."

Based on James Hilton's 1933 novel of the same name, Capra introduces a utopic vision of otherness and escape located high in the formidable Himalayas atop the Valley of the Blue Moon. Like the gentle Buddhism of the Yellow Man before his arrival in London in *Broken Blossoms*, Shangri-La boasts a religion of peace with the requisite modicum of mystery that shrouded most images of Tibet at the time. *Lost Horizon* offers a tale of reverse migration and a pilgrimage of sorts where Robert Conway, a career diplomat and Britain's new foreign secretary, discovers that he is set to inherit the mantle of Shangri-La upon the death of its current benign ruler through a mysteriously hatched plan by Belgian priest Father Perrault, the Buddhist lama Chang, and the young white woman Sondra. Sondra, who was raised in Shangri-La, has read Conway's public writings and fallen in love with him prior to their meeting. It was her efforts that led to Conway's dispatch to Shangri-La. In this imaginative dreamscape of lasting delight tucked away in the highest reaches of the mountains of Tibet, Conway discovers a place that appeals to the dreamer and pacifist he is at heart, despite all the high honors he has garnered in the British Foreign Service. Shangri-La is ruled benevolently with a gentle hand according to a rule of brotherly love by Father Perrault who is on the verge of dying. We learn midway through the film that Conway was hijacked and brought to Shangri-La in order to "ensure that [the] community will continue to thrive" upon the priest's passing.

The staging of this utopic vision as a tonic and salve to the destruction and devastation of war and economic catastrophe in the near impossible to reach Himalayas rests on a construction of Tibet and its Buddhism as a spiritual locale of difference. In this way it comfortably situates itself in the lineage of Orientalist fantasies of far-away places critiqued by Edward Said. Shangri-La, like the Orient itself, is but a "European invention—a place of romance, exotic beings, haunting memories and landscapes" that ideologically reflects the West more than it does its presumed subject.[16] Surrounded by near impenetrable mountain passes, Shangri-La represents the polar opposite of warfare, cultural destruction, and the near apocalyptic fall of the Western world that Father Perrault foresees will decimate Western culture. Surely, the romantic pristine beauty of this Shangri-La serves as fantastical myth that provides a psychological balm for audiences to imagine after World War I and the stock market crash.

As a system of co-citations where scholars build upon a lineage of knowledge regarding the Orient and its difference, Orientalism has far more to do with the geopolitical production of *ideas* about the other that are then invoked as a justification for Western colonial presence in such far-away places. Hence Shangri-La, like many constructed places located in "the Orient," is described as a mysterious land inhabited by guileless children who prescribe to a religious world view of gentleness who are, nonetheless, in need of soft rule, which of course responds to the representations of the other in Asia that were used to justify colonial presence during this same time period. Thus, the myth of Shangri-La takes its place among many a romantic imagining of the Orient that provides a foil to cataclysmic war, capitalistic greed, and brutality, and simultaneously bolsters presumptions of Western superiority. This image of Western wisdom and authority is embodied in the role of Father Perrault as a benevolently-ruling paternal figure and Conway as the worthy son set to inherit the throne of this Oriental colonial paradise. As a British diplomat, Conway's position also reflected the extensive rule of the British Empire, which by the 1920s had already annexed India, Hong Kong, Singapore, Burma, and neighboring countries in Asia and ruled over approximately one-fifth of the world's population. Thus, images of Asia and its inhabitants were often characterized in terms of childlike natives in need of the political and economic support of the benevolent patriarchal European colonizer.

Lost Horizon also opened in the larger geopolitical context of fascism just after the 1936 invasion of Ethiopia by Mussolini and the remilitarization of the Rhineland by Hitler. The break out of the Spanish Civil War in 1936 and the rise of general and dictator Franco also marked this tumultuous global era. On the domestic front, the film opened as Americans struggled through the Depression years and the Great Recession of 1937. Surely, *Lost Horizon's* message of escape, utopia, peacefulness, and kindness offered succor to a beleaguered U.S. audience.

Like the Buddhism projected through the image of the Buddhist priest at the outset of *Broken Blossoms*, the Buddhism projected in Capra's film appears as a kind of amalgam of the Golden Rule and Buddhist teachings of the middle way between extremes. Religion appears as a guiding influence that offers Shangri-La's inhabitants lessons in the ethics of moderation that, according to the Buddha, hinders the development of desires that lead to disastrous consequences. Such Buddhism meshes quite nicely with the Christianity of brotherly love espoused by the Belgian Catholic priest to form a harmonious spiritual hybridization depicted as both accessible and intelligible to a Western audience. While there were many written examples of the magical and mysterious elements of Buddhism in the 1930s through the works of travellers such as the Jesuit missionary to Tibet, Ippolito Desideri who arrived in 1716, *Theosophists* like Madame Blavatsky, and scholars such as Charles Bell and L. Augustine Waddell (who served as consultant to the Younghusband Mission to Tibet in 1903–4), *Lost Horizon* pays curiously little attention to the animistic elements of Tibetan Buddhism that contained both Buddhist and indigenous shamanistic rituals. Instead, *Lost Horizon* proffered a religion based on moderation and kindness that was familiar to its primarily Christian audience in 1937. Thus, it is not Buddhism as a religion *per se* that provides the spirit of difference driving many Orientalist fantasies; it is instead the projection of a magical Tibet imbued with fantasies of immortality, economic stability, and health to hard pressed audiences.

Of course, the timelessness of Shangri-La is not unique to *Lost Horizon*. Instead, Shangri-La is one of many utopic fantasies surrounding Tibet narrated in Orientalist literary and filmic images that have captured the imagination of many a Western reader and filmgoer. In his book, *Prisoners of Shangri-La: Tibetan Buddhism and the West*, Donald S. Lopez, Jr. argues that the hermetically sealed hermit kingdom of Tibet intrigued early Catholic missionaries whose encounter and subsequent descriptions of Tibetan religion and culture set the stage for centuries worth of fascination with all things Tibetan up to the present day.[17] Lopez writes, "Tibet and Tibetan Buddhism have long been objects of Western fantasy. Since the earliest encounters of Venetian travelers and Catholic missionaries with Tibetan monks at the Mongol court, tales of the mysteries of their mountain land and the magic of their strange—yet strangely familiar—religion have had a peculiar hold on the Western imagination."[18] Shangri-La falls squarely into this tradition of describing the enigmatic yet intriguing qualities of Tibet and its Buddhism that must be, according to the logic of Orientalism, protected by European forces, albeit gentle ones in the form of Belgian priests and pacifist British diplomats.

The romance of Tibet, its Buddhism, and the need to protect it from both Western corruption and later Chinese imperialism, finds its cinematic origins in *Lost Horizon*. And like many Orientalist projects of co-citation, the "corporate institution for dealing with the Orient [and Tibet]," proliferated and found its apex in the Hollywood cinematic institution during the 1990s with films such as *Kundun* (1997) by Martin Scorsese which functions as a biopic of the Dalai Lama; *Seven Years in Tibet* (1997) based on the biography of Austrian Heinrich Harrer and directed by French filmmaker Jean-Jacque Annaud which focuses on Harrer's introduction of the young Dalai Lama to the modern world; and *Little Buddha* (1993) by Bernardo Bertolucci, which narrates the diasporic search for a Tibetan lama's reincarnation in Seattle, Washington.

The emergence of these late-twentieth century films about Tibet took place in the context of increasing fears of Chinese geopolitical and economic might. Tibet and Tibetan Buddhism were cast as spiritual caretakers of a land in grave danger of cultural and geographic destruction by the Chinese. Thus, the films are part and parcel of a larger Hollywood corporate institution that relied upon Buddhist texts, autobiographical works of Tibetan Buddhists and travellers to Tibet, and a long lineage of Orientalist writings about this other-worldly nation now in great need of Western protection against the Chinese. While Tibet served as a fantastic other that provided a psychological escape in the nineties for Western audiences, just as it had in the early decades of the century, it confirmed the belief that Tibet's fragile religion and culture were in need of Western intervention. Journalist Orville Schell's study of the virtual reality of Tibet in the media, particularly in film, reveals the early fasci-nation with Tibet as an isolated, ancient, forbidden, and mysterious landscape whose near impenetrability further underscored its difference.[19] As a place of magic and mystery, Tibet manifested itself in the collective imagination as a kind of blank white map that practically invited Western occupation and the race for entry by foreigners such as Alexandra David-Neel, the first European woman to gain access to Lhasa through disguise and subterfuge.[20] According to Schell:

> Tibetan fantasies rooted themselves in almost every form of popular entertainment: in magazines, newspapers, books, comics, children's stories, stage productions, and finally on the screen. When James Hilton's 1933 novel, *Lost Horizon*, was released as a film in 1937, it was the apotheosis of Tibet as fantasy realm. With it, the notion of that land as the paradisiacal Shangri-La entered both the imagination and the vocabulary of Western popular culture, becoming one of the most powerful utopian metaphors of our time. Tibet had now become the last place on earth still abounding in true "mysteries," including lamas who could fly, magicians who could stop rain, oracles who could foretell the future, and yetis, a probably imaginary race of apelike half-human creatures said to inhabit the snowy wastes of the Himalayas and the Tibetan Plateau. If Buddhists saw the world as illusory and deemphasized the difference between dreams and waking consciousness, Westerners blurred the distinction between what Tibet actually was and how they imagined it, or wanted it to be, so that it, too, became the dreamiest of realities. And so, like a split image in the viewfinder of a reflex camera, Tibet developed a divided persona in the public mind of the West. On the one hand, it retained all its associations of being a paradisiacal Shangri-La. On the other, after China's occupation in the 1950s, it also came to be viewed as a victimized land and culture laid waste by an invading colonizing power.[21]

Tibet and its religion thus comingle in the Western psyche as a fount of mysterious wisdom that serves as a counterbalance to a perceived kind of spiritual drought brought about by disillusion with available Western religions and, because of its charismatic pull and its dire straits *vis-à-vis* China required Western protection. This protectionism served to bolster the image of Tibet and Buddhism as a religion on the brink of destruction whose inhabitants contained a knowledge and wisdom that needed saving by the West. Such fantasies of Tibet, according to Schell, belied the impoverished conditions of Tibet, as well as its own history of violence and political intrigue. Instead, Tibet became the opposite of all things the West was not, but with a twist—in order to uphold the romantic fantasy that Tibet offered, it required the support of a paternal savior—the West. Thus, *Lost Horizon*, while presenting the wonders of the Tibetan culture in the high Himalayas, also makes specific note of areas in need of Western intervention in Shangri-La, namely education, modern plumbing, and the guiding influence of European masters.

What makes Shangri-La such a captivating place is not just its supernatural ability to keep its inhabitants young, but also its service as a kind of archive collecting and preserving all the artifacts of Western high culture. While the natives of Shangri-La are all happy workers with little want, Father Perrault has been busy collecting all the vestiges of literary treasure, art, and music from the Western world and has magically transported these pieces to Shangri-La for safekeeping against what he foresees as an orgiastic, frenzied and destructive end for the West. In a private interview with Conway, Father Perrault shares his salvific vision of the West within the secluded mountain peaks of Tibet as follows:

HIGH LAMA: We need men like you here, to be sure that our community will continue to thrive. In return for which, Shangri-La has much to give you. You are still, by the world's standards, a youngish man. Yet in the normal course of existence, you can expect twenty or thirty years of gradually diminishing activity. Here, however, in Shangri-La, by our standards your life has just begun, and may go on and on.

Figure 2.3 Lost Horizon. *Robert Conway meets Father Perrault for the first time*

CONWAY: But to be candid, Father, a prolonged future doesn't excite me. It would have to have a point. I've sometimes doubted whether life itself has any. And if that is so, then long life must be even more pointless. No, I'd need a much more definite reason for going on and on.

HIGH LAMA: We have reason. It is the entire meaning and purpose of Shangri-La. It came to me in a vision, long, long, ago. I saw all the nations strengthening, not in wisdom, but in the vulgar passions and the will to destroy. I saw their machine power multiply until a single weaponed man might match a whole army. I foresaw a time when man, exulting in the technique of murder, would rage so hotly over the world that every book, every treasure, would be doomed to destruction. This vision was so vivid and so moving that I determined to gather together all the things of beauty and culture that I could and preserve them here against the doom toward which the world is rushing.

Father Perrault then reveals his vision of the future following the devastation of the Western world through war:

(pause) Look at the world today! Is there anything more pitiful? What madness there is, what blindness, what unintelligent leadership! A scurrying mass of bewildered humanity crashing headlong against each other, propelled by an orgy of greed and brutality. The time must come, my friend, when this orgy will spend itself, when brutality and the lust for power must perish by its own sword. Against that time is why I avoided death and am here, and why you were brought here. For when that day comes, the world must begin to look for a new life. And it is our hope that they may find it here. For here we shall be with their books and their music and a way of life based on one simple rule: Be Kind.

(pause) When that day comes, it is our hope that the brotherly love of Shangri-La will spread throughout the world.

(pause) Yes, my son, when the strong have devoured each other, the Christian ethic may at last be fulfilled, and the meek shall inherit the earth.[22]

In this dramatic revelation of the purpose behind Conway's presence in Shangri-La, Father Perrault indicates that Shangri-La will protect the West against its own aggression by serving as a treasure trove of the best of Western culture. In return for his benign rule, Conway will be gifted with the mysterious powers Shangri-La has to offer—long life, peace, and the opportunity to live in this beautiful magical paradise with Sondra, the young woman who saw in his writing a man who longed for something different and a "man whose life was empty." Sondra is the main reason for Conway's forced invitation to Tibet and both she and Conway will rule over the new world order foreseen by the Belgian priest. Because of his romantic personality and desire for a world outside of diplomacy and warfare, Conway falls easily into Shangri-La's sway and comes to accept his new role with little resistance.

Conway soon receives the passing of the torch upon the High Lama's death. Prior to his passing, Father Perrault summons Conway into his room to receive his final destiny. The high lama explains, "... I am placing in your hands the future and destiny of Shangri-La. For I am going to die ... I knew my work was done when I first set eyes on you." The lama then explains that he knew that Conway was the rightful heir and states:

> I have waited for you, my son, for a very long time. I have sat in this room and seen the faces of newcomers. I have looked into their eyes and heard their voices—always in hope that I might find you. My friend, it is not an arduous task that I bequeath, for our order knows only silken bonds. To be gentle and patient, to care for the riches of the mind, to preside in wisdom, while the storm rages without.

The lama reveals that Conway is indeed the chosen one and predicts:

> You, my son, will live through the storm. You will preserve the fragrance of our history, and add to it a touch of your own mind. Beyond that, my vision weakens ... But I see in the great distance a new world starting in the ruins—stirring clumsily—but in hopefulness, seeking its vast and legendary treasures. And they will all be here, my son, hidden behind the mountains in the Valley of the Blue Moon, preserved as if by a miracle.

At this final revelatory prediction, the High Lama slowly passes away as the curtains on the windows make a faint flutter. Conway is now the true heir. Thus, the Shangri-La of mystery and magic reveals itself to be an ideal European safe hold for all the best of its culture and civilization, a veritable spiritual colony of peaceful inhabitants under the benign colonial rule of white Europeans.

As noted by the High Lama, Conway will have little trouble ruling over the land, especially since its inhabitants live according to a Buddhist ethic of the middle way between extremes. The religion of Shangri-La, while not explicitly named as Buddhism, is described as a tradition of moderation. Chang, one of the Buddhist lamas who serves as host to the hijacked crew, explains the religion to Conway as follows:

To put it simply, I should say that our general belief was in moderation. We preach the virtue of avoiding excesses of kind every, even including—the excess of virtue itself....

We find, in the Valley, it makes for better happiness among the natives. We rule with moderate strictness and in return we are satisfied with moderate obedience. As a result, our people are moderately honest and moderately chaste and somewhat more than moderately happy.

Buddhism in Shangri-La thus falls neatly within what the Buddha himself referred to as the middle way between opposites. Through such benevolent rule and religious moderation, Chang further notes that there is no need for any kind of policing in Shangri-La. He explains:

We have no crime here. What makes a criminal? Lack, usually. Avariciousness, envy, the desire to possess something owned by another. There can be no crime where there is a sufficiency of everything.

In a humorous man-to-man exchange, Conway asks, "You have no disputes over women?"

"Only very rarely. You see, it would not be considered good manners to take a woman that another man wanted," Chang replies, rather agreeably.

"Suppose somebody wanted her so badly that he didn't give a hang it if was good manners or not?" Conway wonders.

"Well, in that event," Change answers, "it would be good manners on the part of the other man to let him have her ... You'd be surprised, my dear Conway, how a little courtesy all around helps to smooth out the most complicated problems." The power of Shangri-La thus rests in its ability to afford its inhabitants a peace and comradery such that even delicate matters of the heart are solved amiably and courteously to keep the harmony.

Shangri-La as both heavenly realm of mysteries and magic where no one grows sick or dies contains within its snow-buffered walls a utopic vision of otherness that appealed to many audiences who, like Conway, wish for something more in their lives. It is because Shangri-La is so far away that it keeps its potency, for if it was easily accessible it would lose its mystique and ability to transform all those who enter its formidable borders. *Lost Horizon* presents a luscious Hollywood rendition of paradise fictionally located in the Himalayas, replete with talking animals and happy inhabitants toiling away making candles, tending horses, and crafting pots. In this idyllic landscape, life appears simple and free from the threat of war and fear of illness and poverty. Yet what lies beneath this veneer of the spiritual and otherworldly is a Buddhist landscape hidden from the rugged snowy terrain that functions as an ideal colony with a European presence that educates, modernizes, and ultimately controls the native inhabitants who appear docile and childlike.

The great civilizing project of Orientalism is most clearly noted in a scene where Sondra leads the village children in a Christian lullaby as part of their daily school routine. Conway pursues Sondra throughout Shangri-La and finally comes upon her as she conducts the children's choir and disciplines them with the benign rule of her conductor's stick. When Conway takes over to conduct the children so Sondra can make plans to spend the afternoon with him, the children laugh and giggle at Conway's inability to lead. Letting his desire for Sondra get the better of him, Conway quickly dismisses the children from their choir practice and the children suddenly cheer in delight, run down en masse to the lake, strip off their clothing, and jump naked into the water, thus reverting to their primitive, untamed ways. It is through Sondra's guidance and discipline through the Christian lullaby that the children are molded into model colonized citizens, yet as soon as the conductor's stick or the disciplining rod is taken away, the natives run wild and free.

Much like the colonial logic that shapes Orientalism, Shangri-La's children must be protected and educated by the European colonizers for their own betterment. It is worth noting that the inheritance of power in Shangri-La needed to remain within the hands of the white European male and certainly could not be trusted to the indigenous Buddhists like Chang whose robes, carriage, and gait are remarkably similar to those of the Yellow Man. Akin to the failed Buddhist priest in Griffith's *Broken Blossoms,* Chang also embodies many negative characteristics associated with Asian men in the U.S.—inscrutable, untrustworthy, and mildly threatening. Over a lavish dinner, the guests inquire into their safe passage out of Shangri-La, but they receive only veiled responses from Chang to which Lovett remarks, "That's what I mean—mysterious. Mr. Conway, I don't like that man. He's too vague."

In other words, Chang as host is an inscrutable Asian whose motives are questionable and whose trustworthiness is suspect. Returning to his room in his new quarters, Lovett writes in his journal the following reflections about Shangri-La—"This place is too mysterious!"

Yet perhaps what is most mysterious about Shangri-La lies in its ability to transform its new guests brought from Baskul, China via the modern airplane. While the native Tibetans are disciplined through the gently civilizing mission of Father Perrault, Shangri-La also wields its powers of change over the guests by softening their sharp edges and making them more socially acceptable along traditional gender lines. Lovett, teasingly referred to by Barnard as "Lovey" and "Toots," reflects stereotypical feminized attributes such as excessive fussiness, uptightness, a high-pitched girlish voice, and an inability to let loose in this new wonderland. When he first arrives in Shangri-La, all he can do is think about ways to escape, yet he slowly comes to find that he has an important role to play—teaching the village children in school. We are led to believe that this remarkable change of heart takes place after Lovett has too much to drink with the native women who flirt with him and call him "Lovey."

Eventually, he warms to his nickname and begins to flirt with some of the women of Shangri-La. To one of his native admirers he teases with a satisfied grin, "Oh, you call me Lovey, eh? Look at those eyes. There's the devil in those eyes!" Shangri-La has worked its magic by making Lovett more of an "acceptable" man who now expresses sexual desire for women and a masculinity we have yet to see.

When he returns to his room he is seen jauntily writing in his journal, "Feel so good, I could sow a wild oat." Lovett then catches his reflection in the mirror, smirks to himself and then writes "or two." His transformation could not be more obvious, for when he first arrived at Shangri-La he was afraid of his own shadow and was seen jumping at his own reflection in the very same mirror. Now, he is ready to sow his wild oats and begin enjoying himself with drink and with the native girls.

The next time we see Lovett, he shares the wonders of Shangri-La with Chang and claims that he "never for a moment believed that kidnapping story." As a gesture of appreciation for all that Shangri-La has offered him, Lovett declares that he would like to organize classes for the young children in the valley and teach them "something practical" like geology. Lovett has no interest in leaving this magical place and intends to make it home.

Similarly, Henry Barnard, the swindler aboard the ill-fated plane, has transformed from a con artist who had made off with other people's investments during the stock market crash into a benevolent aid worker. Barnard no longer hatches schemes to smuggle gold out of the Valley of the Blue Moon. Instead, during his residence in Shangri-La, he decides that he will create a modern plumbing system in the valley so that the residents no longer have to go to the well for water. Just as the utopic land has done for the men, Shangri-La also transforms the brash white woman Gloria. Prior to her arrival, Gloria was a bleached blond, mouthy, crass woman who scorned all the men on the plane. Condemned to death by her doctor for an unnamed illness, Gloria finds herself miraculously healed upon arrival in Shangri-La. Her convalescence also brings about a freshness in her appearance and she no longer wears the excessive make up she did when she first arrived. She is rendered docile, demure, and worthy of male attention which she readily receives from Barnard, who is the first to point out her natural beauty. Gloria soon becomes the "ideal" woman who allows her man to make decisions for her. When George suddenly rushes into the room to share the news of his escape plans, he is shocked to find that neither Barnard nor Gloria have any intention of leaving the place. In fact, when George asks Gloria join in the escape, Barnard answers for her and says, "Oh, no you don't want to go yet, honey. She'll stick around too." He then looks at Gloria and says, "Is that right?"

"If you want me to!" the now domesticated Gloria beams, and Barnard then promises to take care of her.

Thus, the three figures who are deemed morally suspect—Lovett for his feminine characteristics, Barnard for his reputation as a crook, and Gloria for her outspoken independence—are all tamed by Shangri-La. Not only does this beautiful land offer peace, bounty, prosperity, and the fountain of youth, it also has the power to transform those who transgress normative social codes of the time.

The only two characters who refuse Shangri-La's charms are George and Maria, a young woman brought up in the lamasery who claims that all of Chang's stories of the mysteries of Shangri-La are false. Maria's beauty captures the attention of George who promises to take her away from Shangri-La and the two conspire to hire porters, gather food, and escape. Despite the charms of Shangri-La, neither Maria nor George are taken with its mysteries; instead, they both aid each other in planning their escape.

While Maria and George remain staunchly skeptical of Shangri-La's powers of immortality and good health, Conway finds himself naturally drawn to this magical land and listens with wonder as Chang fills him in about Maria's story of how she was rescued and brought to Shangri-La decades earlier and suddenly asks, "Chang, how old are you?"

"Age is a limit we impose upon ourselves," the mysterious monk replies. "You know, each time you Westerners celebrate your birthday, you build another fence around your mind."

Warned of the threat of leaving Shangri-La, George and Maria persist and serve as the cautionary tale of what happens when one transgresses the boundaries of the Himalayan paradise, for once they embark on the dangerous journey out of Shangri-La they meet with sudden death—Maria reverts to her natural age before George's eyes and dies an old woman on the snowy peaks. George, driven mad by this discovery, falls to his death after Conway agrees to accompany them out of Shangri-La. Maria's instantaneous aging serves as proof that Shangri-La is in fact a magical land and Conway soon fights to return to his rightful place as heir apparent. The film concludes with a final image of Conway at the narrow passageway that leads back to his true home. He has eluded the European aids dispatched to bring him back to London, survived six attempts over the Tibetan mountain passes, escaped guards, learned to fly a plane, stole, and finally after ten months of trying, the heir has returned to usher in a new dawn.

As noted above, *Lost Horizon* set the stage for an American fascination with Tibetan Buddhism and the nation of Tibet, yet the popular filmic images of Tibet that reached their apex in the 1990s following the Dalai Lama's 1989 Nobel Peace Prize also rested on the Orientalist constructions of Tibetan difference that began with the works of early missionaries to Tibet in the late 1700s as well as the written works of nineteenth- and twentieth-century scholars, Theosophists, and travellers, such as Alexandra David-Neel. This popularized image of Tibet as a salvific and timeless land of wisdom survives up to the present day in many Western discourses, but such images have not been met without resistance by the growing number of filmmakers in the Tibetan diasporic community, as well as by non-Tibetans intent on dispelling some of the myths of its difference.

Demythologizing Buddhism through film

Two films directed by the Bhutanese incarnate lama Khyentse Norbu demonstrate the stark contrast between the Western fascination with the romantic images of Tibet and the Buddhists themselves who do not fit the mold of exotic founts of timeless wisdom. Thus, Norbu's 2000 film, *The Cup*, offers the tale of young Tibetan monks in exile in a Buddhist monastery in India who long not for *nirvana*, but for an opportunity to watch the World Cup. The tale involves a humorous process of obtaining the appropriate amount of funds from the monks in order to rent the TV and antennae necessary for the viewing. Ronald S. Green's study of *The Cup* notes that this is a story of Tibetan Buddhism's difficult struggle in exile in India and that perhaps the Tibetan Buddhist monk's life is not as exotic as we might have thought. Instead, Green writes, "we may feel the young monks in *The Cup* should be more devoted to Buddhist training."[23] Khyentse Norbu's 2003 *Travellers and Magicians* critiques the timelessness associated with Tibetan Buddhism by offering the story of Dondhup, a frustrated petty official sent to a rural village in Bhutan, who wishes nothing more than to escape the lush Shangri-La like Bhutanese landscape in order to fulfill his American dream as an apple picker.

The film contains within it a tale of a young man Tashi who, rather than studying diligently at the local religious school, decides to pursue his desire for women and an ordinary life. His desires take him to a dream-like land where he encounters an old woodcutter and his beautiful young wife with whom Tashi has an affair and becomes entangled in a plot to murder the husband. After poisoning the husband with a potion, Tashi suddenly comes to regret his actions and flees the woods, and much to his relief, he awakens and learns the folly of his dream.

Like Tashi, Dondhup comes to question his decision to leave Bhutan in pursuit of his apple-picking dream and comes to see the beauty of Bhutan through his growing infatuation with the daughter of a local paper maker. While one might expect more mysterious and magical films from an incarnate lama of the Tibetan Buddhist tradition, Norbu removes the image of Tibetan Buddhism from its timeless captivity and brings it into the modern present by offering an image of an everyday Buddhism replete with ordinary monks wanting more than Buddhism has to offer, namely the World Cup and a chance to the see the world outside.

The 2005 independent film *Dreaming Lhasa* by directors Ritu Sarin and Tenzin Sonam also serves as a foil to the more Orientalist constructions of Tibet in films like *Lost Horizon, Little Buddha, Kundun,* and *Seven Years in Tibet.* Filmed in the Tibetan language, *Dreaming Lhasa* introduces the complex realities of Tibetan independence and the Tibetan diaspora through Karma, a young Tibetan American woman who comes to India on a grant to produce a documentary about Tibetan monks and nuns who were imprisoned and beaten by Chinese guards while in Lhasa. Karma's work as a documentary filmmaker introduces her to the former monk, Dondhup, who has come to Dharamsala, India in search of a man named Loga as per his dying mother's request. Karma represents the reality of many diasporic Tibetans who have grown up in exile without a clear connection to Tibet outside of their ethnic heritage. Thus, Karma's journey to Dharamsala is based both on a desire to record the stories of the monks and nuns and is also an opportunity to explore her identity as a Tibetan raised in the United States. Her relationship with Dondhup develops as a gentle romance but reflects more of her growing sense of ease with her identity as a Tibetan. While she has a daughter with a non-Tibetan in New York, Karma's affections for the former monk allow her to overcome the anxiety of authenticity when she is not sure if she is Tibetan and if she will actually be accepted by the larger Tibetan community whether in Tibet or in exile.

Karma's role as documentarian also introduces the story of a young disillusioned Tibetan exile named Jigme who grew up in Dharamsala as a displaced member of the Tibetan community in exile in India. Jigme soon falls for Karma and, despite her unrequited love, his work with the filmmaker ignites his political investment in the Tibetan Independence movement.

While *Dreaming Lhasa* is more concerned with explorations of an imaginary homeland for Karma and Jigme and Dondhup's dreams of a free Tibet than with a narrative film about Buddhism, its lack of explicit attention to Tibetan Buddhist difference is what makes it such a powerful counterexample to other more Orientalist depictions of Tibet and its inhabitants as somehow otherworldly, more spiritual, and in dire need of saving by the West.

While there is tendency to presume that American audiences have now moved beyond the Orientalist versions of Buddhism made popular through the silver screen and that its legacy has waned, a look at more contemporary Buddhist films indicates otherwise. In the following chapter, I examine the fascination with Zen Buddhism in three American films, *The Big Lebowski* by the Coen brothers, *Ghost Dog* by Jim Jarmusch, and *Zen Noir* by independent filmmaker Marc Rosenbush. These films capitalize on the inherited images of Buddhism's otherness. Although the particular school of Buddhism differs, Zen Buddhism appealed for many of the same reasons that Western audiences hungered for the romantic and mysterious versions of Buddhism found in *Lost Horizon* and, to a lesser extent, *Broken Blossoms*. Zen's rhetoric of antinomianism, its appeal for oneness, the significance of the present moment, and its apparent disregard for capitalism and the ravages of modernity captivated audiences so much so that Zen became a well-known symbol of a cultural iconoclasm made popular by the Beat generation up until today. The romance of Buddhism thus continues to attract followers through filmic imaginings of its otherness that offers a new identity. As we shall see in the following chapter, the Buddhism of contemporary films no longer imagines a faraway Buddhism that cannot exist in an American context. Instead, the new generation of American-made Buddhist films make it possible to imagine oneself as a Buddhist monk (albeit a noncelibate one) struggling to make sense of a world gone awry.

3

Zen Appetites: Consuming Religion and Otherness through Film

The construction and imaging of Zen Buddhism for popular consumption in Asian and Western films occupies a well-worn place in the long lineage of Orientalist fantasies of distant geographies in time and space made popular in the U.S. through films like *Broken Blossoms* and *Lost Horizon*. Fetishized and commodified, Zen Buddhism's emphasis on nonduality, experiential insight, and its characterization by Chinese patriarch Bodhidharma as a "special transmission outside of words and letters," has provided much creative fodder for directors East and West. Whether projected as a palliative tonic for a mass-mediated, time-bound (meaning bigger, better, faster, more) U.S. American culture or an Edenic utopia in rapidly post-industrialized Asian nations, the global appetite for Zen exoticism has arguably gone viral. Much like *Broken Blossom*'s idealized Buddhism on the distant shores of China and *Lost Horizon*'s magical Tibetan Buddhism hermetically sealed in Shangri-La, more recent American-made Zen Buddhist films share a popular fascination with Buddhism's purported difference and, as I argue, contribute to the undue airspace and attention given to exotic Buddhism and an abstract unraced and ungendered (in other words, an unproblematic, overly simplified) kind of Buddhism put forth in popular culture and its mediated images. Such emphasis on Zen exotica further suppresses our ability to see a more complex, forthrightly lay-centered lived Buddhism. In this chapter, I analyze three American films in order to highlight the trajectory of a racialized Buddhism as it appears in more contemporary Western iterations heavily influenced by early Buddhist films in the U.S.

What makes Zen Buddhist films from the latter half of the twentieth century up until today distinctive is the relative ease with which Zen Buddhist practice and a Zen identity can be taken up to express an American iconoclasm and spirit of rebellion made popular during the countercultural movement. While Zen has attained a cultural chic and purchase in contemporary American culture, its mediation through films such as the Coen brothers' 1998 cult classic, *The Big Lebowski*, Jim Jarmusch's 1999 independent film, *Ghost Dog: The Way of the Samurai*, and Marc Rosenbush's 2005 comedy, *Zen Noir*, continues to capitalize on Orientalist notions of Buddhists as heroic if not timeless, illogical, antinomian figures whose Zen makes them savvy, iconoclastic arbiters of cool. That is, there is a spirit of Zen hipness that permeates these films as the main characters easily adopt Buddhist identities that appeal because of the cultural heterodoxy they embody.

"The Dude" of *The Big Lebowski* is an unemployed, middle-aged slacker who spends his nights in a bowling alley spouting out Zen-like aphorisms in a slow-paced drawl. The Dude has become an icon of a hip Zen Buddhist in the popular imagination who, in doing nothing, accomplishes everything. In *Ghost Dog*, the protagonist fashions himself in the image of a Samurai warrior, spending his days nearly invisible in Jersey City where he works as a contract killer for a decaying breed of Mafiosi. Leaving no trace of himself like many a good Zen Buddhist, Ghost Dog hybridizes Zen, the warrior codes of the Samurai from Japan, and contemporary hip hop culture to combat the alienation of African American men. His hipness derives from his ability to kill only out of loyalty to his retainer Louie, to sacrifice his own life out of his Samurai code of honor, and to befriend and transform the life of a young Haitian American girl through the gift of books in place of the sword.

The detective of *Zen Noir* manages to overcome his linear overly-rational thinking to embrace the oneness of Zen taught to him by an elderly Japanese Zen master who instructs him through unconventional means, such as pelting him with oranges so that he wakes up to the ultimate oneness of reality. Yet despite the trendiness and rebelliousness of Zen Buddhism that has charmed many an American filmgoer, such films are also implicated in a complex process of racialization that perpetuates the myth of Asians and Asian Americans as mystical and unintelligible characters, obscures the nonmeditative ordinary practices of Buddhists, and subtly elevates the Euro-American Zen practitioner over his or her Asian and Asian American counterparts. The slacker ease and humor of the Dude, the cool hipness of Ghost Dog, and the over rationalism turned to illogical wisdom of the detective appeal to audiences looking to borrow such Buddhist difference, and for freedom from rules in their own lives.

In the following chapter, I explore the elements of an abstract (abstracted from raced and gendered Buddhists) Zen Buddhism commodified for public consumption. This neo-Buddhism rests on an unspoken omission of certain forms of ordinary lay Buddhism that do not bolster the image of the exotic or the hip *un*chaste Buddhist monk. Instead, the popular Zen films that appeal to cultural iconoclasm are ones that rely on well-established models of Buddhist mysteriousness in the West discussed in the previous chapter that perpetuate the racial life of Buddhism.

The Big Lebowski

I dig the Dude; he's very authentic. He can be angry and upset, but he's comfortable in his skin. And in his inimitable way, he has grace. He exudes it in every relationship: an unexpected kindness, unmerited good will, giving someone a break when he doesn't deserve it, showing up even when he has a bad attitude just because it means so much to the rest of the team. Hugging it out instead of slugging it out.[1]

—Jeff Bridges

In January 2013, the actor Jeff Bridges, still affectionately referred to as "the Dude" (the quintessential Zen slacker in *The Big Lebowski*) appeared on The Daily Show with John Stewart to promote his book *The Dude and the Zen Master* co-written with Bernie Glassman.[2] What followed was a humorous and kinetic exhibition of the popular stereotype of the Zen master—the Buddhist of irreverent wit and mystery that holds pride of place in many Western images of Buddhism. During the interview, Stewart queries The Dude about what it means to be a Zen Master to which Bridges replies rather quizzically with his well-known smooth drawl, "I'll tell you how I know … and I am going to make you a Zen master now and perhaps you can do this during your moment of Zen. It's really simple, ready? Stay right where you are. Hah!" At this pretend magical moment of mind-to-mind transmission of Zen wisdom from master to disciple, Bridges nonsensically pulls a clown nose out of his pocket and places it atop Stewart's nose. Bridges thus proclaims, "Boom man. That's it. You're done. That's all it takes," and unwittingly reconfirms the public perception of Zen's otherness and irrationality. At this stage of the interview, Stewart's frustration becomes my own as we both want more clarity of meaning behind what it means to be a Zen master.[3] Surely it can't be so simple.

Stewart continues to ask about the meaning and purpose of Zen to which Bridges reveals, "By the way, in Buddhist circles the Dude is considered a Zen master." He then recounts the Dude's receipt of the Zen Master title by Roshi Bernie Glassman over dinner when the two met in person for the first time. Out of nowhere, Bridges explains, the world-renowned Zen master Glassman suddenly announces the uncanny similarity between the last name (Coen) of the directors of *The Big Lebowski* and the Japanese *koan* or mental puzzle used in Zen practice. Although the story elicits laughs from the audience, Stewart then delivers a most telling line when he acknowledges, "I gotta tell you. That's a pretty weak tea to go on." It is the frivolity, the free spiritedness, and lack of rootedness in any kind of practice, locale or even history that makes Bridges's Zen a weak tea. The verbal abstraction, the lack of clarity of meaning, the inability to remain rooted in his seat, and the cool vibe Bridges emits while on TV express a Zen -light that appeals to wider audiences because it seems to require so little to be a Zen Buddhist—all one seems to need is an appetite for the zany. Such an abstracted disembodied Zen, I argue, is one that invests in a commodified religion that contributes to the obscuration of the vitality of an ordinary lay Buddhism on the ground and also hides the very reality of a raced and gendered Buddhist pluralism.

Through *The Big Lebowski*, audiences are introduced to the Dude, a middle-aged, long-haired, unemployed white man who spends most of his time drinking White Russians and hanging out in a bowling alley with his two league partners, Vietnam veteran Walter (played by John Goodman) and dimwitted Donny (played by Steve Buscemi). As the film begins, the actor Sam Elliot narrates the story of the Dude as a tumbleweed rolls along on screen, carried gently through the streets of Los Angeles as it makes its way to the ocean only by the force of the wind. Like the ideal Taoist sage who goes with the flow and the Zen Buddhist who is open to all possibilities, the tumbleweed represents Bridges's character, the Dude, who is first seen wandering around the local Ralph's market dressed in rumpled Bermuda shorts, an open threadbare brown robe, and sunglasses in search of milk for his ubiquitous White Russian. When he returns to his filthy apartment, he is quickly attacked by two assailants who beat him and repeatedly plunge his face down the toilet demanding he produce the money that his wife owes to a fellow named Jackie Treehorn. In what turns out to be a case of mistaken identity, the Dude, surprisingly composed after his brutal beating, attempts to explain that there must be another Lebowski because he doesn't have that kind of money, doesn't have a wedding ring, and leaves the toilet seat up (a sure sign of his bachelorhood). After getting a good look around the shabby apartment, the two attackers realize their mistake and the Asian American assailant unzips his fly and proceeds to urinate all over the Dude's carpet. It is at this moment that the Dude truly bemoans this intrusion and, as he later explains the offense to his bowling partner Walter, he utters the famous quote, "Yeah man, it [the rug] really tied the room together."

Later, when he finally meets the millionaire Jeffrey Lebowski, the Dude explains that all he really wants to do is have his rug replaced. Following their meeting, the Dude grabs one of the Big Lebowski's carpets and heads home; however, he is soon entangled in a wild goose chase for the Big Lebowki's wayward young wife (played by Tara Reid) through the remainder of the film.

After a series of comical errors involving money drop-offs, encounters with various nihilist thugs, and finally the death of his bowling partner Donny, the Dude returns back to his ordinary life and can be found once again bowling and living life like a free, unburdened tumbleweed going with the flow, open to all experiences.

The film concludes with a dialogue between the Stranger, the cowboy who narrates the opening of the story, and the Dude. The Stranger sits at the bowling alley bar, orders a sarsaparilla and bids the Dude farewell and good luck in the bowling tournament:

> The Stranger: "Take it Easy Dude."
> The Dude: "Oh, yeah."
> The Stranger: "I know that you will."
> The Dude: "Yeah well, the Dude abides."
> The Stranger: "The Dude abides."
> "I don't know about you, but I take comfort in that. It's good knowin' he's out there. The Dude: Takin' her easy for all us sinners."

According to Bernie Glassman, the film's conclusion provides one of the most important Zen teachings as he likens the Dude to a *mensch*, a real human being. Bridges elaborates on this famous quote and explains, "And *The Dude abides*... True abiding is a spiritual gift that requires great mastery. The moral of the story, for me, is: be kind. Treat others as you want to be treated."[4] Be kind, treat others as you want to be treated—these are the very same descriptions of the central teachings of Buddhism found in both *Broken Blossoms* and *Lost Horizon* that reflects a distillation or simplification of the teachings to a creed that can be found in just about any religion and code of ethics. What makes the Dude a Zen Buddhist is not the teaching of kindness, but rather, an embodiment of the iconoclasm and mysteriousness associated with Zen Buddhists in popular culture that appeals to a wider American public.

In *The Dude and the Zen Master*, Bernie Glassman offers a Zen interpretation of another one of the Dude's most famous quotes in the film that audiences hear on the Dude's answering machine. Relaxing after another day of dashing about Los Angeles while trying to save his own life and the life of the Big Lebowski's wife, he soaks in a candlelit tub, smokes a joint, and becomes one with the sounds of whales on his tape recorder. The phone begins to ring nonstop. Refusing to leave this quiet reverie, the Dude lets his phone ring until the message machine picks up and the Dude's recorded voice says, "The Dude is not in." Glassman whimsically notes that when the Dude states that he is not in, he is in fact expressing one of the central tenets of Zen Buddhism, which is no self and no ego attachment. If the Dude is not in, he is not individuated. Rather, the Dude understands the Buddhist teaching of the interdependence of all phenomenon. If he is not in, he is then unattached to his self and ego desires. Therefore, he is one with all things. He is therefore empty of individual existence, which, as Glassman notes, is enlightenment.

"My definition of enlightenment," Glassman writes, "is realizing the oneness of life. And whatever you exclude and call *not me*, or whatever you're not dealing with, is going to thwart you."[5] Glassman's very simple Zen intepretation of "The Dude's not in" reflects his intention to introduce Zen Buddhism to popular American audiences through the language and culture of its time. Hence, *The Big Lebowksi,* much like the variety of *sutras* in the Mahayana canon suggests, are all like fingers pointing to the moon in the direction of enlightenment. Nonetheless the freedom from convention reflected in *The Big Lebowski* and *The Dude and the Zen Master* ought to give us pause, especially when thinking about introducing Buddhism to American audiences in the "parlance of the time," as the Dude likes to say. An uncritical reading of the Dude's Zen produces a blind spot regarding the politics of recognition and the privilege afforded to white men and the power of their image.

While the efforts of Bridges and Glassman are laudable, they also belie a rather uncritical and unselfconscious adoption of a Zen Buddhist identity that obscures the fraught history of the racialization of Asian and Asian American Buddhists as perpetual foreigners and embodiments of the Yellow Peril. While one might wish to argue that the very fact of Buddhism's popularity among white males demonstrates its widespread acceptance in the U.S., the WW II-era legacy of Buddhism as un-American still makes it challenging and threatening for some Asian Americans to make such easy and forthright declarations of their Buddhist identities. One cannot help but wonder why it is so easy for men like Bridges to adopt a Buddhist identity in public while for others, the risk is to great. I suggest that the difference hinges upon white privilege, white supremacy, and anti-Asian and Asian American sentiment. While the spirit of Zen has produced many appealing images of Buddhist difference in film and other media, it behooves us to reconsider bell hooks's admonition to think critically about our looking relations and ask, whose Buddhism do we see on the screen and why? Whose Buddhism is missing and why? Such questions help uncover the myriad ways that Buddhism has been implicated in the powerful intersections of religion, race, and gender.

And yet, while there is much to lament about the irreverent Zen that Bridges displayed on television, there remains something commendable about the collaboration between Bridges and Glassman that warrants closer attention for a re-visioning of Buddhism. Jeff Bridges and his co-author Bernie Glassman offer a slightly more detailed interpretation of the Zen qualities of the Dude in their book that proves quite helpful for understanding the Dude's appeal in popular American culture and to decipher some of the near unintelligible verbal meanderings of Bridges during his interview. The book itself records a series of exchanges about Zen in general and some of the key *koans* of Zen Buddhism that Glassman finds in *The Big Lebowski*. In Bridges's introduction to the book, he recounts the exchange the two have over the Zen nature of the film:

> [Glassman] "*The Big Lebowski* is filled with koans, only there in the 'parlance of our time,' to quote the Dude."
>
> "What are you talkin' about man? What do you mean?" I asked him.
>
> "It's filled with 'em, like: *The Dude abides* – very Zen, man; or *The Dude is not in* –classic Zen; or *Donny, you're out of your element*, or *That rug really tied the room together*. It's loaded with 'em."[6]

Bridges seems genuinely surprised by Glassman's likening of the Dude to a Zen Master, but realizes later on that Glassman wants to teach Zen Buddhism to the wider American public in the "parlance of the time," which itself is a very Buddhist method of skillful means (*upaya*) where one teaches according to the needs of the listener. My critique of this approach to Zen is that it rests upon and perpetuates an implicit and unspoken assumption of a white male Buddhist as the most recognizable form of Buddhist. Because *The Big Lebowski* achieved its own cult status among many filmgoers of its time, Bridges notes that it seemed the perfect vehicle "in making Zen more accessible to our times and culture, relevant and down-to-earth, and Glassman felt that *Lebowski* did that big-time."[7] Yet, while Bridges's explanation of Zen through the role of the Dude borders on the superficial offering of simplistic aphorisms and phrases like "Hope you dig it," his explanation of the purpose of both the book and *The Big Lebowski* prove quite useful for thinking about the power of film to remake Buddhism, despite the director's original intentions. Bridges explains:

> To me, this book is sort of like a snakeskin. A snakeskin is something you might find on the side of the road and make something out of it—a belt, say, or a hatband. The snake itself heads off doing more snake stuff—getting it on with lady snakes, eating rats, making more snakeskins, et cetera.
>
> I look at movies the same way. The final movie is the snakeskin, which can be pretty interesting and valuable. The snake is what happens while we're making the movie—the relationships, the experience. I try to open

wide and get really connected with the people I'm working with—the director, the cast, the production crew—all of us cooking in a safe and generous space, trying to get the job done. And we have to get that fire going as soon as we can, because our time together is finite, two or three months, maybe six. That's all the time we've got to come up with what we intend. Or, every once in a wonderful while, with something that transcends all our desires and intentions[8].

What appeals to me most about Bridges's otherwise troubling approach to Zen is his emphasis on the ability to utilize texts and films for something beyond their original intention. Such a claim points to the possibility of re-visioning popular images of Buddhism through film itself, even when one may find the film frustrating. Much like a snakeskin can be turned into a belt or purse that completely transcends the snake itself, a film can function as a reflection of pop cultural understandings of religion, but can also point to something beyond the image itself. In this manner, Bridges's view of film resonates nicely with Michael Bird's approach to film as hierophany, a "disclosure of the transcendent or sacred precisely through the material of reality," or the material reality of film that is both rooted in, yet points to something beyond it.[9] It is this something beyond that I am most intrigued by, for it indexes both the reality of the film and, at the same time, seeks to transcend the limits of the film to remake and re-vision the tradition it purportedly reflects. Both Bridges and Bird highlight the power of film to point to something beyond its own form in order to make reality anew.

The conceit of film as a kind of "cinematic theology" that "does not exhaust reality but rather evokes in the viewer the sense of the ineffable mystery," offers a partial explanation of how *The Big Lebowski* becomes the core of a new popular American online religion called Dudeism.[10] According to the Dudeism website, Dudeism is:

An ancient philosophy that preaches non-preachiness, practices as little as possible, and above all, uh... lost my train of thought there. Anyway, if you'd like to find peace on earth and goodwill, man, we'll help you get started. Right after a little nap.[11]

As an amalgam of ancient Taoist and Zen teachings applied to a contemporary slacker context, the Church of the Latter-Day Dude offers online ordinations and reflects the popular fascination with all the mysteriousness of Buddhism noted in the previous chapter, but in a more kitschy and humorous mode. While I don't consider Dudeism to be a serious religion, I do find that it reflects the appeal of a film like *The Big Lebowski* for a popular audience still in search of otherness and difference; Buddhism and other Asian religions are thus made relevant and virtually accessible in the present without doing much more than, as the introduction to Dudeism states, taking a nap.

Ghost Dog: The Way of the Samurai

Jim Jarmusch's 1999 film, *Ghost Dog: The Way of the Samurai*, features Forrest Whitaker as a modern-day hit man living as a quasi-monastic Samurai warrior for a low-pedigree Italian-American mobster. Jarmusch creatively adapts the Samurai code of conduct known as *bushido* that was heavily influenced by Zen Buddhism for the contract killer known by friend and foe as "Ghost Dog" for his untraceable hits. Throughout the film, Jarmusch weaves Tsunetomo Yamamoto's eighteenth-century book, *Hagakure: The Book of the Samurai* into the story through verses that appear on screen to mark each new scene. Ghost Dog narrates the verses as the audience simultaneously reads the text, thus creating an explicit connection between the two. In this way, spectators are drawn into the unfolding of this film of an African American turned hit man whose identity as a Zen-inspired Samurai warrior brings him great success. But his success comes to an end when he kills the lover of the Mafia boss Ray Vargo's daughter, Louise. Although contracted to kill only Handsome Frank for his dalliances with Louise, Ghost Dog encounters her as soon as he shoots Handsome Frank dead.

After he encounters the daughter, she gives him her worn copy of the *Rashomon*, written by Ryūnosuke Akutagawa in 1915, that relates a story of a single event interpreted differently by multiple people. The placement of the book in the film represents Ghost Dog's Zen understanding of the relative and illusory nature of individual points of view. He receives the book, pockets it, and then leaves the house with Louise still inside. The next day, after confirming Handsome Frank's death, Ray Vargo puts a hit on Ghost Dog out of a twisted sense of loyalty to Handsome Frank whom he had ordered dead. The remainder of the film presents Ghost Dog's Zen quasi-Buddhist ethos as he embarks on a series of killings to protect himself and his Samurai "master," Louie, a tired looking member of the aging ill-fated local Mafia. What makes Whitaker's character so appealing for viewers is his ability to become a nearly invisible man whose barely noticed maneuvers allow him to elude his enemies and serve as a Samurai retainer who intuits the Zen concepts of no self and emptiness.[12]

Viewers first encounter Ghost Dog as he sits in his dilapidated rooftop temple-like shack where he spends much of his time contemplating *The Hagakure*. Alone on the rooftop (similar to the ubiquitous, mediated images of monks meditating on isolated mountain tops), Ghost Dog's only companions

Figure 3.1 Ghost Dog: The Way of the Samurai. *Ghost Dog reads the* Hagakure

are the carrier pigeons he carefully tends on the roof outside the shack. Jarmusch immediately establishes a connection between Ghost Dog, Zen Buddhism, and Asian cultures as the camera slowly moves through his temple highlighting a makeshift Buddhist shrine complete with lit candles, a bookshelf loaded with Asian texts, and wallpaper composed of old Asian language newspapers. Amidst his Buddhist paraphernalia are the modern-day versions of the Samurai sword—a veritable panoply of semi-automatics and, we later discover, a hidden cache of rifles artfully concealed in the floor of his shack and accessible only by carefully manipulating a series of wooden slats in the floor. As a self-styled Samurai, Ghost Dog lives according to the tenets of *bushido* or "way of the warrior," the ancient Samurai code exemplified by the heroes of countless popular legends and myths, and conveying an ethos of self-discipline, self-sacrifice, single-mindedness, unhesitating obedience to one's lord, and utter fearlessness in the face of death.

As he prepares himself for a hit, Ghost Dog narrates the following passage from the *Hagakure* that appears on the screen. Thus, the audience reads along with Whitaker the following verses:

The Way of the Samurai is found in death.
Meditation on inevitable death should be performed daily.
Every day, when one's body and mind are at peace,
one should meditate upon being ripped apart by arrows,
rifles, spears, and swords, being carried away by surging waves,
being thrown into the midst of a great fire, being struck by lightning,
being shaken to death by a great earthquake,
falling from thousand-foot cliffs,

dying of disease or committing seppuku at the death of one's master.
And every day, without fail, one should consider himself as dead.
This is the substance of the Way of the Samurai.

The passage itself introduces the audience to Ghost Dog's veneration of the Samurai code, a code adopted after nearly being shot to death by two white thugs in an alley. We later learn that Ghost Dog, saved from an almost certain death by one of the Mafia gangsters, Louie, disappeared only to emerge a few years later at Louie's doorstep declaring he was Louie's retainer and protector.

Jarmusch offers a creative twist to the story by showing two separate scenes of the same event. In the first scene, Ghost Dog falls asleep on his roof as he dreams about that day—he dreams that as he is being savagely beaten and one of the white men pulls a gun on him, Louie comes to the rescue and draws a gun to save Ghost Dog. In the next scene, Louie tries to explain to the Mafia boss how he met Ghost Dog and narrates the day when he comes to the alley where Ghost Dog is brutally beaten and the white man points the gun directly at Louie and *not* Ghost Dog. Louie then protects Ghost Dog by accident. This difference of interpretation reflects the relativity of perspective hinted at in Louise's copy of the *Rashomon* she bequeaths to Ghost Dog. Saved from death, Ghost Dog becomes the retainer who trains his body and mind through Zen meditation and martial arts so that he can become a modern Samurai.

Ardently dedicated to Louie, Ghost Dog has trained himself to become a highly skilled Zen practitioner whose mind will not waver from his utter devotion to his master, for he has mastered the complete death of self-attachment. Quoting the *Hagakure* on the ethics of *bushido*, he recites, "If one were to say in a word what the condition of being a Samurai is, its basis lies first in seriously devoting one's body and soul to his master. Not to forget one's master is the most fundamental obligation for a retainer." By considering himself dead, he thus embodies the Buddhist teaching of no self as he quotes the central tenet of the *Heart Sutra* found in the *Hagakure*:

Our bodies are given life from the midst of nothingness. Existing where there is nothing is the meaning of the phrase, 'Form is emptiness.' That all things are provided for by nothingness is the meaning of the phrase, 'Emptiness is form.' One should not think that these are two separate things.

It is this understanding of no self and nonduality that allows Ghost Dog to remain invisible as he carries out his hits and gives his full devotion to Louie no matter the consequences. He is ready to give his life as easily and swiftly as he performs his hits on the Mafia members who want him dead.

Figure 3.2 Ghost Dog: The Way of the Samurai. *Ghost Dog worships before a hit.*

Ghost Dog's actions are performed in a highly ritualized manner reminiscent of the routinized behavior of Zen monks living in monasteries. As he prepares to leave his shack for the evening, he prepares his briefcase of weapons, bows to the shrine he has built outside his shack, and slowly walks through the city streets seeking his targeted mode of transportation, an expensive car. Ghost Dog, in having a Samurai and Zen identity, has no identity, which allows him to pass by unseen by shopkeepers and other bystanders. Cloaked in a dark hooded sweatshirt and shielded by darkness, Ghost Dog lumbers along as his large body seamlessly maneuvers through his ritual of stealing cars. Once he locates a car (a Mercedes, which he later replaces with a BMW), Ghost Dog operates a makeshift device that allows him to disarm the car's alarm and silently break into it and immediately plays a hip hop CD that he has brought along with him and places carefully into the stereo. Each movement made in this music sequence is deliberate, repetitive, and serves to draw a connection between a Zen monk's ritual behavior and the new identity appropriated by Ghost Dog.

While Ghost Dog embodies the Samurai spirit in his contracts and imagines himself as if dead, his relationship with his best friend Raymond, a Haitian immigrant ice cream truck worker, and Pearline, a young Haitian girl, reflect another side of his Zen identity. In a serious of comical scenes, Ghost Dog and Raymond speak in English and French, neither understanding the other's language. Yet the two magically seem to understand exactly what the other says. Their relationship reflects the characterization of Zen as "a special transmission outside of words and letters and a directing pointing to the nature of man." The transmission outside of words and letters refers to an experiential understanding in Zen that does not rely on reading scripture.

Instead, the mind of enlightenment is one that is directly experienced and intuited. Jarmusch captures the spirit of the saying brilliantly through their nonverbal communication. Ghost Dog also reflects the role of the Zen master in passing down his wisdom and knowledge to a worthy disciple. While Ghost Dog always carries a black briefcase loaded with weapons for his contracts, the young Pearline constantly totes around her own kind of briefcase, a lunchbox filled with classics like *The Wind in the Willows*, *Frankenstein*, and *The Soul of Black Folk*.

If Ghost Dog defies the stereotype of the violent and criminal black gangster, Pearline defies the debilitating stereotype of disaffected, uneducated black youth, for in her briefcase she carries books, the weapons of knowledge that will protect her from the violence and poverty of her neighborhood. The two warriors join together in a master-student relationship, and Pearline connects with Ghost Dog on a mind-to-mind level just as Zen masters who pass their wisdom down to their worthy students.

Ghost Dog is a cool-headed, impossible-to-trace hit man who, unlike his bumbling mafia enemies, never appears ruffled, yet he also exhibits a deep care for his companions, both animal and human. He has a particular affinity for birds and bears, which reflects a Zen attunement to nature. He also has a strong sense of duty and protection over Raymond and Pearline. Prior to sacrificing himself in true Samurai fashion for the last scene by emptying his gun of bullets and engaging in a Western shootout scene in broad daylight with Louie, Ghost Dog makes sure to give Raymond a finely tailored suit that he stole for a disguise during the last big shoot out at Vargo's mansion. He then locks his gun and all of his money inside his briefcase and gives Raymond the key. He then saunters into the sunlit street at high noon, heading directly toward Louie. Ghost Dog already knows that Louie has to kill him to protect himself from Louise, the new head of the Mafia family, so he lets Louie take him out old-school style by approaching his master with an empty gun that Louie thinks is loaded. Once shot, he reassures Louie that it's okay and then he gives Pearline his copy of the *Hagakure*, thus symbolizing the mind-to-mind transmission from master to student. His task complete, Ghost Dog dies a noble death for the sake of his master.

Because Zen is often presented as a timeless, formless alterity in Buddhist film, Jarmusch deploys its difference to great effect to artfully critique racial stereotypes, create new American myths of cultural and racial identity, and play with notions of cultural hybridity. The appropriation of a particular eighteenth-century Japanese Samurai code, and the musical score by RZA and members of the Wu Tang Clan (known for their interest in Asian cultures and martial arts) effect an Orientalized and romanticized version of a Samurai/Zen blend that accomplishes two ends—one that is seemingly cutting edge and forward thinking in its racial implications and another that reproduces age old negative images of Asians and Asian Americans. Jarmusch's use of Japanese religion in the form of the *Hagakure* and its continual references to Zen concepts of nonduality and selflessness anchor the film in a uniquely Zen atmosphere where a black hit man self-styled as a Zen Buddhist monk takes up the gun as sword and expresses his fealty to his master.

Considered a "postmodern pastiche" that blends a number of myths both literary and cultural such as the eighteenth-century Samurai code, hip-hop culture, stereotypes of Italian- American Mafia, and television cartoons like Betty Boop and Ren and Stimpy, the film itself blends, hybridizes, and appropriates Zen Buddhism and romanticizes Asian culture.[13] In his essay, "Ghost Dog: The Deconstruction of Identity," Paul Bowman observes that "... the film directly proposes that through an encounter with a *translated* Japanese text, and through *fantasy* (identification with a fantasy social position—one *cannot be* a Samurai outside of feudal Japanese social relations), and the *discipline* of martial arts, a black youth from violent ghetto streets can 'become' for all intents and purposes, a ninja...."[14] For Bowman, self-invention through martial arts and the adaptation of an ancient text to contemporary times enables Ghost Dog to prevail and reinvent himself despite living in the ghetto surrounded by violence and poverty.

Yet, as Ghost Dog accesses this exotic identity of ancient Samurai warrior/ Zen monk, one is left to wonder what effects this exercise in identity re-formation might have on constructions of Asians and Asian Americans in popular culture. In other words, what are the effects of appropriating exoticized forms of Asian and Buddhist identity without offering a more complex image of Asians and Asian Americans themselves? Such a question is related to the similarly uncritical adoption of a Zen Buddhist identity by privileged white males like Bridges and the attribution of a Zen identity to slackers like the Dude. What, if any, image of Asians and Asian Americans does Jarmusch offer up in a film that borrows so heavily from Japanese Buddhism? He offers up a tired stock image of an Asian man with some secret magical martial arts prowess Ghost Dog observes while walking through the city streets in daylight. Pausing in front of a parking lot, he watches a thief on the verge of robbing an elderly Asian American man. Rather than immediately moving in to save the man, Ghost Dog remains aloof and observes the encounter in a detached manner. Just as the thief is about to attack, the old man suddenly turns around and levels a powerful roundhouse kick and subsequently beats the would-be robber in a highly stylized martial arts fashion reminiscent of the prowess of Bruce Lee. In pointing to this scene, I am not arguing that there should be more Asian and Asian American faces in Jarmusch's work. Instead, I argue against the continually reproduced stock image of the otherness of Asians and Asian Americans who possess a martial arts skill powerful enough to ward off would be assailants.

And yet Jarmusch's adaptation of the *Hagakure* offers alternatives to trenchant stereotypes and myths past their shelf life in American culture such as the "Hollywood-racist stereotype of the young African-American who sleeps through the day and steals cars and kills people at night."[15] The protagonist Ghost Dog is a widely read hit man who has not only read American classics, but also has a cultural literacy that far extends what the Hollywood image of the young black man would allow. Self-educated, loyal, controlled, reserved, and compassionate, Ghost Dog appropriates a Zen Buddhist persona to combat racism, poverty, and alienation. Thus, his adoption of a Buddhist identity (albeit one funnelled through the violence and moral codes of the Samurai warrior) functions as a form of self-invention and self-protection against the racialization of African American men through an ancient Samurai culture and ethos easily accessed by adopting Zen practices and a Samurai identity in the present.

While the projection of his warrior Zen monk identity appeals to audiences taken in by the hipness of such hybridization, the appropriation and adaptation of the past into the present or, to put it differently, the other into the here, also freezes images of Asia, Asians, and Asian Americans into a reified construction of otherness. Thus, even while deploying Buddhism to combat racism against African Americans, Asians and Asian Americans are still rendered invisible, or worse, can only be seen through the darkness of mystery.

Zen Noir

Marc Rosenbush's 2004 independent film *Zen Noir* is a classic noir "who dunnit" that is far more interested in exploring the "who" of the "who dunnit" than whatever it is that was done. Rosenbush juxtaposes a Western, left-brain mode of thinking that seeks answers outside the self against the Zen form of thinking that posits no distinctions between past, present, and future, inside or outside, self and other. A low budget, independent American film, *Zen Noir* casts a down-and-out gum-shoed detective mourning the death of his wife and unborn child as a Zen acolyte in a mysterious temple headed by an "Oriental Monk" par excellence. As *Zen Noir* makes clear, Zen is imminently usable in film and other forms of representation as a powerful tonic for psychological stresses where the Zen monk as therapist is cast as religious hero who acts as a source of wisdom, compassion, and antidote to whatever ails the Westerner.

Zen Noir opens in typical noir style by laying out a mystery to solve but with a twist—a drunken nameless detective (his namelessness is reminiscent of Ghost Dog's invisibility and the nameless monks in *Spring, Summer, Fall,*

Winter... and Spring to be encountered in the following chapter), suffering from the death of his wife, gets a mysterious phone call to come to a Buddhist temple to solve a mysterious murder. The nameless detective rushes off to the temple only to find that none of the residents of the temple are aware that a murder has even taken place. The temple residents include a white femme fatale named Jane whose head is shaved bald (we later learn that she is bald because she has cancer and that she has escaped to the temple searching for a way to come to terms with her impending death), another white monk who is also nameless (although he later pokes fun at the detective's attachment to individual names by claiming that he is actually known as "Articulate Lotus Flowing From the Source"), and finally, the mysterious iconoclastic Japanese Zen head monk—who is, of course, also nameless.

While Jane serves as the typical femme fatale whose definition of a lay Buddhist is one "who can still get laid," and lures the nameless detective out of his mourning, at least temporarily, by sleeping with him, it is the elderly Zen master who imparts the deepest lessons of impermanence, interdependence, and the nondual nature of reality to the grieving detective. As the embodiment of an illogical yet profound wisdom, the antinomian monk employs unusual methods of teaching. The monk teaches through the use of oranges, which are placed in various locations in the temple and in various states of decay throughout the movie. In fact, the film's opening shot offers a close up of an orange encircled by a flame. Up close, the dimpled skin begins to resemble the shaved head and hair follicles of a tonsured monastic. So, from the beginning, the orange is cast as teacher and symbol of a deeper Zen wisdom of interdependence and the self.

The master works to impart the wisdom of interdependence and the appreciation of the present moment throughout *Zen Noir* as he proceeds to pelt oranges at the detective. This pelting of fruit is much like the use of a meditation stick by the master who may strike the student when the muscles grow tired and the mind wanders. The deepest transformative moment for the detective, though, comes when the master calls him to sit and just enjoy an orange with him. While eating orange slices together in the *zendo*, the left-brain detective implores of his master, "Why does everything I love have to die?"

The master imparts the following enlightening Zen lesson in broken English, dropping his grammatical articles much like Yoda in the Star Wars series:

Nature of Life to end. Life of nature to end. Body of nature to change. Loved ones of nature to change. You meet Jane, fall in love, eat orange together. Good. But one day change, Jane die. You eat orange alone. Very sad.

Long time ago my master, wise man, very kind. We sit eating orange together. Every bite not just orange, entire world.

Look, what you see? Orange? Okay. What else? Skin? Juice? Good. But must look deeper. What else? Death, orange, dead insect, dead people, all dead! But all still right here. This orange now every bit, every taste, not just orange … Entire Universe!

As the monk speaks, a bamboo flute plays Asian music in the background, symbolizing the detective's mental transformation as he comes to see that the orange itself reflects the entirety of reality and its interdependence. The Zen master continues:

So, sitting and eating, master and me. The telephone rings. Fire, big fire! Father, sister, whole village gone! Such pain! So Unfair! Family! Why? Start to shake, start to cry, crying, screaming, tearing robe and whole time still eating orange. Piece in mouth, next piece, next piece, next, no taste now, no worry now, just fire, eating, fire, screaming, pain, until master stopped me, grabs hand and look with burning eyes… "You gonna eat orange or freak out?! Pick one."

Master very wise, very kind. Fire happen but orange still there. Must not lose orange, so holding orange, loved ones here. What to do? What to do? Ate orange very slow, then cry, great pain, many tears, first day of life but best orange I ever had.

Upon receiving the deepest insight into the nature of reality and imper-manence, the detective bows to the master and, having finally managed to contort his body into the lotus position, he sits next to the master in meditation and when the master has finally imparted all of his Zen wisdom, he falls over dead and it is the nameless detective who takes up the mantle of Zen.

Marc Rosenbush's *Zen Noir* posits a Buddhism that is timeless, pure, illogical and, therefore, a perfect antidote to Western culture and Western modes of thinking associated with the pitfalls of the modern world. Rosenbush's pure unmediated experience of Zen serves as the perfect tonic for such excesses and idealizes Zen for Western consumption. Yet the detec-tive's implied succession as the head monk of the temple also reflects an uncritical acceptance of the ease with which one can take up the reins of the temple and adopt such an identity.

Jane Iwamura's critique of the emblem of Buddhism and the icon of the Oriental monk offers one of the few noteworthy interventions against the racialization of this emblem in American popular culture. She argues in particular that it is the Euro-American [read: white] neophyte who stands to not only inherit the role of head Buddhist, but also to do so in a more effective manner than his or her master. Such is the implied message of *Zen Noir*. Iwamura argues:

> The Oriental Monk figure is portrayed as a desexualized male character who represents the last of his kind. Passing on his spiritual legacy to the West through the bridge figure represents his only hope for survival. Hence, this narrative implicitly argues that Asian religions are impotent within their racial context of origin, and are only made (re)productive if resituated in a Western context and passed on to white practitioners who possess the daring and innovative sensibilities that their Eastern counterparts presumably lack. In this way, the icon of the Oriental Monk and its contemporary narrative—a construction of "racist love"—may be more insidious than negative stereotypes informed by "racist hate," as it allows for the recognition of peoples and cultures of Asian heritage while simultaneously subjecting them to a narrative of their own obsolescence.[16]

It is not just that Zen Buddhism and its masters come to America to introduce a new mode of thinking and practice that challenges authoritative conceptualizations of religion, but rather, Zen is then appropriated by the white American and offers a more authentic virile version than his or her preceptor precisely because the white American is not Asian.

When paying close attention to the racialization of Buddhism in the West, one might easily dismiss *The Big Lebowski*, *Ghost Dog*, and *Zen Noir* as films that capitalize on the Orientalist construction of Zen's otherness and near unintelligibility, and presume their popularity comes from a strictly Western obsession with the exoticism of Asian Buddhism. One might also make the assumption that the Buddhist tradition lies largely in the hands of men on the quest for enlightenment based on what these Zen films project. However, such assumptions belie a similar phenomenon that takes place in films directed and produced in Asia that also reference similar images of Buddhism's curiosity; in other words, it is not merely the case that Western Buddhist films exploit the mysterious image of Buddhist monastic difference. Instead, as I show in the next chapter, the image of the exotic monk is alive and well in Asian-produced films, such as South Korean director Kim Ki-Duk's 2003 *Spring, Summer, Fall, Winter... and Spring*, which projects the Buddhist monk as a symbol of premodernity and difference whose Buddhism remains incompatible with the present day. Unfortunately, in such a magical world of mysterious monks who seem to exist in timelessness, women have curiously little visibility and voice. And their Buddhism is for the most part absent.

4

Plus ça change, plus c'est la même chose: Women as Snares of *Samsara*

"Look at this dressed up body, a mass of sores, supported (by bones), sickly, a subject of many thoughts (of sensual desire). Indeed, that body is neither permanent nor enduring."[1]

Despite the extensive monastic attention paid to the troubling allure of women, Buddhist discourses on the body found in the verse from the *Dhammapada* above commonly refer to the body as a skin sack or a malodourous sieve leaking substances putrid and foul. In the *Anguttara Nikaya Sutta* of the Pali Canon, the elder monk Sariputta informs the Buddha of his own spiritual maturation. He states:

> Just as Lord, a man might attend a cooking pot full of fat, riddled with holes, perforated all over, oozing, and dripping, even so Lord, I attend to this body of mine, riddled with holes, perforated all over, oozing, and dripping.[2]

Here Sariputta disavows the purity and containment of his own body for specific soteriological ends—the uprooting of desire, detachment to the self, and the subsequent development of moral virtue. Confirming this rather unpleasant yet spiritually edifying view of Sariputta's own body, the Buddha then likens the body to "a boil that has been gathering for many years which might have nine open wounds" that constantly seeps filth.[3] He then exhorts his disciples, "Therefore monks, you should be disgusted with this body."[4]

But what exactly is wrong with the human body and why must it always be viewed as repulsive? What are the effects of such hostility toward the physical body in general and female bodies in particular? As I show in this chapter, the Buddha's message about the inherent impurity of the body focused specifically on women's bodies as a way to divert a monk's attention from the alleged charms of their beauty to that of the foulness contained within. In so doing, the monk could then uproot his desire for the beauty that so entices him because after meditating on female bodies in various states of decay in cremation grounds he realizes that, in reality, beauty is nothing but a duplicitous façade covering up the festering substances within. The problem with such aversion therapy, however, is that such assignations effectively efface the presence of women as religious agents with their own agency, religious aims, and ordinary desires that are not necessarily counter to a spiritual life.

While such early Indian Buddhist attitudes toward women's bodies might appear rather antiquated today, an analysis of contemporary Buddhist films indicates otherwise. In this chapter, I offer an analysis of the internationally renowned *Spring, Summer, Fall, Winter... and Spring* (2003) by well-known Korean director Kim Ki-Duk that reveals the uncritical reproduction of the textual portrayal of women as the snares of *samsara* or mantraps that keep a man from spiritual liberation and the use of the female body as a catalyst for male transformation. Furthermore, I argue that such images of women as mantraps and catalysts rests on the obscuration and suppression of any positive subjectivity and agency on the part of women who are not just marginalized but considered incapable of spiritual development and mere props for a monk's edification.

Such vivid excoriations of the physical body in a religious tradition that emphasizes the qualities of loving kindness, compassion, and the interdependence of all phenomena certainly command attention and explanation, for they seem rather misplaced. Such contradictory sentiments leave us to wonder where these negative valuations of the human body originated. According to Susanne Mrozik's study of the ascetic discourses found in Buddhist texts, these admonishments regarding bodies are intended to eradicate attachment to the more base material desires and, through the embrace of the impure body, monks are rendered more spiritually pure because they have detached themselves from both excessive self-regard and any attachment to desire.[5] Such a task never proved easy for monks; thus, the Buddha devised a number of meditative techniques to accomplish such a challenge.

One of the essential problems with the uncritical adoption of the extreme language of impurity that characterizes such bodily discourses in Buddhist texts by contemporary filmmakers is that it precludes the possibility of imagining a more ordinary embrace of the body. Is it not possible to imagine a lay Buddhism that can include both a spiritual quest, and an acceptance of the sensual body? As it stands in the texts, few opportunities exist to theorize sexually positive relationships and a healthy embrace of the body as it is. Perhaps most disturbing about these textual attitudes toward the body is the turn from somewhat neutral characterizations of impure male bodies like Sariputta's to far more negatively charged descriptions of impure and disfigured female bodies that are presented in various states of decay as objects of contemplation for the explicit moral edification of the monks.

Early Indian Buddhist literature's extreme descriptions of the physical body as a "mass of sores" reflects an abiding monastic preoccupation with asceticism and celibacy to control the ignition of desire and thirst (*tanha*), which is said to fuel the cycle of *samsara* or rebirth. According to the Buddha, desire or thirst for positive experiences and the avoidance of negative experiences are the inevitable spiritual downfall of monks and nuns who become overly attached to what they misperceive as permanent. In the first sermon the Buddha gave to his disciples, he taught the Four Noble Truths, namely: In life there is suffering; Suffering comes from thirst or desire; There is a way to end suffering; The way to end suffering is through the Noble Eightfold Path. What is of most concern for monks like Sariputta is the eradication of desire. According to Walpola Rahula, the Buddha taught:

> It is this "thirst" ... which produces re-existence and re-becoming ... and which is bound up with passionate greed ... namely, (1) thirst for sense-pleasures ... (2) thirst for existence and becoming ... and (3) thirst for non-existence.[6]

Thirst or desire most commonly impeded monks' efforts to remain celibate. Thus, the rules of comportment found in the *Vinaya* or monastic codes of the Buddhist canon include many precepts regarding restraint of the senses and the avoidance of unwholesome contact with others. One method of drying up desire focused on the practice of viewing the body as loathsome so that one would no longer be attached to its sexual desires. Encouraged to view their own bodies as impure, monks like Sariputta identify with the abject unclean body in order to effect what Susanne Mrozik refers to as materialization of virtue.[7] That is, conceptualization of the body as foul could propel a monk along the pathway to purity or Buddhahood precisely because through the embrace of the abject body image the monk disassociates from his gendered male body that constantly seeks sensual pleasure. However, a careful reading of canonical Buddhist texts suggests, perhaps not surprisingly, a preference for imagining female bodies as dirty, loathsome, abhorrent, and by extension, material embodiments of the immoral. As he meditates, the monk shifts his gaze from his own body to that of a woman whom he then deconstructs through the process of meditative contemplation.

As a result and by extension, lay Buddhist women are thus cast as the physical embodiments of the very desire and thirst that were and must be eradicated by monks on the pathway to enlightenment. This representation is all the more troublesome, given that women serve as some of the most generous donors to the monastic institution. Yet what more effective way to uproot the deeply entangled roots of sexual craving within the monk's psyche than to visualize the purported cause of that suffering (women) as foul, impure, and ultimately dangerous? According to this logic, not only are female bodies rendered dirty but, as I show below, they also take on moral attributes of duplicitousness and evil and are assigned to roles of temptresses, mantraps, and female demons to be avoided at all costs. If the monk is unable to avoid his lust for such women, then he had better imagine her in various states of decay and foulness in order to transform his desire.

Ascetic discourses in Buddhist canonical texts attest to an anxiety over maintaining appropriate social boundaries between the monastic and lay world. These boundaries are constantly threatened, however, by the rules of monastic dependence. The laity provides the monks with food, clothing, and other material support, just as the monks provide the laity with opportunities for merit-making. This close proximity between the monks and the laity inevitably brings the monks into the presence of women, which in turn may lead to sexual desire—for which the Buddhist texts provide a tidy solution—imagine the women as foul and loathsome.

Yet for all the concern of the impurity and putrid essence of the female body, there is little or no corresponding representation of the male body as morally bankrupt and contaminating. The medieval Indian Buddhist hagiographical texts studied by Liz Wilson confirm that while the Buddha did indeed refer to men's bodies as weeping boils, it is his description and attitude toward women's bodies that receive the most explicit and graphic treatment.

For example, Buddhist canonical texts and commentarial literature make much of the story of Prince Siddhartha's Great Renunciation as he flees the confines of his palace and sets off to attain enlightenment and become the Buddha. Having spent the day experiencing first-hand what comes to be known as the four sights (old age, sickness, death, renunciation) that give him insight into the true nature of reality, Prince Siddhartha returns to his palace only to see his life and, in particular, his harem women, as embodiments of the illusion of permanence. During the day, the women delight with their most agreeable and beautiful bodies but, as the *Lalitavistara* recounts, on the eve of his departure, Prince Siddhartha comes to imagine his harem as cadavers strewn about in a cremation ground. In the biographical text of the Buddha's life, deities have cast a sleeping spell over his women in order to get him to renounce his carnal pleasures. As they fall to the ground unconscious, the deities ask, "How can you find pleasure in the midst of this cremation ground [*śmaśāna-madhye*] in which you live?"[8]

The prince looks about him and sees his beautiful women positioned like corpses with mouths agape, drooling, and their limbs akimbo. Such a vision inspires disgust and despair over the true nature of reality and compels the Prince Siddhartha to contemplate the impermanence and horrors of ordinary sensual life. The *bodhisattva*, declares to the deities, as he prepares to renounce the life of pleasure, "I really do live in the middle of a cremation ground."[9]

Another account of this event by the poet Asvaghosa notes that when the *bodhisattva* encounters the spectacle of women lying about the palace in various states of disarray, he:

> was filled with contempt. "Such," he concludes, "is the real nature ... of women, impure ... and monstrous ... yet a man, deceived by dress and ornaments, succumbs to passion for women."[10]

Much like the Buddha's own experiences, monks like Kulla in the *Theragatha* are encouraged to gaze upon the festering dead bodies of women so they come to see the true nature of the bodies that had previously held them in their *samsaric* charms. The Buddha exhorts the monk Kulla who is lustful of women thus:

> See Kulla, the abject, foul, putrid body
> Oozing, dripping, cherished by fools.[11]

Such meditations upon the foul decaying body are classified under the category of *asubhavana* or "meditation on foulness." In these meditations, the meditator contemplates a corpse in order to provoke the state of *samvega* which Wilson translates as "the shock of experience."[12] The state of shock functions much like aversion therapy whereby the foolish monk meditates upon a decaying female corpse in a cremation ground, perhaps even poking the bloated body with a stick so that its maggots and putrid effluvia spew forth. Through this contemplative practice conducted over the course of a few days, the monks are taught the nature of decay and impermanence as they are forced to meditate upon the very object of their lust to discern what it was that they were so fond of in the first place. These bodies, as Wilson's study suggests, become charming cadavers whose previous beauty withers away into festering corpses all for the spiritual maturation of men.

Such charming cadavers offer one of the most extreme yet effective forms of object meditation and learning for the monks. But they leave little for women to contemplate, having been reduced to nothing but a meditational prop without a recognizable face, body, and self or subjectivity, much less a voice of their own. Given the grave moral danger associated with women and their sexualized bodies, it is instructive to examine one such story in early Indian Buddhist literature to demonstrate how aversion therapy works for the monks who are attached to women and how such therapy renders women simultaneously excessive and obscured.

The story of Sirimā

The commentaries on the *Dhammapada*, one of the pithiest of the texts in the Theravada Pali Canon, introduces the instructive story of Sirimā, a beautiful young former courtesan who unwittingly attracts the attention of a young monk who encounters her during one of his daily alms rounds. In this text, Sirimā is introduced as a wealthy, generous laywoman who offers the monks delicious foods and garners much attention for her beauty and charms. The monks are so taken with her that stories of her beauty and generosity are circulated until all the monks are tantalized by her beauty and awakened sexually just by hearing about her. One monk is so taken by her reputation that he purposefully seeks her out just to get a glimpse of her. So besotted is he that he goes to visit her even while she is sick. Despite her tired and haggard appearance, the young monk is immediately enticed by her beauty and unable to quell his passion. Knowing the perilous fate of this poor hapless monk, the Buddha then devises a scheme to make a public display of Sirimā's body after she dies from her sickness in order to serve as the ultimate object lesson in uprooting desire. After Sirimā died, the Buddha instructs the king that there would be no cremation; instead, her body would be displayed in the charnel ground protected from birds and dogs. According to the text:

> Three days passed one after another. On the fourth day the body began to bloat, and from the nine openings of her body, which were like gaping wounds, maggots poured out.[13]

Her body soon bursts open and is likened to a cracked rice vessel. The king then makes a pronouncement that all should come to the charnel grounds to observe her body. The young monk hears Sirimā's name and rushes over to the cremation grounds only to learn that she is for sale for one thousand in cash, but no one is willing to buy her for any price. It is at this moment that the Buddha declares:

> Now there is no one who will take her even for free. Her beauty has perished and decayed." Saying, "Monks, look at this diseased body," he

spoke the following verse [*Dhammapada* 147]: "Look at this decorated image, an elevated mass of wounds. This diseased thing is highly fancied, (although) it's neither permanent or stable."[14]

While the Buddha advised some monks, including his cousin and attendant Ananda, to avoid women at all costs, he advised others like the besotted monk above to make use of the woman's body as a powerful lesson in impermanence. Encouraged to engage in meditation on death, the young monk comes to see that the source of his desire and passion is nothing but a rotting corpse.

Such are the lessons of life and death that must be experientially understood by monks in order to experience liberation from the cycle of birth and death. As many Indian Buddhist texts remind us, such liberation comes in the form of the woman whose body decomposes into nothingness as the monk's mind fortifies in spiritual strength. Such practices of extreme asceticism have the effect of consigning women to the realm of the sensual where they become foes to be vanquished if the monk is to succeed. But such meditational uses of the female body in the process of decay have more than just an obscuring effect on women. The extreme practices of dehumanizing women also make it near impossible to find any semblance of subjectivity and positive sense of self for these lay woman who are continually offered up as bait, snares, and lessons in *samvega* by the Buddha. We might then ask what the stakes are for ordinary lay Buddhists who are women when they cannot find any semblance of whole selves in such texts (and in the films I discuss below) and why it is that their diminishment is what leads to the edification of the monks.

Classified as sexually dangerous, their sighting can give rise to a kind of moral panic by monks whose ability to control their sexual urges are weakened by the women's sexual allure. In the monastic codes known as the *Patimokkha*, Venerable Sudinna is chastized by the Buddha for returning to his wife and having sex with her so that she might have a child. According to the text, the Buddha exhorts:

It would have been better, confused man, had you put your male organ inside the mouth of a terrible and poisonous snake than inside the vagina of a woman. It would have been better, confused man, had you put your male organ inside the mouth of a black snake than inside the vagina of a woman. It would have been better, confused man, had you put your male organ inside a blazing hot charcoal pit than inside the vagina of a woman.[15]

So frightening indeed is the body of a woman that the monk risks more danger to himself by having sex with his former wife than he would if he were to put his penis in the mouth of a snake. Because the extreme Buddhist discourses on asceticism envision women as objects of monastic transformation, the textual excoriations of the female body and sexuality leave little opportunity to imagine women or men in the Buddhist social world as ordinary sexually engaged people. Instead, their healthy sexuality and sense of self is sacrificed for the monastic order at women's expense. In fact, as we shall see in the film *Spring, Summer, Fall, Winter... and Spring*, women's sexuality ends up, as bell hooks puts it, sacrificed at the altar of patriarchy and, as I argue, at the altar of ascetic male virtuosity.[16] There are very few instances where one can even imagine otherwise in so strict an understanding of desire and thirst as antithetical to the religious life.

Spring, Summer, Fall, Winter... and Spring

While such unsavory treatments of women might seem entirely antiquated and easily dismissed as vintage sexism, a close reading of contemporary configurations of Buddhism in film suggests otherwise. There are a number of startling and uncanny similarities between early Indian Buddhist descriptions of women found in canonical literature and contemporary Buddhist films such as Kim Ki-Duk's *Spring, Summer, Fall, Winter... and Spring*. This and other contemporary Buddhist films often portray women as dangerous mantraps that must be guarded against lest they incite a damaging and dangerous lust in the hearts and minds of monks. By and large contemporary Buddhist films encourage that very same dehumanizing male gaze examined by feminist film scholar Laura Mulvey in 1975.[17] What is perhaps most troublesome about such viewing relations is simply that they reflect an unquestioned inheritance that goes back far longer than the history of mediated images. This matter is not just a modern visual phenomena nor just an odd historical issue that we have surpassed. Rather, such an unwitting inheritance, I argue, forecloses the possibility of imagining a diverse Buddhism past and present that includes multiple religious actors both monastic and lay, male and female. In the remainder of this chapter, I take up Kim Ki-Duk's 2003 film *Spring, Summer, Fall, Winter... and Spring* as an emblem of such a damning inheritance that perpetuates the view that authentic Buddhism is really for the monk who lives a celibate life separate from the terrible beauty of women. Women in Kim's film are but mute objects of the male gaze and catalysts for the development of a male spiritual virtuosity. Like their textual ancestors, women entice with their bodily wares and, unless vanquished through death, will continue to trap their men in an endless round of rebirth.

What sets the film apart from its textual antecedents, however, is that Kim also incorporates sex as a necessary stage in the monk's development and moral training. Unlike the ascetic discourses found in Indian Buddhist texts, *Spring, Summer, Fall, Winter... and Spring* holds out the possibility that sexuality can be a profound teacher advancing the monk toward his spiritual awakening so long as he abandons the woman afterwards. That is, the monk first experiences sexuality in response to the body of a woman and only after having sex with her does he realize the folly of desire. Much like the lay woman Sirimā who was unceremoniously abandoned in the cremation grounds to rot in front of the eyes of discerning monks, Kim's young monk also abandons the object of his lust but only *after* they have sex, marry, and he murders her. He, too, leaves her for dead like the many women lying about the cremation grounds and learns experientially what his master warns, "Lust awakens the desire to possess. And that awakens the intent to murder." Kim's woman is a reimagining of an ancient materialization of dangerous sexuality that entices men from the path of purity. In her death, the woman vanishes from the story and from the spectator's mind like an apparition once her *dharmic* lessons are imparted. Conjured for the edification of the monk, the apparitional woman disappears from the screen leaving no trace. In a man's Buddhist textual and filmic world, women have no real place. After ensnaring their men and imparting lessons on the dangers of desire, they are left for dead.

Spring, Summer, Fall, Winter... and Spring immediately captivates spectators with its idyllic vision of pristine beauty in which nature and its rhythms provide the backdrop for Kim's monastic tale. As the word "Spring" appears on the screen, an ancient *deva* (protector) gate slowly opens to reveal a Zen Buddhist temple floating atop a tranquil lake. Kim explicitly uses theatrical elements in his film to artfully mark the Buddhist passage of cyclical time with intertitles, as "Spring" is followed by "Summer," "Fall," "Winter," "... and Spring." In this way, viewers are brought intimately into this otherwise secluded locale far from any nearby town. Two monks, an older master and a young boy, are seen engaged in their daily rituals as the master teaches his disciple the lessons of *karma* and *samsara*.

As a reference to Buddhist concepts of emptiness and illusion, Kim also utilizes props such as freestanding wooden doorframes, beams, and aging gateways painted with traditional Buddhist guardian protectors that the characters walk through as if they were real entryways into sleeping quarters and meditation halls. The monks use ancient stone mortars and pestles to pulverize plants that are squeezed through muslin cloth twisted tight with branches to extract medicinal herbs. Kim's explicit use of traditional implements also denotes a stark contrast between a rapidly modernized Korean economy and society and the idealized nostalgic world of monks. However, modernity soon encroaches upon Kim's monastic paradise through the intrusion of a young woman, and later, two gun-wielding policemen whose weapons are placed in stark relief against the abbot's more naturalistic implements such as handmade paintbrushes and paints.[18] Rather early in the film, Kim evokes a sense of nostalgia and the idealization of Buddhism as a social critique of modern technology.

Kim Ki-Duk's visual nod to the pre-modern Zen world of South Korea expresses an intimate and sensual portrait of Buddhism, constructed out of exaggerated notions of Zen's affinity with nature. From the lush green trees that encompass the peaceful mountain lake upon which floats a temple raft to the poignant shots of an elderly monk and his boy acolyte foraging for special mountain herbs to turn into medicinal poultices, Kim's film offers audiences an experience of Zen life characterized by natural beauty, a reverence for simplicity, and a portrait of emotional nurturing as an aged, wise monk takes a young, orphaned boy under his wing to raise as a son and transform into a monk isolated from society. Under his tutelage, the young monk who remains nameless throughout the film thrives in nature as he begins to learn the lessons of *karma* and *samsara*.

Spring, Summer, Fall, Winter... and Spring invites spectators into an intimate space where the father-son relationship between monk and disciple unfolds in a seamless trajectory marked by little verbal communication. The film beckons the audience to participate as voyeurs as we watch the disciple mature from an isolated, charming quasi-son and his all-knowing father who manages to see without being seen and who teaches the young boy critical Buddhist lessons of cause and effect, the weight of one's karmic actions, and the possibility of redemption. Redemption by the father is not, of course, a Buddhist teaching, but rather a Christian motif introduced by Kim, himself a Protestant Christian. Thus, the fictional Buddhist temple floating on a lake whose architecture is based on illusory walls and gates demarking empty spaces reminiscent of theatre props, also serves as a dual icon of a Buddhist Shangri-La and a Christian Garden of Eden.

Divided sequentially according to the seasons, Kim's film explores both the cycles of rebirth that characterize Buddhist notions of time as well as a repudiation of linear time based on a progression from past, present, and future. As referenced in the title of the film itself, in this Zen world, one moment flows into another seamlessly and without end. Time moves in a never ending circularity; because this Zen time does not connote the "march of progress," it lends itself well as a foe to the rapid modernization and economic upheaval of South Korea that took off in the 1980s. The Buddhist temple and Zen aesthetics reflected in Kim's film contribute to the spectacular visions of beauty offered in this ode to the past and, as Hyangsoon Yi notes, "primitive" and "prelapsarian" fantasies. Yi argues:

> Zen monasticism is envisioned as an organized practice of noble primi-
> tivism that is fully in tune with nature and is unencumbered by the frenzy

of modernity. This mystification uncovers a profound sense of loss and frustrations Koreans feel about their contemporary existential conditions. Factors that have formed these conditions include the all-out economic development, oppressive socio-political climate, and competitive modern education, among others.[19]

That the temple is accessible, however, indicates that the icon of transcendence can in fact be polluted by encroachment of the contemporary, and that, as a result, Buddhism cannot exist successfully in the modern world without losing some of its otherworldly exoticism.

Spring

In Act I of Spring season, the young monk learns his first lesson about cause and effect and suffering. The young boy wanders seemingly alone throughout this beautiful landscape; for entertainment he ties small stones onto animals to serve as weights they must bear. In this natural setting the boy tethers a fish, a frog, and a snake to various stones without a care to the effects of his actions, leaving them to struggle and suffer on their own. He cackles gleefully as his victims slither and writhe in pain. The elder monk observes his young charge in the midst of torturing the animals, yet withholds his judgment and punishment until night time when the boy sleeps, for he knows that it is better to experience what the animals felt in order to understand the pain he inflicted. Thus, as the boy sleeps, the wise old monk gathers a large flat stone and tethers it to the boy's back with rope, which will serve as the first object lesson in the young monk's experiential curriculum—by causing the suffering of others, he will reap negative consequences.

In the morning, the young boy is forced to feel the weight of this burden on his back as he wakes up, hobbles outside his sleeping quarters, and begs the master, "Master, there is a stone on my back. Please take it off."

The wise monk continues with his work without looking up and asks the boy if the stone torments him.

The young monk responds, "Yes Master."

The wise monk then asks the boy if he did the same to the fish, the frog, and the snake to which he replies, "Yes Master."

The boy is then forced to stand up and feel the heaviness of this burden and imagine what it must have been like for the animals he captured. The boy is then told to find the animals and free them but he cautions the acolyte, "But if any of the animals, the fish, the frog, or the snake is dead, you will carry the stone in your heart for the rest of your life."

Figure 4.1 Spring, Summer, Fall, Winter... and Spring. *Boy learns karmic lessons.*

Naturally, the boy then returns to the scene of his crimes and discovers that he has killed two of the animals. The fish's corpse bobs on top of the stream, its body anchored by a stone. The snake lays dead in a twisted bloody knot illustrating its struggle as it died. The frog, however, manages to live and is freed from its burden by the young monk who has learned his karmic lesson as he sobs in remorse over his actions. The boy's youth is thus marked by invaluable lessons of cause and effect by his Buddhist master in the quiet of the natural world, free from the intrusions of the modern world. But his greatest transgression in this idealized world unfolds with the arrival of a young woman to his floating temple on the lake.

Summer

Act II of the film opens with another intertitle indicating that it is now "Summer." As a foreshadowing of his own sexual awakening, the young monk stares mesmerized by the vision of two snakes copulating while a rooster (symbolizing greed in Buddhism) pecks away on the deck of the floating temple. The young boy has matured into a teenage boy in the next chapter of his life, when a young girl wearing a simple white dress and accompanied by her mother encroaches upon the Edenic temple topos. The young girl does not speak and is brought to the temple in order to heal an unknown illness, which her mother attributes to a lack of peace in her soul or some sort of spiritual malaise. Again, here we see the Buddhist temple associated with the premodern and, therefore, a salve for modern living. Although dressed as an innocent young girl, the unnamed girl quickly becomes the snare of *samsara* as a temptress who sexually awakens the young monk. As summer progresses, the young monk pursues the young woman who entices with her body and her glances yet never utters a word, not even when the monk reaches out to grope her breast when he discovers her undressing inside the temple. In fact, it seems the young girl welcomes the role of temptress as she lifts a blanket off her body to welcome the monk into her bed in the middle of the night. Although the young couple believes that they are keeping their forbidden trysts from the elder monk, the wise old monk remains alert but passive as he knows that experience rather than intervention will serve as the best teacher.

Soon, however, the wise monk believes that his charge has learned enough about sexual desire and decides that the young woman should be expelled from the temple. Bringing them both into the temple, he asks the young girl if she is still sick and she replies, "No."

The master then utters, "Then it [sex] was the right medicine. Now that you have recovered, you can leave this place."

The young woman's mysterious illness is apparently cured by having sex and she is cast out of the utopic mountain temple. That is, the woman is healed and brought to health by engaging in the act that according to Kim renders her whole—sex. The young monk, on the other hand, having experienced sex for the first time in his life, is not so easily satisfied and panics over the loss of this young woman.

The elder then knowingly warns him, "Lust awakens the desire to possess. And that awakens the intent to murder."

Figure 4.2 Spring, Summer, Fall, Winter... and Spring. *The girl entices the monk.*

At the conclusion of Act II, we see the young woman cast out of utopia wearing blue jeans and a t-shirt instead of the simple girlish white dress she wore when she first arrived. Smitten like a fool, the young monk then abandons the temple in pursuit of the young woman, carrying only the rooster and the temple's Buddha statue in his rucksack.

From the wise old monk's response it is quite clear that it is the encroachment of modernity and its ills in the form of the young woman coming to the isolated Buddhist temple that ushers in the "Fall" that drives the young acolyte to the brink of insanity. The young monk's lust is catalyzed by the silent young woman's enticing body and brings him to fulfill the master's sage-like prediction heard throughout Buddhist texts about desire inevitably leading to suffering. What Kim's vision of Buddhism also shows us, however, is that women cannot exist without sullying the landscape and polluting the mind of the young boy who has grown into a hapless teenager whose lust is awakened by the mere presence of a woman. Kim offers an androcentric vision of the idealistic monastic life, one separated from samsaric urban life and free from the intrusions and machinations of women. Such a story of male temple life with a symbolic father and son is offered as the monastic ideal reminiscent of early Indian Buddhist communities, where women took the fall for the lusty minds of men and were rendered polluting influences to the monasteries.

Fall

Act III ushers in the Fall where we find the aging master sitting with a cat reading the headlines off the newspaper that covers his rice cakes. The headline reads, "Man Flees After Murdering Wife." Somehow, the wise old monk foresees that his acolyte will return to the temple and pulls out the boy's old monastic robes and lays them out for his impending arrival. Fall thus brings the young man back to the temple although this time he comes as a violent fugitive crazed by love. He has escaped the city where he pursued his first love, for he has fallen prey to the snare of *samsara* and the prophecy of murder came true. In a jealous rage, he has murdered the young girl who had become his wife.

The old monk takes the young man back and simply utters, "The world of men has grown tiring for you huh? ... Didn't you know before what the world of men was like? We have to let go of the things we like. Is it so unbearable for you?"

This reference is the last we hear of the young woman who, like Sirimā of the ancient texts, has no voice and is now dead. Kim's young woman receives the same treatment here as women in early Indian Buddhist texts.

She comes to sully the purity of the temple and tempts the young monk to the point of murder. Once she provides the necessary lessons in the follies of desire, she is simply killed off. The young man, however, is welcomed back to the temple much like the prodigal son and is given the task of cleansing the anger in his heart by carving out the characters of the famed *Heart Sutra* on the deck of the floating temple with the knife he used to kill his wife. Once he completes his task, he surrenders readily to the two policemen who pursue and find him at the temple. The elder monk invites the policemen in, knowing they will take his former disciple away to prison. Yet he has compassion for his spiritual son who had been so tragically tempted. Women, it appears, do not matter much in this Buddhist world. The master's lack of concern over the girl indicates that it is an almost natural course of events; the murder of the woman is thus recast as a necessary catalyst propelling the monk on in his journey to enlightenment. That we know nothing more of her shows indeed the ambivalent attitude toward women that is of course reflected in the Buddhist texts and reproduced in film. Rather than learning about the source of a woman's desire, we merely learn how a young girl becomes the object and instigator of the man's transformation.

The remainder of Fall shows the elder monk predicting both his own death and the return of his spiritual son after serving time in prison. As the elder monk prepares to die, he again lays Buddhist robes and a rosary atop his own bed for the young monk to don once he returns. Building an elaborate funerary pyre atop an old row boat, the monk places Chinese characters for "shut" over his eyes, ears, nose and mouth. We are then witness to the spectacle of the elder monk's self-immolation as he burns on the pyre. As soon as he is engulfed in flames atop the floating boat, the director cuts to an image of a snake swimming away from the pyre representing the reincarnation of the monk. It is in this instance, however, that the Zen association fails, for in Buddhism, the snake represents one of the three Buddhist poisons of greed, aversion, and delusion. Therefore, it would be an entirely unsuitable form of rebirth for an enlightened master.

Winter

Act IV returns us to temple several years after the young monk has served his jail time. The floating temple is now locked in ice as the acolyte returns an older man who now takes over the temple after collecting the master's relics from the frozen funeral pyre and placing them into an ice Buddha sculpture he has chiseled by hand. It is during this period of time that the monk curiously trains himself in martial arts as the audience is treated to a view of the director who now plays the monk artfully sculpting Buddha images out of ice and performing magnificent gravity defying splits in midair.

Winter also brings another woman to the temple. This time, we find a mother who brings her infant son to the temple for the monk's keep. The woman covers her face under a purple silk scarf so that the monk cannot see her identity—nor can the viewer. Because her face is veiled, viewers have no idea if she may in fact be the reincarnation of the monk's former wife. Like the young girl who tempted the monk in the Summer season, this mother also lies in the same bed in the temple and inspires the monk's curiosity. She raises the blanket to invite him in just as the young girl did. Kim intentionally confuses the viewer and makes an explicit connection between the mother and the young girl for even as the mother lays in bed, the camera moves to the elderly master's old bed where we find the reincarnated monk as snake observing the scene all over again. While we are led to believe that the woman wishes to cover her face with the scarf out of shame, and because such an image introduces an enticing ambiguity, one cannot help but also see that in Kim's vision of Buddhism, women not only lack voice, they also lack an identity; all we know of these women is that after serving their purposes, they are killed. For just as the unfortunate wife was murdered by her Buddhist husband, so too, does the woman who has brought her child to the temple meet her death when she falls through a hole in the ice made by the monk to wash his face. The viewer is left intentionally bewildered and unsettled about the woman as Kim eludes to a connection between the murdered wife and the mother. Are they the same person? Has she been reincarnated? Is the young boy the monk's son? Has he killed again? While it may be the case that life outside the

Figure 4.3 Spring, Summer, Fall, Winter... and Spring. *The mother brings boy to temple.*

temple in the real world is associated with a kind of spiritual alienation that only temple life can cure, it also appears that with the death of the mother and the arrival of a new orphaned monk Kim closes the monk's karmic loophole.

Spring

Spring, Summer, Fall, Winter...and Spring concludes in many ways precisely where it began with the new head of the floating temple caring for the newly-orphaned monk. Much like in the opening scene, the young boy engages in the same kind of antics that the older monk did in his own youth—torturing animals. This time, the boy stuffs rocks in the mouths of the same animals. To further underscore the cyclical nature of Buddhist time, the young acolyte is now played by the very same actor who plays the boy in the original Spring. Perhaps the lesson here is that history continues to repeat itself while its lessons remain unlearned. Simplicity, pure experience, naturalness, and antidote to contemporary woes, Zen Buddhism again takes form as a symbol of premodernity in Korean filmmaker Kim Ki-Duk's sensory delight.

But what about the women? While the monks vanquish their seducers, the women fare far worse—they die without any possibility of spiritual liberation and redemption for their actions. Because of the foreclosure of the possibility for female liberation and their inevitable death, such "charming cadavers" serve as cautionary tales of Buddhist lay women's sexuality gone awry.[20] The film reaffirms the textual perspective that women bind men to samsara and yet, unlike the canonical texts, Kim's film holds up the possibility that were it not for the women's seductive powers, the monks might never reach enlightenment and liberation. Thus, the women are the necessary antagonists in Buddhist films—men fear them, are seduced by them, and fall madly in love with them. In so doing, the men are driven to murder, experience desire and remorse, and therefore mature on the path to liberation, while women in the Buddhist world seduce with their duplicitous bodies and minds, trap their men, and are ultimately killed off.

Women are then an impermanent yet fortuitous object lesson in the monks' mental development and spiritual purification. There is a lamentable lack of healthy, unpunished, ordinary female sexuality and religious flourishing both in *sutras* and in films that cannot but perpetuate a Buddhism with limited vision. Such partial visions leave in place a troubling form of religion that attends only to the male monastic rather than the lay Buddhist woman as religious actor. Such visions leave many unanswered questions in their wake—What kind of Buddhism is rendered here? Is it a Buddhism of plurality or one of limited vision? What are the effects of the narrow focus on monasticism and ascetic discourses that vilify the body—and women's bodies in particular? Is there another way to imagine Buddhism such that it meets the religious aspirations of its nonmonastics? What happens if we change the protagonist from a monk to that of a Buddhist nun who also returns to the ordinary world and engages in sexual activity? Must she necessarily be deemed impure and incapable of spiritual enlightenment? Or—might there be another way to imagine her actions as those of a compassionate *bodhisattva* whose spiritual salvation lies in being part of the very world of desire? In the following chapter, I attempt an answer to such questions as I reread the negative associations of women with dangerous sexuality through the 1989 Korean film, *Aje Aje Bara Aje* (*Come, Come, Come Upward*) to counterbalance an otherwise debilitating view of women's agency, and spiritual capacity for enlightenment.

5

Coming Down from the Mountaintop: Engaged Buddhism in the World

Throughout the previous chapters, I have argued that many Buddhist films have contributed to the racialized view of the religion as an exotic tradition of mystery and near unintelligibility populated by monks who cannot coexist with the ordinary world. In so doing, I noted that the image of faraway utopic mountaintops makes it virtually impossible to imagine a Buddhism that is part and parcel of the everyday landscape inhabited by ordinary Buddhists struggling to transform suffering of self and other. In the chapter that follows, I take up the question of how one might begin to reimagine Buddhism so that it is removed from such a limiting otherworldliness and grounded in normative nonmonastic life. Toward that end, I examine two South Korean films produced in 1989—*Aje Aje Bara Aje* by internationally acclaimed director Im Kwon-Taek, and *Why Has Bodhidharma Left for the East?*, an international box office success by the artist Bae Young-Kyun.

Both films feature monastics on the quest for enlightenment who ultimately discover that liberation from the world of suffering only comes when they can let go of their attachments to the goal of *nirvana*. By solving the answers to the *koans*, mental puzzles that defy easy logic, the protagonists break through dualistic notions of self and other through the guidance of their respective Sŏn masters. Both characters come down from the mountaintop into the messy chaotic world of *samsara* where they are destined to attain enlightenment. The deployment of *koans* in these two films can perhaps best be understood as the gift of narrating their whole selves into existence following their grappling with the seeming discrepancy between lay and temple life. These films therefore offer fascinating explorations of the significance of everyday life as the ground for enlightenment, and counterbalances to what has become the stock character of Buddhism in many films—the antinomian iconoclastic monk whose mysterious fountain of wisdom continues to capture the imagination and yearning of many a filmgoer.

The first section of this chapter addresses *Aje Aje Bara Aje* (*Come, Come, Come Upward*), which narrates the experiences of a young female nun who descends the mountaintop temple and becomes a laywoman whose engagement in the world through intimate relationships with men transforms her into an earthly *bodhisattva*. The bulk of this chapter focuses on her development as an earthly *bodhisattva* to draw attention to the significance of women and the laity in the Buddhist world. In the latter section of the chapter, I address *Why Has Bodhidharma Left for the East?*, a Sŏn Buddhist film about the experiences of a monk whose entry into the monastic life begins only after he abandons his family in the quest for enlightenment and as an escape from the *samsaric* life. He soon discovers that he cannot progress in his practice until he lets go of his attachment to the goal of liberation and ultimately returns to the world of suffering into order to transform the world and himself simultaneously.

Aje Aje Bara Aje

Indian Buddhist literature abounds in stories of the bodily sacrifices and self-mutilations that underscore the spiritual heroics of *bodhisattvas* or buddhas-to-be who cast their bodies down at the feet of starving animals and humans for their consumption. A series of such dramatic bodily performances are found in the past-life stories (*jataka* tales) of the historical Shakyamuni Buddha that are used as narrative didactic techniques and, as Ranjini Obeyesekere puts it, lessons on "how to be good Buddhists."[1] In one such previous lifetime, the Buddha was born as the *bodhisattva* Rūpāvatī (Beautiful Woman), a self-sacrificing woman who slices off her own breasts as a gift of food for a starving mother so that she won't devour her newborn son. Transforming herself into nourishment for the suffering mother, Rūpāvatī's act of compassion and gifting of herself signifies a profound understanding of the suffering of all sentient beings as well as the depth of her commitment to save others. Upon saving the poor mother from the act of murder and infanticide, Rūpāvatī's body is restored anew and she is predicted to full enlightenment in the future.

Such stories of the radical acts of somatic compassion performed by *bodhisattvas* indicate that bodies can indeed be used for positive ends in Buddhist traditions. Yet, must bodies always be sacrificed in the quest for salvation? Is there a way to imagine a somatic compassion that has far more to do with the gift of the living body through intimacy than with the giving away of one's body through self-sacrifice? Can such intimate expressions of compassion themselves be the grounds for enlightenment and spiritual maturation?

In Im Kwon Taek's film, *Aje Aje Bara Aje*, a young woman devotes herself to the monastic life by becoming a nun who, despite her best efforts at asceticism, attracts the romantic attentions of a stranger who doggedly pursues her after she saves him from hurling himself from a cliff in an attempted suicide. For having attracted a man, she is consequently punished by her fellow sisters who banish her from the mountain. Although she is expelled from the nunnery, Soon Nyo soon becomes an earthly *bodhisattva* who engages in radical acts of somatic compassion akin to *bodhisattvas* in Mahayana Buddhist texts—that is, she engages in relationships of intimacy and care with alienated and broken individuals in order to effect their transformation and her own enlightenment. Although her sexual methods may seem unconventional by most orthodox Buddhist monastic standards, her compassionate activity in the form of companionship, love, and caregiving result in an awareness that, ultimately, there is no distinction between the ordinary world and the monastic world and that everyday life is the most effective training ground for enlightenment. Her realization, which is solidified after observing the death and cremation of her previous abbess and watching the nun's body reduce to ashes, reflects the Mahayana Buddhist teachings of emptiness and no individual self.

Aje Aje Bara Aje's opening shot allows spectators an ethnographic gaze into the daily functioning of a Buddhist nunnery with its monastic compound adorned with Buddha statues, reliquaries, nuns in meditation, and pious lay women working the temple grounds.[2] Scenes of temple life on the mountain

Figure 5.1 Aje Aje Bara Aje. *Soon Nyo becomes a nun*

are framed by the background chanting of the famous *mantra* at the end of the Mahayana Buddhist text, the *Heart Sutra* (*Banya shimkyung* in Korean), "*Aje Aje Para Aje Para Seung Aje Moji Sa ba ha...*" While English translations of the film's title are translated as "Come, Come, Come Upward," this literal translation cannot convey the religious significance of the *mantra* and its use as the initial audio framing device of the film. Without a Buddhist interpretation and nuance of this title, the viewers lose some of the key Mahayana Buddhist standpoints of the film—emptiness and interdependence.[3]

In contrast to the English translation, the Buddhist reading of the title is based on the Sanskrit translation of the *Heart Sutra*. This reading translates loosely as "Gone, Gone, Completely Gone," a translation that while interpreted literally in a number of different renditions, clearly references the Buddha and his experience of ultimate enlightenment. As I show in this chapter, the explicitly Mahayana Buddhist origins of the title reflect the depths of Soon Nyo's spiritual realization that affect her own enlightenment as she learns to fuse the gap between self and other, *samsara* and *nirvana*. Her enlightenment comes not as a nun living in a monastic community apart from the world, but rather only when she descends the mountain to engage in the world and can finally answer her abbess's *koan*—"Between your spirit that stays here and your body rambling around in the world, which one is real?" This *koan* was given to her as she was sent back down the mountain to "kill the immature Buddha" within herself. Although expelled from monastic life, Soon Nyo later becomes a *bodhisattva* par excellence who, in rejecting the life of asceticism, becomes a laywoman and wife to three struggling men at different times. Through these relationships, Soon Nyo embodies the ideal of somatic compassion, not through sacrificing her life or even her sexual pleasure. Instead, she engages in mutually enhancing relationships of intimacy that bring each of her husbands to spiritual wholeness and further her own spiritual development toward enlightenment as a lay woman. While one might assume that women are once again represented merely through their sexuality, my concern is less about the sexual activity of the *bodhisattva* and more about the agency and subjectivity that is hinted at through the derivation of pleasure for one's own sake.

Soon Nyo's sexual intimacy may seem antithetical to the Buddhist life, but as I argue in this chapter, her sexuality symbolizes an engagement in the ordinary world that assists in her progress toward enlightenment. Her figurative foe in the film comes in the form of another seemingly wiser young nun named Jin Sung who serves as her guide when she first enters the monastic life. Jin Sung knows all the rules of comportment for the monastic life and avails herself of every opportunity to admonish Soon Nyo for her shortcomings. Yet, despite her advanced experience as a nun, the temple's abbess later sends Jin Sung from the monastery to study at the university. The abbess views this assignment as an antidote to Jin Sung's over-attachment to asceticism, orthodoxy, and separation from the ordinary world which could hinder her ability to advance toward Buddhahood. Thus Jin Sung reluctantly heads down the mountain and enrolls in university, but later returns with an even greater fervor for asceticism and isolation. Im counterbalances the prevailing popular construction of Buddhism as a religion of meditation and isolation represented by Jin Sung with this tale of the interconnectedness of all beings and the need to engage in the messiness of ordinary life both to heal and be healed through the contrast between the two women.

What I find particularly intriguing about Im's film lies in his juxtaposition of the two nuns on a similar quest for *nirvana*—the protagonist Soon Nyo who later transforms into an earthly lay *bodhisattva* gifting her body in the care of men, and her spiritual opposite, Jin Sung, who rigidly adheres to sexual purity and avoidance of the nonmonastic world. The tension between these two nuns reflects the differing attitudes toward sexuality in Buddhist *sutras* that Im deploys for his commentary on Buddhist social responsibility. On the one hand, nuns like monks are required to take vows of asceticism and uproot sexual desire through celibacy. On the other hand, the ability to deploy desire and sexuality for the sake of enlightenment also emerges as a potent source of spiritual power. Through Soon Nyo, audiences have the fortuitous occasion to reimagine Buddhism through *Aje Aje Bara Aje*'s emphasis on the practice of compassion in everyday life where destroying the roots of desire are not held to be the pinnacle of virtue. Instead, immersion in ordinary struggles and the honing of the capacity for compassion with and through the body are tantamount to enlightenment and liberation.

While much has been made in feminist critiques of Buddhist literary associations of female bodies with containers of filth and snares of *samsara*, the story of Rūpāvatī noted above demonstrates that Indian Buddhist discourses on female bodies also depict them as potential sites of ethical transformation.[4] Thus, the texts themselves are neither uniform in their interpretation of bodies nor entirely negative with regard to women. It is the textual engagement with the liberating potential of gifting the body for the transformation of the other that concerns this chapter. I read Buddhist textual acts of compassion of *bodhisattvas* like Rūpāvatī alongside film as radical acts of somatic compassion to save others and enlighten the self. In so doing, I not only utilize Buddhist texts to interpret film but I also utilize film to create alternative images of Buddhism that position the practice of everyday Buddhism as a productive site of enlightenment. Such an interpretation signifies a lay Buddhism wherein women's practices are not overlooked, but rather are approached as sources of liberation. Toward that end, I engage in a heterodox reading of the sexual ministry of Soon Nyo as an instance of *bodhisattvic* compassion. Rather than approaching Soon Nyo's expulsion from her Buddhist nunnery and subsequent sexual relationships with men as indices of sexual impurity as most of her fellow nuns have, I read her sexual engagement with lay men as enhancing both for herself and for the recipients of her companionship. Such an interpretation of sexuality as somatic compassion emerges as a logical extension of what is gestured toward, but not fully articulated in, Buddhist *sutras*—that is, a female lay religiosity whereby the female body becomes the site of spiritual liberation of self and other. Her actions will be read as examples of an ordinary Buddhism freed from the overlay of heroic expectations associated with the monastic virtuosi.

While Soon Nyo's main method of compassionate activity is expressed through her sexual interactions with men, my aim is to neither to advocate for enlightenment through sexual activity alone nor to merely continue to conflate women with sexuality and body. Rather, my intent is to articulate a space in the Buddhist social order and popular imagination for the theorization and embodiment of lay Buddhist women's religiosity. When adequately addressed, such an approach has the potential to transform and counter the negative constructions of women and the laity in Buddhism. In this way, Soon Nyo's sexuality is not to be read as a strictly physical or psychological liberation; instead, I approach her sexuality as a metaphor for a new kind of Buddhism located in and accepting of the body rather than in opposition to it. This approach to the body in Buddhism, while similar to Tibetan Tantric traditions that locate enlightenment within the body, differs in that it focuses on ordinary laywomen as the subjects and agents of spiritual transformation. Rather than articulating a Buddhism that transcends sexuality, my reading of *Aje Aje Bara Aje* finds resonance in Buddhist textual sources such as the *Gandavyuha* (*Entry into the Realm of Reality*) and commentarial literature referenced later in this chapter that highlight female *bodhisattvas* who bring men to enlightenment without sacrificing their own lives. In so doing, I approach Buddhist *sutras* and film as mutually dependent and referential texts and I move interpretively between the two for this re-visioning of tradition. Therefore, it seems fitting that this chapter focuses on the development of Buddhist film as a spiritual technology that reconstructs received images of religion, self, and other anew.

Bodhisattva bodies enticing others to the *dharma*

Susanne Mrozik's analysis of early medieval Indian Mahayana Buddhist texts devotes sustained attention to what she refers to as the bodily "materialization of virtue," an ethical prescription where *bodhisattvas* are encouraged to cultivate bodies that act as catalysts for the enlightenment of others.[5] In her reading of the *Compendium of Training* composed by Indian scholar Shantideva in the seventh or eighth century, Mrozik argues that the body becomes the locus of practice for the *bodhisattva* who purifies his or her body in order to "cook" or "ripen" others.[6] Rather than assuming that bodies are antithetical to mental transformation, Mrozik argues that bodies are positively performative in the Buddhist context—that is, bodies are cultivated by *bodhisattvas* as tonics and cures for those who interact with them through the physical act of touch. Through such interaction beings emerge ethically transformed.

Mrozik's analysis proves particularly constructive for interpreting and highlighting the compassionate acts of women and female bodies in Buddhist films precisely because she locates the association of the body of a spiritually pure being like a *bodhisattva* with a purifying sexuality; that is, the body of a *bodhisattva* can be used as a sensual and sensory enticement for the moral edification of others. Unlike the examples of bodies as disgusting containers of filth in the Buddhist worldview studied in the previous chapter, here lust and sexuality are productive and generative when the object of the being's lust is the *bodhisattva* who can deploy desire and sex for ethical effect. As Mrozik notes "... bodhisattvas make vows to produce bodies whose very taste, touch, and sight transform living beings, physically and morally."[7] The production of pleasing bodies indicates a sexual pleasure that can be deployed for spiritual ends, for as Mrozik explains:

> Base cravings such as those for meat or sex, which under other circumstances might have negative karmic effects, here have marked positive effects. Bodhisattva vows transform the arena of sensual pleasures into one that is physically and morally productive. These vows produce bodhisattva bodies which, like "well-prepared, boiled rice without husk-powder" convey both benefit and pleasure on living beings.[8]

Sex in the texts is therefore not uniformly negative; instead, when deployed for the right reason, sensual pleasure can be quite constructive for one's salvational goals so long as the intention is pure.

The utilization of the body as transformative gift for others' consumption and subsequent psycho-spiritual healing finds clear articulation in the sexual ministry of Soon Nyo. Through Im's lens, Soon Nyo's interactions with men are to be read as both a question and a response to whether Korean Buddhism adequately responds to the needs of contemporary men and women while remaining isolated on mountaintops from the people.

Mahayana Buddhist texts such as the *Gandavyuha Sutra* (*Entry into the Realm of Reality*) and the *Vimalakirtinirdesha Sutra* (*The Holy Teaching of Vimalakirti*) argue against the ultimate distinctions between *nirvana* and *samsara* and also validate the female body as the locus for advanced spiritual development. Im employs this Mahayana textual view through the symbol of Soon Nyo and her compassionate activity through her body to support his insistence on a Korean Buddhism that serves humanity through social interaction. The ascetic nun Jin Sung's rigid asceticism and desire to remain isolated from ordinary society reflects earlier Indian Buddhist texts such as the *Theragatha* (Verses of the Elders) that denigrate women's bodies as impure, full of sexual desire, and the perpetuators of the cycle of *samsara* or suffering. Discussing the significance of the Mahayana standpoint in his film, Im explains:

> The Buddhism Korea accepted was the Mahayana sect, whose objective is to bring ordinary people to enlightenment. Many monks, however, do not follow the precepts of Mahayana Buddhism and communicate to ordinary people. They live as Hinayana hermits in the mountains. If reality is painful for most people, then it is necessary to share ordinary people's pain and struggle by following Mahayana Buddhism. I made *Come, Come, Come Upward* to ask how the monks could separate themselves from ordinary life and follow Hinayana Buddhist ways.[9]

Im's vision of Buddhism necessitates an active social engagement with the world of suffering rather than an isolated effort to eradicate individual desire. In this manner, his film reflects a concern with the ordinary world and serves as a text or Buddhist *sutra* that can revise the way Buddhism sees the ordinary and is seen by a larger audience.[10] My particular fascination with this film emerges both from Im's impetus to narrate a socially engaged Buddhism into existence and my own hope that Buddhism can flourish more fully with a less rigid view of what Buddhism should look like. As I show in this chapter, through films like *Aje Aje Bara Aje* that propose an alternative means of being Buddhist, we might imagine a Buddhism that encourages both an engagement with, rather than a denial of, the senses *and* the practice of compassion through ethical interaction with others.

Mahayana texts such as the *Śikṣāsamuccaya* and the *Gandavyuha* invert the notion of a polluting female sexuality to a liberatory female sexuality, a textual device that I utilize in this chapter to underscore the value of a female lay Buddhism which is often ignored in larger discourses of Buddhism in both Asian and Western film. From the Yellow Man in *Broken Blossoms* and Father Perrault in *Lost Horizon*, to the young lustful monk in *Spring, Summer, Fall, Winter... and Spring*, the detective in *Zen Noir*, and Jarmusch's hit man in *Ghost Dog*, the male Buddhist monk figure appears as the focal point of Buddhist practice. Films like *Aje Aje Bara Aje*, however, allow for moving beyond the perceived center of Buddhist life to the margins where the Buddhist laywoman ordinaire is upheld as an enlightened *bodhisattva* who transforms self and others through her embrace of the ordinary body rather than its transcendence through meditative practices. It is this vision of Buddhism in film that proves most suggestive and useful for a nuanced reading of tradition that also counteracts some of the fantastical images of monks found in the films discussed in early chapters.

Film scholars such as David James tend to prioritize the connection between nationalism and Buddhism in *Aje Aje Bara Aje* over any specifically salvational concerns.[11] James establishes Im's oeuvre firmly within the historical framework of South Korea's political liberalization and relaxation of censorship laws that allowed filmmakers to explicitly represent and critique the exploitation of the working class in the 1980s.[12] According to James, Im deploys this new freedom of expression through the figure of the heroine Soon Nyo who administers to the needs of the displaced, the working class, and other embodiments of *han* or national sentiments of loss and rage in response to colonization and other political traumas.[13] James sees the director's oeuvre as a confrontation with alienation and his "attempt to turn the colonized Korean film industry into a vehicle of national culture."[14]

While acknowledging the critical value of such analyses for understanding the filmmaker's pivotal role in Korean national identity and cinema, this chapter foregrounds the religious implications of Im's cinematic work. My interest in doing so is not so much to posit a facile distinction between religious and national identities but rather to explore the film's latent and explicit interpretation and presentation of a central Buddhist question of how one attains enlightenment—through asceticism or through radical embodied compassion? *Aje Aje Bara Aje* has not been approached by scholars such as James as a strictly Buddhist film *per se*, yet I propose just such a reading that takes seriously the Buddhist ethical and philosophical dilemmas posed by Im.

While the relationship between religion, nationalism, and film is indeed complex and integrated, I depart from the tendency to analyze instances of Buddhism as examples of nationalism alone in order to approach *Aje Aje Bara Aje* as a primary source for remaking and re-imaging Buddhism. As a scholar invested in a feminist and racially liberatory approach to Buddhism, my reading of film as religious text imagines new roles and places for women in Buddhism that heretofore have been left undertheorized and undervalued in canonical texts, institutionalized Buddhism, and on screen.

Mahayana Buddhist discourses on bodhisattva bodily sacrifice and bodily ripening thus converge in my analysis of *Aje Aje Bara Aje* to imagine anew the significance of an everyday lay Buddhism where female bodies are not burdened by the historical preoccupation with their spiritually polluting effluvia, but rather are given new meaning as catalysts for enlightenment with and through their bodies. Soon Nyo's sexual ministry is therefore explicitly read against the grain as a Buddhist ethics of care that responds to the needs of lay society and rests on the bodily performance of the *bodhisattva* who gives of her body to the pleasure and transformation of the displaced men she encounters. Of course Soon Nyo's acts of bodily sacrifice can simply be read as yet another Buddhist rendering of the female body as a mere catalyst for the enlightenment of men, yet I generate possibilities of a more complex understanding of the conceptualization of female bodies in *Aje Aje Bara Aje* by recourse to the very Mahayana teachings that reflect nuanced views of sexuality as enlightenment lessons for both the male recipient and the female bodhisattva.

Although Soon Nyo deploys her sexuality to liberate *han*-filled men in nationalist terms or *dukkha*-filled men in Buddhist parlance, when seen through the lens of Mahayana teachings, such a technique is indicative of the bodhisattva's prediction to enlightenment and she will not digress back to an ordinary level of consciousness.[15] That is to say, Soon Nyo's transformative effect on men can take place precisely because she is destined to achieve full enlightenment. In my reading of this bodily performance, priority is given to the use of the body as gift as a metaphor for the body as the ground for everyday enlightenment. An important distinction remains, however, between the Mahayana *Compendium of Training* that elaborates on *bodhisattvas* and sexual pleasure and my own reading of Soon Nyo as one such *bodhisattva*, and that difference is one of sex. The majority of *bodhisattvas* whose bodies bring both sexual desire and spiritual development to the opposite sex are male. There are few opportunities to imagine female *bodhisattvas* that do not induce negative forms of lust. Instead, female *bodhisattvas* and their pleasing *bodhisattvas* are believed to have warranted their beauty through meritorious actions in their past lives; however, when men admire and lust after them, the karmic consequences accruing to men are consistently presented in a negative light.

I depart from such an interpretation and approach Im's film as a *sutra* or text that can help redefine the parameters of female sexuality and female *bodhisattvas*. Instead, I approach Nyo's sexuality as both indicative of her own spiritual attainments as well as spiritually productive for the men with whom she interacts. Rather than bringing them to enlightenment in some distant future, she transforms them by liberating them from alienation and isolation. Therefore, my approach to Buddhist film and women's capacities align more closely with the views held by the *Gandavyuha* that presents female *bodhisattvas* as spiritual friends and enlightening companions. One such enlightening woman is the courtesan Vasumitrā whose famed beauty transforms men. She explains:

To gods, in accord with their inclinations and interests, I appear in the form of a goddess of surpassing splendor and perfection; and to all other types of beings I accordingly appear in the form of a female of their species, of surpassing splendor and perfection. And all who come to me with minds full of passion, I teach them so that they become free of passion.[16]

Thus the example of Soon Nyo as female bodhisattva proves most generative for imagining (and therefore realizing) everyday enlightenment in the very messiness of *samsara* that monastic Buddhism encourages one to escape.

Earthly *bodhisattva*

Im Kwon-Taek clearly establishes Soon Nyo's transformation into an earthly *bodhisattva* when she hears the cries of a suicidal man. While all the other nuns working the fields ignore his cries, Soon Nyo alone moves quickly to save him. When he returns later to the temple in pursuit of her, he cries out, "I was reborn because of you. You are a mother to me!" References to the maternal qualities of the nun here are reminiscent of the nurturing and salvational qualities of the *bodhisattva* Kwan Um (Kuan Yin in Chinese), believed to save all sentient beings in times of crisis. The man's plaintive cries for her companionship and care quickly extend beyond the maternal and into the sexual as he continues to hound her—eventually becoming her husband.

In later expelling Soon Nyo, the abbess, Eun Hyo Sunim, assures her that, "The mountain isn't the only place for asceticism. I am sending you away but not for good." She then gives Soon Nyo the *koan* to contemplate as a laywoman, an indication of the head nun's faith in Soon Nyo's future enlightenment.

"Between your spirit that stays here and your body rambling in the world, which is real?" she rhetorically asks Soon Nyo. The abbess then promises they will meet again once Soon Nyo discovers the true nature of her self. The abbess's remarks indicate that she predicts enlightenment and liberation for the young nun, but not in the traditional role of a celibate nun. Instead, she is encouraged to immerse herself in the muddy, dirty, and chaotic world of the city or *samsara*. Yet, as she discovers, the murky world she has entered is the very ground for her to practice and solve her *koan*. This realization comes not so much from meditative contemplation but rather from active engagement in the world of suffering. Yet it is not mere suffering that Soon Nyo experiences; she also experiences sexual pleasure, love, and companionship. Such experiences are not asceticism but, as her abbess told her, there are other ways of being Buddhist and becoming enlightened. Soon Nyo's subsequent experiences of joy and sexual pleasure thus counterbalance *Spring, Summer, Fall, Winter… and Spring*'s images of dangerous female sexuality as cautionary tale.

According to David James, Im Kwon-Taek often utilizes women as icons of Korea's historical exploitation (colonialism, military rule, etc.) by presenting them as victims of sexual violation, a move that also serves to titillate the spectator.[17] James's argument can easily be supported by the two emotionally fraught scenes of sexual violence and aggression in *Aje Aje Bara Aje*. In the first, Soon Nyo is raped by the man she saved (and later married) and in the second, the pious Jin Sung is nearly raped by a self-castrated monk she encounters dwelling in a cave.

The first rape scene transpires shortly after Soon Nyo has left the mountain and boards a bus headed for the city where she will begin her new life. But no sooner does she board the bus, than she is met by the very same man whose attentions led to her banishment. Despite her desire to remain sexually pure, the man takes her to a restaurant and forces her to drink alcohol. Staggering out of the restaurant in a drunken state, she is escorted to a motel room. Once in the room, she passes out and the man tears the nun's robe from her body. He then rapes her while she lingers in and out of an alcohol-induced haze. Abruptly awakened to consciousness, she cries out and desperately reaches for the knit cap her abbess had given to her to hide the fact that she was once a nun. She quickly covers her tonsured head in shame as her transition into her lay life begins through sexual violence.

Unfortunately, Im offers us little time to come to terms with the sexual violence in the film as the very next scene brings us to the happily married couple living in a shanty town just outside the coal mine where her rapist-turned-husband has the first respectable job he has ever had. After laying claim to the young woman through an act of sexual aggression, the man is made anew and transformed through her care. While there is no getting around the fact that the nun was raped and forcibly laicized, it is still worthwhile to note Soon Nyo's later capacity to initiate and experience sexual pleasure as an enlightened being. In other words, her subsequent sexual relationships are mutually enhancing and not considered detrimental to her religious life. Similarly, one can look to her subsequent sexual intimacy as a metaphor for a Buddhism characterized by integration in everyday life.

The second sexually violent scene takes place in an isolated cave that Jin Song visits in order to deepen her practice of meditation and strict asceticism. While there, she encounters a Buddhist monk who taunts the nun for her excessive attachment to sexual purity. In a highly charged moment of sexual aggression, the monk suddenly grabs the young nun and removes his garments as if to rape her. However, instead of raping her, he forces her to gaze upon his genitals, which have been mutilated by the monk himself.

Forcing Jin Sung to witness the follies of overattachment to sexual desire by gazing upon his self-castration, he uses his body as a cautionary tale against the constant obsession with the need to uproot sexual desire. As he warns her, regardless of the depth of his practice of asceticism, desire will continue to grow despite one's best efforts to eradicate it at its roots. In addition to serving as a warning against over asceticism, David James notes that this scene also inverts patriarchal power for:

> [it] is the man, not the woman, who is positioned as the object of gaze, and when the woman looks, what she sees is the mark of his castration, his lack of a phallus that figures the impotence of meditational asceticism and self-mortification.[18]

Im utilizes this deeply troubling scene to reinforce his belief that ascetic practices that isolate Buddhists from society are but hindrances to spiritual progress which the director envisions communally, especially when overemphasized at the expense of social engagement. Sequestration in mountains, caves, and temples holds very little potential for social transformation by monks and nuns who, according to Im's vision of Buddhism, should take part in the world by working to address its ills. Despite her most ardent efforts, Jin Sun fails to make any progress on her path to enlightenment, not because she does not have the disciplinary strength, but rather because her discipline has alienated her from any genuine care for the world of the suffering.

Soon Nyo, however, becomes an earthly *bodhisattva* to three separate men, all of whom eventually die transformed and brought to wholeness despite their afflictions. Her interactions with all three men reflects both her own desire and her pleasure as well as the healing powers of companionship that reflect her spiritual-social commitments. While Soon Nyo's method of bedding several broken men seems controversial when viewed through the lens of asceticism, Im offers a fascinating, if not problematic, account of the enlightening activities of this earthly *bodhisattva* who, like the audience of Shantideva's texts, gives her body for the consumption and edification of others. Unlike the mute, faceless women in Kim Ki-Duk's film, Soon Nyo is afforded a religious agency when she experiences a spiritual awakening the likes of which cannot be found for women in *Spring, Summer, Fall, Winter... and Spring.*

When her first husband is suddenly killed in a mining accident and Soon Nyo subsequently has a miscarriage, she offers her compassionate care to a double amputee by becoming his wife and bringing him to psychological fulfillment and wholeness through her companionship. Upon his death, she then travels to a remote island where she befriends, and ultimately marries, another widower she meets at a hospital, becoming the mother to his young son. While such activities seem antithetical to the enlightened life, Soon Nyo's development into an enlightened being comes precisely when she loses her attachment to the distinctions between purity and impurity, propriety and impropriety. Her embrace of the world of *samsara* and her compassionate care through the form of her companionship become the practice of her *koan*, a *koan* that ultimately dissolves the bonds between self and other, dissonance and consonance. She is constantly sought after by suffering men wherever she goes and her abbess knows that her care and her enlightenment are deeply interconnected. That self that is the true self can only be found in the complete giving up and surrender of herself for the sake of the other. Only then will she ultimately discover that the two (self and other) are one and the same. This is the essence of realization of the true self and Buddha nature for Mahayanists.

Soon Nyo's descent from the mountain thus signifies a move from an isolated temple that is too caught up in its own purity into the murky and desperate world below. Yet this messy world is the very ground for the transformative efforts of the *bodhisattva*. As Soon Nyo explains the course of her post-monastic life to the ascetic foil Jin Sung (who fails in her own development because she is too attached to notions of purity), she makes a critical connection between the compassionate activities of the *bodhisattva* who embraces others in whatever manner suited. She explains to Jin Sun, "... I don't regret my life in which I gave my heart and my body to such people. Living, happiness, and unhappiness are all the same in essence ... I never gave up ... Whenever I met a new man I did my best as if I was a virgin. I hope that it might be asceticism." In this scene Soon Nyo shows that much like the *bodhisattvas* in Shantideva's text, she recreates herself for the others' and her own care and salvation without attention to the illusions of propriety.

What makes the example of Soon Nyo so different from her textual predecessors is Im's insistence that the audience not only witness the suffering she endures during her rape but also her sexual pleasure and that she not be hindered in her spiritual development for having such experiences. Instead, her subsequent experience of sexuality is taken as normative rather than extraordinary or antithetical to the religious life. While Im's film does not engage in the explicit, and at times rather graphic, sexuality that we find in films like *Spring, Summer, Fall, Winter... and Spring*, what he does offer is the camera's focus on Soon Nyo's pleasure while having sex. One night after celebrating the successful management of a viral outbreak in the community, Soon Nyo and her husband Song, an ambulance driver, retire to their apartment straight into bed. Rather than treating the act of sex as intrinsically harmful, Im's camera lens focuses on Soon Nyo's pleasure, an important choice that allows audiences to see that even a Buddhist laywoman like Soon Nyo can have a normal and healthy sexuality that includes self-fulfillment. Unfortunately for her husband, the viral epidemic has taken its toll and just as he climaxes, he dies. While his death might appear a warning against

Figure 5.2 Aje Aje Bara Aje. *Soon Nyo (left) recounts life as earthly bodhisattva to Jin Sung (right).*

Buddhist sexuality, the emphasis on Soon Nyo's own pleasure, as well as her development as a *bodhisattva,* mitigate against reading her sexuality as strictly negative. Instead, Im advocates for us to read her sexuality as an example of her engagement and embrace of the world. He is not advocating solely for female sexuality, but rather for transcending traditional Buddhist interpretations of sexuality as a hindrance.

Jin Sung, the ascetic Buddhist nun devoted to her abbess and the quest for enlightenment does not fare as well in the development of the wisdom and compassion necessary to experience *nirvana.* Instead, she becomes the symbolic contrast to Soon Nyo's embodied engagement in the world. Unlike Jin Sung's isolation in the nunnery, Soon Nyo's practice of Buddhism immerses itself in the world of men and women, for as one lay Buddhist teacher remarks, "Buddhism must be with the people." In other words, the Buddhism that is currently practiced on mountaintops must thus be purged of its "Hinayana" aspects. Im illustrates the shortcomings of an ascetic Buddhism which he believes must be revised in order to provide a structure of social interaction with the ordinary world much like he imagines the Christians have done. Im's critique of an isolated Buddhism is also echoed in the words of a male student activist who pursues the ascetic nun during her brief stint in university and asks: "What is your purpose? To ignore the poor, to hide deep in the mountain and discipline yourself? For Buddhism to build a stronghold in the current age, you have to get together with poor farmers and city laborers to lead their spiritual ways...It's the only road to salvation." Indicating the rise of Christianity and the need for Buddhism to compete on the religious front, he notes, "Christianity lifts the burdens of the people; what will Buddhism do? Read scriptures?" Jin Sung clearly misses his point about the socially engaged nature of religious institutions when she simply responds, "We need to free our lives," and implies that each individual must do this on her own. Her narrow view reflects the Mahayana stereotype of what has come to be known as "the lesser vehicle" of Buddhism which maintains that one attains enlightenment on one's own and not through the salvational and compassionate activities of the *bodhisattva*.

The student activist who doggedly pursues Jin Sung reflects Im's belief that Buddhism must transform into a more socially-engaged tradition. The student speaks against the Buddhism represented by the ascetic nun who argues throughout the film with Soon Nyo about the purpose of the Buddhist life. The ascetic nun is filled with visions of an idealistic world of mental purity, a world that is unsullied by the *samsaric* nature of the cities. Thus her attachment comes in the form of attachment to *nirvana*, just one side of a coin whose opposite is *samsara*. Her attachment to her rigid vision is her downfall as she is unable to develop her mental understanding and come up with an answer to her given *koan*, "Why does [Bodhi]dharma have no beard?" She spends many meditational retreats at her temple and even meditates in a cave for three years without any further development along the way. Soon Nyo, however, solves her *koan* because she lives her Buddhism in the context of others, which demonstrates the dissolution between self and other that is essential to enlightenment.

The contrast between Soon Nyo and Jin Sung in their methods of practice and attitudes toward social engagement also shows up in their continual disagreement over their respective interpretation of early Korean Buddhist statues that were erected around their temple. Examining the folk features of the Buddha statues, the ascetic nun dismisses them as ugly, thus indicating an unenlightened mind that makes distinctions and one that clings to the sense of superiority of the monastic life. In response, Soon Nyo mocks her in a fashion very similar to what one finds in Mahayana *sutras* where monks like Sariputra who represent the lesser vehicle are often made out to be fools in a dialogical duel between different philosophical systems.

"Maybe an ugly heart only sees ugly faces in the stones," Soon Nyo suggests.

"Criticizing the heart can be another egotistic attachment," the ascetic nun tersely responds, "Ugly face should be said to be ugly."

Soon Nyo then compares the statues of these Buddhas to the concept of Buddha nature that Mahayana theory espouses when she retorts, "What if a person who has found Buddha is a poor farmer or ignorant person's face, picked up a chisel, carved away and resulted in these?"

"You must not desecrate the holiness of our religion," Jin Sung admonishes her in response. "The reason why we lead this ascetic life is to be pure like Buddha, and don't we become Buddha ourselves when our minds are pure?"

"The farmer and peasants who carved the Buddha out of stone have pure hearts like the Buddha and the soil they live off is the equivalent of heaven, don't you think?" Soon Nyo responds.

"That is nonsense and misdirected thought," the ascetic nun coldly replies.

Soon-Nyo's comments indicate that the Buddha's face and the face of the peasants are superimposed to show the value of the peasants and their inherent Buddha nature which reflect the teachings of the *Heart Sutra* as well as other famous Mahayana Buddhist texts such as the *Gandavyuha* noted earlier.

While the philosophy of Buddhism calls for the emptiness of all distinctions and the centrality of compassion in the Mahayana school, Im argues that Buddhism has not fulfilled its vision. Rather, in Korea, most monks and nuns have avoided getting their hands dirty and involved in social justice and social welfare precisely because they believe that to become enlightened means to let go of all attachments to family and to friends. For Im, however, what is necessary is a movement off the mountains into the muck of everyday life in order for a more meaningful transformation of society and individuals to take place. Thus, the mantra "gone, gone, completely gone," which means to move beyond clinging to thoughts and ego attachments, even attachments to Buddhist asceticism, is a necessary move that Buddhism must make in order to remain relevant to contemporary society. He is not interested in a Buddhism that is full of exoticized monks and nuns on high mountain tops separating themselves through deep ascetic practices. Rather, his vision of Buddhism advocates for an immersion into everyday life with and through engagement that involves the senses rather than denying them.

Im's vision of Buddhism as a social justice movement is one that must be purged of its magical notions of holy monks and nuns tucked away in meditation. Meditation must be the root of social action and not its antithesis. At the conclusion of the film, Soon Nyo returns to the temple as her abbess lies on her deathbed waiting her disciple's return. The abbess recognizes that Soon Nyo has developed through her compassionate engagement in the world and implores the nuns to allow her to remain living near the temple as a laywoman. Jin Sung does not fare as well in her assessment by the dying abbess who sees little spiritual progress in the ascetic nun. The abbess then passes away and is set ablaze on a funeral pyre surrounded by her devotees as her body eventually reduces to ashes.

Soon Nyo observes the entire cremation of the abbess and in that process comes to the final answer to her *koan* that her teacher already intuited—that she herself has always had the capacity for enlightenment or the Buddha nature within herself. The difference between Soon Nyo and Jin Sung lies in how they honed their understanding. Soon Nyo's wisdom was honed through continued interaction with the world of suffering and led her to the following discovery:

Sunim between my soul left with you and the body out in the world, neither is my substance. I knew too late that I finally have the real self when and only when the two are in the same boundary.

In other words, ultimately there is no self and no distinction between all phenomena. Instead, all things are empty of inherent existence as the title of the film and the mantra in the *Heart Sutra* indicates. Thus, her sexual intimacy with men is not in any way a hindrance to her enlightenment. Instead, as James notes:

Her sexual munificence is metonymic for her general social ministry and it is the source of her own spiritual development. This allows the film to assert a redemptive humanism, founded in female sexuality ...[19]

The criticism Soon Nyo receives for her presumed transgressions with men simply cannot stick because it is her very method of engagement that leads to her enlightenment. Reflecting that, "Something that is in the rough may be more pure as the lotus blooms in the mud," Soon Nyo has realized that her true self is beyond distinctions of good and bad. Ultimately enlightened by the abbess's lessons, and out of an act of great devotion to her master, she decides to erect one thousand pagodas in honor of her teacher, housing in each one the master's relics. Jin Sung, however, remains untransformed and ever more dogged in her attachment to asceticism and purity.

Aje Aje Bara Aje explicitly calls into question and critiques the historical and often exoticized view of Buddhism as an otherworldly tradition. The image of Buddhist monastics as holier and more sacred than the laity is thus inverted in this film. As per Soon Nyo's example, it is only those who are willing to get dirty, and engage in all kinds of emotional turmoil and partake in the delusional world who will emerge enlightened. If, according to the teachings of Mahayana Buddhism, there is no individual self, then how can enlightenment be an individual achievement? It must be shared and attained by selfless compassion through worldly engagement.

Why Has Bodhidharma Left for the East?

While *Aje Aje Bara Aje* focuses on a nun sent down the mountain against her wishes who achieves enlightenment once she is laicized, her example is by no means widespread in the Buddhist world. The tension, however, between attaining enlightenment with or without the masses is certainly posed as a perpetual dilemma in many Korean Buddhist films, even ones with male protagonists who become monks for all the wrong reasons and attain liberation only when they re-enter the ordinary world. Such is the case with the next film, which examines the challenges and obstacles to enlightenment even for monks who live in isolation devoted only to attaining *nirvana*. The opening of Bae Yong-Kyun's 1989 international art house success, *Why Has Bodhidharma Left for the East?* begins not with a moving image or even still shot, but rather with a textual passage that reflects the significance of experience and the Sŏn emphasis on a special transmission outside of scriptures. The movie thus begins with the well-known *koan*, "To the disciple who asked about the Truth, without a word he showed a flower." The text itself of course references the famed story of the mind-to-mind transmission of the *dharma* in "The Flower Sermon" where the Buddha holds out a flower and only Maha Kasyapa responds with a smile.[20] The nonverbal actions of the Buddha reflect the quintessential Zen response to how to understand the truth, a truth that cannot be contained in words, for language and its concepts can distort the pure experience of truth. Bae thus establishes his film in the lineage of Zen's mind-to-mind transmission exemplified in the Flower Sermon and later reflected in the *Platform Sutra* where Hui-Neng is said to have secretly received the *dharma* transmission as the Sixth patriarch from the Fifth Patriarch Hung-jen.[21] The film centers on the distortions that the mind creates through dualistic phenomenon and the importance of letting go of attachments to the ego self.

The particularly Zen introduction and *koanic* title of the film establishes this film as distinctly Buddhist in pacing, theme, narrative, form, and content—these filmic qualities come from the director's personal study and practice in the Korean Sŏn tradition. Commenting on Zen's function in the film, Bae explains:

The action takes place around a monastery where an old Zen master lives. The central interest of this work is absolutely non Zen in [and] of itself—in effect, Zen assumes the role in this film of an environment of profound significance. I chose this setting because it is of great interest and beauty and is perfectly suited to express my search for life's meaning. Zen is not a theology of supernatural revelation and one can scarcely find any religious dogma in it. I am persuaded, however, that in Zen there is an awareness of the universal problem of humanity—the search for the existence of the Self and the enlightenment of the soul.[22]

Rather than the extensive use of dialogue to express the dilemma of the self, Bae utilizes dramatic effects from nature itself such as the often volatile wind rustling through trees, still water in reflective form, and violent waterfalls continually plunging downward, to express the mental states of the three monks inhabiting the mountain hermitage that serves as the film's *mise-en-scène*. His depiction of the elements of water, wind, fire, and earth also reflect the harmonious relationship between the monks and the natural world. In her study of Bae's work, Hyangsoon Yi notes comparisons between transcendentalism and the organic quality of the film where nature and humanity seem to coexist interdependently. She observes, "[t]here is no dramatic action in this type of quotidian reality. Small and sparse in its setting and *mise-en-scène*, the film nevertheless generates a mysterious sense of expansiveness."[23]

Bae introduces us to the monastic hermitage atop a mountain far away from the distractions of women. The women who appear in the film are briefly seen as examples of the world of suffering living at the base of the mountain in a dilapidated poverty stricken town. The film centers primarily on Kibong, a discontented young man who comes to the mountain hermitage to escape the world of suffering below. Attached to the notion of householder life as a sorrowful existence, Kibong ordains with the hope that he can achieve liberation and enlightenment by cutting off all attachments to his previous life including a blind elderly mother and a life of poverty. Foreshadowing his desire for freedom through the severing of familial ties, a street vendor is seen wandering into Kibong's ramshackle dwelling looking for used items chanting, "Sell your old objects, sell your obligations ..." encouraging Kibong to abandon his home. Yet, even after he enters the monastic life, he is plagued by a continuing Confucian guilt over abandoning his widowed mother and sister, but he remains unable to see that world as one worthy of his full participation. Thus, when asked by the youngest monk in the hermitage, Haejin, why he wished to ordain, he responds, "There is no peace or freedom in the world." Like many monks, Kibong mistakenly assumes that liberation is possibly only through escape from the world and through the rigors of meditation. Like Jin Sung in *Aje Aje Bara Aje* discussed earlier, Kibong clings too tightly to false notions of purity that can only be found through escape from ordinary life.

It is here where we see that Kibong, like Jin Sung, is in fact overly attached to the distinction between freedom and entrapment, *nirvana* and *samsara*. He erroneously assumes that the life of a monk will automatically bring the freedom he seeks when in fact, as his master implores, it is not the world below the hermitage that is the problem. Rather it is the false ego self that keeps Kibong from freedom. The master Hyegok thus sets Kibong straight when he replies, "It's because people do not have enough heart to hold all the things in the world. In fact, they have enough heart but it is full of the idea of the self." Kibong's central dilemma and problem of the self is that he presumes that freedom and escape are the same thing. As such, it is up to the elderly master to guide Kibong through the gift of a *koan*, namely, "When the moon takes over your heart, where does the master of my self go?"

Throughout the remainder of the film, Bae traces Kibong's faltering spiritual development and lackluster intuitive insight into his *koan*. Despite many attempts at intensive meditation and engaging in extreme ascetic practices such as meditating with a stone on his head and even forcing his body to remain still upon a rock in the midst of a raging water fall, Kibong discovers like the Buddha that such extremes only bring more suffering. In fact, not only do such extreme ascetic practices prove inadequate, Kibong also has to be saved by his master from the river, an act that sets in motion the death of the master Hyegok.

Kibong's breakthrough only occurs when he realizes that he is far too attached to the notion of escape from *samsara* in the pursuit of an ill-formed understanding of freedom. Rather than escaping the slums of *samsara*, Kibong must learn what his Master teaches him while he is dying. That is, "to leave is to arrive; to arrive is to leave." In other words, enlightenment and liberation cannot be attained through escape from worldly entanglements. Rather, it is within the world of entanglements and *samsara* that *nirvana* and *samsara* are experienced as one. Although doggedly pursuing an answer to his *koan*, it is only when given the final *koan* by the master Hyegok that Kibong finally attains realization. The final *koan* given by the master is that of cremating his body and scattering its ashes within a day and a half of the master's passing. That is, only through doing can Kibong experientially intuit the gift of the *koan*.

Through the final act of carrying his master's body upon his back, constructing a funeral pyre, lighting the pyre, observing the cremation, sifting through the ashes for relics, grinding them up, and finally scattering the powdered remains to the elements does Kibong finally understand the folly of his own conventional thinking. As he spreads the ashes of the cremated master and observes the remains scattering in the wind and dissolving into ponds of water to be eaten by fish he learns that the self is none other than not self or as the master put it, part of the entire universe. Thus, his attachment to the distinction between home and temple, *samsara* and *nirvana*, escape and freedom, gradually lessen as the film concludes with his journey back down to the world of suffering, where he can learn to open his heart to love all beings. His insight is thus akin to another Buddhist monk he meets who, having learned the way, proclaims:

Figure 5.3 Why Has Bodhidharma Left for the East? *Kibong spreads his master's ashes*

> I became a hermit to free myself from the dust and the dirt of the world, looking for perfection. But I realized that it was impossible without loving the garbage and the dust of the world, even life's passions. If it's easy to fight against reality and fate, it is difficult to love them. What a beautiful world when you know how to love it!

Kibong's ruptured self and psychological crisis over abandoning the world and selling his obligations comes to resolution at the film's conclusion only through the ritual and bodily practice of his *koan* which sends him back down the mountain into the ordinary world. Through his descent from the hermitage, Kibong reveals the failures of monastic life as a guarantee of freedom and liberation. In so doing, Bae Young-kyun also inverts the monastic hierarchy over the ordinary lay world. He has curiously little to offer with regard to women's spiritual capacity, yet his film goes far in constructing an alternative to the idealized meditating monk.

The Buddhist worlds reflected by both Im Kwon-Taek and Bae Young-Kyun are problematic in so far as they conceive of a chasm between the world of *samsara* and that of *nirvana*. Both Soon Nyo and Kibong struggle over their ill-conceived attachments to the salvational goals of liberation from the ordinary world, but upon solving their *koans*, each respectively recognizes and affirms their necessary place in the world of *samara*. Yet, as it will become apparent in the following chapter, not all Buddhists are so preoccupied and troubled by escape from *samsara* or ever really dedicate themselves to the pursuit of *nirvana* at all. Instead, many Buddhists, particularly in Asia, have very little interest in escaping the everyday world at all. In fact, most Buddhists are far more concerned with making this very world more livable and less troublesome while they are still in it. In the following chapter, I introduce another way to be Buddhist—one that does not concern monastic life at all and one whose Buddhism is subtle, profound, and almost imperceptible for those who are unfamiliar with its practices. Rather than a Buddhism of monks, nuns, and meditation, the Buddhism that occupies the next chapter is one of the laity and rests less on escape from the world and more on settling into the world and oneself.

6

The Ordinary as Extraordinary

In Yōjirō Takita's 2008 Oscar winning foreign language picture, *Departures* (*Okuribitu*), cellist Daigo Kobayashi loses his job in Tokyo after his orchestra folds, and he returns to live in his childhood home in Yamagata with his wife, Mika. Unemployed, he responds to an ad in the paper looking for someone to help out "assisting departures." Thinking that he will have a job in the travel industry, Daigo quickly responds to the ad, dresses sharply for the interview and, much to his shock, discovers that the NK Agency that posted the advertisement actually stands for *nōkan* or "casketing a corpse." The job he has applied for *is* in some ways about departures, but not of the travelling sort. Instead, the job consists of helping out with the departed as a *nōkanfu* or "Buddhist mortician." Desperate for a job and lacking any other opportunity, the cellist turns Buddhist mortician when hired by Mr. Sasaki, who pays him a substantial sum in cash before he has even left the office. Bewildered, and ashamed, Daigo hides his new job from his wife. Eventually, however, Daigo ignores the stigma of working with the dead and embraces the role of preparing their bodies for cremation for the sake of the departed and the living.

Departures asks us to imagine the transformation that takes place for the *nōkanfu* and the mourner alike through the ritual of encoffinment. Daigo quickly immerses himself in his new role as an apprentice and joins Mr. Sasaki on a series of jobs—first he plays a corpse for an instructional video on encoffinment, and then tags along to his first official job, which is a particularly grotesque one. An elderly woman has passed away alone in her apartment and her body was not discovered for over two weeks. Horrified by the stench of the corpse and the gruesome state of her decaying body that lay in a bed surrounded by filth and covered in maggots, Daigo is revolted and wretches uncontrollably. It is up to Mr. Sasaki to remain calm and collected, for he knows the significance of providing the dead with the appropriate burial and because he himself understands that life and death are on a continuum.

This vivid scene in the film is based on a similar image in a journal entry written by Shinmon Aoki in his book, *Coffinman: The Journal of a Buddhist*

Mortician that includes attending to the corpse of an elderly pensioner who had died alone months before.[1] He describes approaching the bed where the decomposing corpse lay when his eyes suddenly fixed on the maggots writhing all over the bed, the floors, and the body itself. After spending an hour sweeping up the maggots in order to begin to prepare the body, and even more time sweeping the maggots after the body was placed in the coffin, Aoki realizes that the source of great disgust he felt was nothing more than another form of pulsating life. Rather than rejecting them as something foul, the mortician recognizes that the maggots are also living beings and part of the larger cosmos. He recalls:

> As I was sweeping them together, I got a better look at the maggots' individual existences. I noticed some were trying to crawl up the pillars to get away. A maggot is just another life form. And just when I was thinking that, I was sure I saw one of them glow with light.[2]

As a reflection about the interrelatedness of all phenomenon and their mutual dependence, Aoki recalls that just as what he had seen in fireflies and in the faces of the dying, a light emits from the living bodies of maggots, denoting that they too are part of the totality of existence and oneness. Therefore, it makes little sense to assume that they are different, abject, filthy, and impure. Instead, like Mr. Sasaki, Aoki maintains a calmness and equanimity in the face of death and the maggots that feed on the departed. Thus, an understanding and acceptance of the inevitability of death allows him to continue with his work without attachment to the fear that death instills.

While the title itself suggests that the *nōkanfu* cleans, dresses, and places the deceased in a coffin to prepare for its subsequent cremation and send off to the next world, in this chapter I propose that *Departures* functions primarily as a filmic meditation on Buddhist concepts of presence, the interrelatedness of all phenomena, and the expression of gratitude. While these concepts are found in all forms of Buddhism, they take on a particular valence in the Jodoshinshu ("True Teaching of the Pure Land School"), the Buddhist tradition in Japan that grounds practitioners in the practice of everyday life infused with compassion (literally meaning to "experience with another"), the experience of connection to something greater than oneself, and interdependence.[3] *Departures* establishes a powerful yet gentle counterbalance to the rigors of monastic life, the challenges of meditation, and the exotic Buddhism projected in many of the films studied thus far.

Takito's film demonstrates one of the central teachings in the Shin Buddhist tradition—deep reverence and appreciation for this very life with all its vicissitudes and an affirmation of the self with all of its karmic limitations. *Departures* thus draws audiences away from the mountaintops and into family homes where mourners experience what highly acclaimed Shin Buddhist scholar Taitetsu Unno refers to as a:

> deep appreciation for the preciousness of this fragile life on earth, prompted by an awareness that death can instantly end this human life, a life that can never be repeated in eternity.[4]

Unno also notes, "Buddhism does not negate life but affirms life, including everything within it—despair, frustration, and anger ..."[5] Shin Buddhism does not encourage the experience of transcendence but rather that of settling into the here and now as "a true, real, and sincere human being."[6] The Buddhism of this Japanese film unfolds in stark contrast to the romance of Buddhist otherness and encourages wider audiences to see ordinary lay people engaged in the quotidian as religious practice. It is also a Buddhism that focuses on the development of compassion and the heart through interrelatedness rather than the disciplined restraint of the body through asceticism and the cultivation of a pure mind in isolation. The heroism of Shin Buddhism is to live grounded in this *samsaric* world and "to manifest compassion in everyday life, beginning with members of our own families and extending it to all of society," and to recognize the obstacles to this compassion generated by "one's own self-centered ego."[7]

Daigo Koboyashi and his boss, Mr. Sasaki, draw the grieving into a new relationship with the deceased, one that can best be described by what I call the first *sincere* greeting—a ritualized moment of heartfelt encounter when the bereaved let go of previous regrets and accept the departed as they truly were in life. As I show in this chapter, *Departures* is a reflection upon that moment of embrace of the authentic self and other that dissolves barriers between self and other, good and bad, life and death. In other words, the ritualized encounter between the departed and the living creates an opportunity for the mourner to resolve former resentments and conflicts to experience the departed anew.

One of the most important ritual tasks of the *nōkanfu* is to apply *shini-geshō* or "death makeup" to the corpse to make it beautiful so that it appears that the person died a peaceful and calm death.[8] The *nōkanfu* elegantly transforms the corpse and restores it to its previous appearance while alive. When complete, mourners once again see their loved ones face to face. When the *nōkanfu* restores the faces of the deceased, the mourners greet their loved ones and see them as they were, rather than as the embodiments of disappointment, shame, or even anger they might have brought the living prior to their deaths. Thus, the *nōkanfu* as ritual specialist draws the mourners and the dead alike together in a moment of presence that allows the mourners to experience the rebirth of the deceased into their hearts as they prepare to say goodbye.

Death teaches us how to live

As is well known in the Buddhist tradition, death can sometimes be the most effective *dharma* teacher—one does not have to learn how to magically overcome death or transcend this worldly life in order to experience *nirvana*. Instead, one accepts its inevitability. The Buddhist story of Kisa Gotami serves as a universal tale of the depths of grieving that come from the experience of death and its unavoidability.[9] Kisa Gotami comes to the Buddha distraught over the death of her only child and begs for medication to bring her son back to life. Seeing her despair, the Buddha advises her that she will be able to get the medicine if she gathers mustard seeds from the homes of the villagers. But he adds a provision—the mustard seeds must be obtained only from households that have not experienced death. Kisa Gotami of course runs throughout the village searching frantically for such seeds only to discover that death visits everyone and is an unavoidable consequence of life. Kisa Gotami thus learns the true nature of reality—impermanence and its universal applicability. Returning to the Buddha without seeds, the grief-stricken mother comes to accept the inevitability of death and later attains liberation from *samsara*. Through his work as a Buddhist mortician, Daigo encounters the reality of death on a regular basis which effects a turn toward responsiveness and responsibility to be present to life as it unfolds even unto death.

As a caregiver whose compassionate activity extends to both mourner and the mourned, Daigo comes to an acceptance of the vital role he plays in the spiritual lives of his clients and settles calmly into the life he has now—not the previous life of a cellist that he lost, nor the life that beckons into an unknown future. According to Taitetsu Unno, everyday life in the world as opposed to the faraway temple is where one works for transformation. He writes:

> The practice of Shin Buddhism does not require a special meditation hall or a cloistered retreat because everyday life is our *dojo*, the training place for compassion to others, beginning with our family members... Among the most challenging tasks awaiting us in this *dojo* of everyday life is that of the caregiver. Fraught with all kinds of challenges, difficulties, and demands, it is one of the most stressful tasks that await some of us. Anyone who meets the challenge and provides care for the need is a bodhisattva, whether the person knows anything about Buddhism or not.[10]

It is everyday life with all of its *samsaric* ups and downs that provides the perfect place for spiritual growth and discipline. The challenge of caregiving is to give of oneself without attachment to the fruits of one's own labors.

It is the giving *without* the expectation of return that is perhaps the most demanding action to perform. Daigo's transformation from cellist to *nōkanfu* offers a profound meditation upon the significance of ordinary life that affirms life's fragile beauty and the importance of a deep embrace of one's own life and the lives of others as they truly are. Such an acceptance gives rise to what Mark Unno calls a perspectival awareness and existential understanding of all life as interrelated and non-dualistic.[11] This awareness of interdependence develops into an expression of sincere gratitude for all the causes and conditions that have shaped one's life up to the present moment. Thus, as *Departures* suggests, the present moment and one's ethical engagement with the ordinary *samsaric* world becomes the training ground for spiritual maturation.

Unlike the Buddhist films discussed in earlier chapters, the Buddhism revealed in *Departures* has little use for the sensational or lackadaisical approach to Zen or the iconoclastic or the rigorous ascetic life. Instead, the Buddhist practice of *Departures* is a mindset of openness, an acceptance of one's ego limitations, and the recognition of one's valued place in, and responsibility to, the other in the larger cosmos. In this way, Shin Buddhism reflects the Buddhism of social integration and transformation found in Im Kwon-Taek's *Aje Aje Bara Aje* and Bae Young-Kyun's *Why Has Bodhidharma Left for the East?*, where the everyday life becomes the ultimate place of enlightenment. Like the nun turned laywoman, Soon Nyo, and the monk Kibong who descends the mountain for the suffering world of *samsara*, Daigo recognizes the role the Buddhist mortician plays in the care of the grieving. In so doing, his job as the *nōkanfu* is one best understood from an ethical standpoint where he becomes a caregiving *bodhisattva* for the sake of the other.

Despite what many films project, meditation is not a central practice in all forms of Buddhism; rather, as Taitetsu Unno notes, "[t]he Shin Buddhist path makes no undue demands on its followers, physical or otherwise, except one: *the giving up of the ego-self."*[12] However, this ego-self abounds in self-concern and conceit which makes it near impossible to give up. What is of utmost concern in this widely practiced tradition is the concept of relationality and the deep understanding of the connections between self and other. Unlike the ascetic traditions that claim the householder life full of desire and struggle, this form of Buddhism is "a path of supreme optimism, for one of its basic tenets is that no human life or experience is to be wasted, abandoned, or forgotten, but all shall be transformed into a source of vibrant life, deep wisdom, and compassionate living."[13]

One does not take vows in Shin Buddhism like a monk or nun in Theravada or Zen Buddhism. The most recognizable form of ritual in the tradition is that of chanting the *nembutsu* or the name of the Buddha, "Namu-Amida-Butsu" which Jeff Wilson translates as "I take refuge in Amida Buddha."[14] According to Wilson, a Shin practitioner, "we don't think of nembutsu as a mantra, a prayer, or a formal practice designated to generate enlightenment."[15] Instead, the practice of the nembutsu awakens one to less egocentric ways of living and points the practitioner toward what is known as "the entrusting heart, the heart that is rooted in gratitude and considerate awareness of others."[16] In reciting this name, Shin Buddhist engage in a continued practice of recognizing that the self is embraced and transformed by none another than Amida Buddha, the Buddha of Infinite Light and Infinite Life. Although such a recitation might appear literal in that one chants for salvation by Amida Buddha, Shinran Shonin, the founder of Shin Buddhism, maintained that the *nembutsu* forged a connection between the self and other or Namu (self) and other (Amida Buddha) that over time comes to be understood as a relationship of oneness where the self is none other than Amida Buddha or the other.

While other Buddhist schools involve more formalized ritual actions, Shin Buddhism emphasizes humility, the deep appreciation of the fragility and beauty of life, and the practice of compassion. Compassion is understood in terms of its meaning, "to experience with another." Daigo's role as the *nōkanfu* is to practice such compassion selflessly through the care and reverential handling of the bodies of the deceased. In *Departures*, much is made of the significant affirmation of life and its unrepeatability that comes from the encounter with death. For Daigo, compassionate activity also serves to awaken his understanding of nonduality or the lack of artificially-constructed boundaries between self and other that give rise to one's own ego calculations and demands.

The Shin Buddhist tradition is attributed to the life and works of Shinran Shonin (1173–1263) a former failed monk turned layman who left the monastic life because he felt that it was impossible to overcome the ego-self no matter how rigorous his practice. According to Shinran, chanting the name of Amida Buddha served as a foundational ritual practice that can be done anywhere and anytime by anyone and was aimed at commoners over the monks and nuns in meditation halls. Taitetsu Unno explains:

This practice of recitative *nembutsu* ["name of the Buddha"] changed the course of Japanese Buddhism, for the monastic paths, patronized by the imperial court and the nobility excluded the masses until Hōnen founded the independent Jodo School. Then the gates of liberation and freedom were wide open, welcoming those who had hitherto been excluded: women of all classes; hunters, butchers, and fishermen, who took life to make a living; peasants and merchants, considered ignorant and "bad" in the eyes of the upper classes; and monks and nuns who had violated precepts.[17]

Neither meditation halls nor the monastic life are considered the most opportune places of worship for Shin Buddhist practitioners, for such efforts are seen as expressions of self-power (*jiriki*) rather than other-power (*tariki*). Self-power connotes a belief in one's own ability to cure one's ego attachments and desire, which Shin Buddhists believe to be extremely difficult because it is so difficult to overcome the self. According to Unno, self-power was identified with "the difficult path of Sages" by the sixth-century Chinese monk T'an-luan and referred to the idea that through discipline and asceticism one can achieve enlightenment. Other-power, however, reflects the belief in powers other than one's own ego to experience liberation from suffering; in other words, Shin Buddhist teachings emphasize the deep recognition of the interdependence of all phenomena so even one's own liberation rests on countless other beings in the universe.

Infinite light

In his edited collection of lectures in *Devotional Cinema*, filmmaker Nathan Dorsky states:

> Devotion is not an idea or a sentiment. It is born out of the vastness and the depth of our view. Out of darkness, behind all light, this vastness abides in nowness. It reveals our world. It is accurate and humbling and yet, for all its pervasiveness, it is not solid.
>
> That the ineffable quality of vision can be expressed by projected light within darkness gives film great power. When a film is fully manifest it may serve as a corrective mirror that realigns our psyches and opens us to appreciation and humility. The more we open to ourselves and are willing to touch the depths of our own being, the more we are participating in devotion. Similarly, the more film expresses itself in a manner intrinsic to its own true nature, the more it can reveal to us.[18]

While not speaking explicitly about Shin Buddhism, Dorsky's attention to light, nowness, appreciation, and humility bears a striking resemblance to Shinran who also taught that a deep reverence for life and a recognition of one's ego limitations are the central aspects of a religious life. Dorsky's emphasis on light also plays a crucial role in the Shin Buddhist tradition that reflects the compassionate activity associated with Amida Buddha who represents infinite light and infinite life. Amida's infinite light represents the compassionate activity in the world that illuminates the darkness of all beings and places in the universe and which brings that darkness or brokenness into wholeness.

Dorsky's comments above note that the visceral effects of film can imbue a sense and appreciation of nowness in the viewer, a nowness that finds its corollary in Buddhist understandings of the present moment. Dorsky also argues that film has a remarkable ability to invoke a sense of absolute time, a time beyond the relativity of calculation and division into short measures along an ultimately immeasurable continuum. How fitting then to examine the role that film can have on the religious imagination. Through an appropriate and well-executed balance of shots and cuts, angles, and pacing, one can experience film devotionally—that is, through the body and senses to see the world as it is but at the same time, to see it anew without the burdens of preconditioned thoughts and judgment. Dorsky's study of the devotional aspects of cinema is suggestive for reading the young coffinman's gradual growth, awareness, deep appreciation, and experience of nowness that grows out of Daigo's experiences of the interrelatedness of all beings.

When viewed as a technique to cultivate nowness, *Departures* transforms the viewer's usual vision of reality from a series of discrete moments along the continuum of time to a perspectival awareness of the oneness of all phenomena and the significance of this very moment in life. The central object for transformation in this film is the matter of caring for the dead. As noted in Chapter Four, *Spring, Summer, Fall, Winter... and Spring* shows us that there is no better teacher and reminder of the march of relative time than death. Gory images of bloated corpses rotting away in cremation grounds and full of maggots abound in Buddhist literature to remind us that death will come no matter the person, that impermanence and decay are inevitable. As the *Diamond Sutra* states:

> As stars, a fault of vision, as a lamp,
> A mock show, dew drops, or a bubble,
> A dream, a lightening flash, or cloud,
> So should we view what is conditioned.[19]

Mr. Sasaki reflects a seasoned ritual specialist who became a *nōkanfu* when he prepared the body of his beloved wife who died almost a decade earlier. There is both a somberness and a reverence that Mr. Sasaki displays in the fetching and preparation of the dead for each eventual cremation. The reverence is both for the dead and the living, for in this acceptance of death, he loosens fear's grip of the unknown and the unfinished life and in so doing he gains a deeper appreciation for life, its fragile nature, and the beauty found in its impermanence. The equanimity Mr. Sasaki displays—no matter how gruesome the condition of the body—demonstrates that he has accepted all that life entails: the awful, the beautiful, and the routine. He guides Daigo through his apprenticeship with care and gentleness and seems to know that Daigo is fated to this job despite its negative reputation in Japanese culture. Writing about the transformation of awareness that emerges through the practice of encoffining, Shinmon Aoki explains, "First we lose our attachment to Life; at the same time we lose our fear of Death. Finally, we feel peaceful and serene inside. Forgiving of all things, we enter a state where we hold all things in gratitude."[20]

Once Daigo accepts his job and settles into his natural ability as caregiver to the deceased and the grieving survivors, he experiences a calmness and sense of real purpose to his work as he washes, dresses, and places the bodies of the deceased into pristine coffins on their way to cremation. The embrace of the liminal and polluting job of the coffinman also signifies that he has let go of his attachment to judgments and dualistic thinking that maintains boundaries between the pure and the impure, the self and other.

In exploring the explicitly Buddhist teachings that *Departures* inspires, one encounters the art of living with humility, gratitude, and wonder that comprise the spiritual life, and not meditation or asceticism. *Departures* is a remarkable film precisely because its Buddhism is not based on highlighting the heroic virtues of monks; rather it is the quotidian and ordinary that is revealed to the viewer as full of deeper meaning. But what is this deeper meaning? For Daigo, the deeper meaning has more to do with a radical acceptance of self and other as they are—full of regrets, mistakes, unattained fancies, *and* undeniably interconnected. It is this oneness of humanity with all of its petty desires that both Daigo and Mr. Sasaki are able to intuit through the care and embrace they receive from others. It is from the senior coffinman that he learns a true taste of life as it is—a life that holds the deepest sorrow and the deepest joy together as one experience not to be avoided or clung to in desperation.

In a humorous and intimate scene, Mr. Sasaki invites Daigo into his private indoor garden office on the top floor of the NK Agency. This scene unfolds in the context of verdant life with an abundance of green plants, flowers and death. In his upstairs oasis, the master coffinman also has a framed photograph of his wife; thus life and death come together in a seamless way in the coffinman's space. Mr. Sasaki invites Daigo to sit down to lunch, for he knows that Daigo suffers from his wife's abandonment and waivers in his commitment to the job. As he grills puffer fish roe on his tabletop hibachi, its bloated sack emits a delicious smell. Mr. Sasaki offers some to Daigo and then pauses to relish the intoxicating scent before quickly slipping the piping hot roe into his mouth. Closing his eyes, he savors the taste and in sheepish delight utters that it tastes so good, "I hate myself." While the scene itself is quite humorous, it conveys a critical lesson in the appreciation and embrace of the absolute value of the present, an understanding he then passes down to his protégé. The master coffinman appreciates the experience so much precisely because it will never happen again in the same way. His remark that it tastes so good that he hates himself reflects how deep the appreciation of something transitory can be.

The joy and appreciation that comes from this single moment in time reflects what is known by the Japanese aphorism, *ichigo-ichiye* which can be translated as "a whole lifetime in a single encounter."[21] The sheer delight that the puffer fish bestows comes from the very fact that that moment of taste will never happen again in the same way. The beauty and the joy in life come from the fact that each moment will never be repeated; attention to the present moment thus frees one's calculating mind from living forever future forward and liberates one's remorseful mind from excessive attachment to the past. Therefore, in that moment of presence, one can really live. The concept of *ichigo-ichiye* illuminates some of the most important ritual moments of the beautiful encounter between the departed and the living engineered by Daigo while he continues to develop his skills as a compassionate caregiver for the bereaved.

Daigo's next job after having lunch with his boss brings him to the home of a widower and his young daughter who mourn the loss of their beloved wife and mother. The husband observes as if in respectful shock as Daigo cleans her body and pays the greatest attention to even the smallest details with great delicacy. Watching Daigo as he deftly removes the woman's dressing gown under a silken cloth that is artfully draped over her body so that the mourners do not see her pale skin is akin to watching him play his childhood cello with a reserved passion. The film intersperses past memories of his

Figure 6.1 Departures. *Mr. Sasaki eats grilled fish roe.*

playing as his fingers gracefully hold the bow that he elegantly and deftly moves across the strings while the fingers on his other hand dance atop the strings to release the suppressed sorrow, shame, and disappointment through the haunting music that emerges from the instrument. Although he might play a concerto over and over again, it will never sound the same each time; hence, his love of the music and the music's beauty attains its value from the fact that it cannot be repeated. In just the same way, Daigo prepares the wife's body by washing it with a gentleness and reverence as he skillfully arranges a Buddhist rosary between her fingers. He then prepares to apply makeup on the wife's face and turns to ask the family for her favorite lipstick in order to make her look as she did when she was alive. The husband is startled by this request, but the young girl intuits the reasoning behind the request and brings back her mother's lipstick.

As Daigo applies the makeup we hear him explain through voice over, "One grown cold restored to beauty for all eternity. This was done with a calmness, a precision ... and above all, a gentle affection." Once her face is complete, her young daughter suddenly recognizes her mother and jumps up in tears crying out for her. It is this moment when the widow also encounters his wife again and in that single moment he remembers his entire lifetime with her. As Daigo departs, the husband rushes out to bid farewell and sobs as he finally recognizes and truly encounters his wife Naomi again. Daigo has made this moment of recognition possible. The widower then explains to Daigo through his tears, "She never looked so beautiful," and offers a gift of dried persimmon. They bow to one another and Daigo returns to the car and together with Mr. Sasaki shares in the pleasure of eating the dried fruit in silence as an expression of appreciation, gratitude, and respect for the bereaved.

Acceptance

In his journal, Shinmon Aoki notes that mourners' farewells also serve as an invitation to engage in life as authentically as possible. This authenticity emerges from an acceptance of oneself and another as he or she truly is. For Aoki, the coffining business and preparation of the dead brings him into contact with the despair and humiliation surrounding his profession, and at the same time with the experience of what it means to be accepted as one is.

He experiences this sense of deep acceptance when he prepares the body of a former girlfriend's father. As his sweat drips down his brow while he slowly and meticulously lifts, cleans, and swaddles the body, he is suddenly awakened by the symbolic embrace of the ex-girlfriend who wipes the sweat from his brow with a cloth. Rather than resolutely accepting the impure position of the coffinman, Aoki experiences what it means to have pure acceptance and the experience of deep compassion. Remarking on the experience of looking into this woman's eyes as she wiped his brow, he notes:

> Even her sitting by me to wipe the sweat away, all the way through the procedure, was a gesture of no ordinary dimensions. And she did this right in front of her husband and relatives. I felt there was something there that transcended the trivial world of scorn or pity or sympathy, that even went beyond the relationship between man and woman.

> I felt that she showed me she accepted my total existence just as I was, no more no less, and so thinking I began to feel good about myself. And I began to feel I could continue in this line of work.[22]

Despite all the social taboos associated with dealing with the dead, Aoki's recollection of this moment of radical acceptance of the self gestures toward a Buddhism that is not just about transcending one's defilements. Rather, this form of Buddhism cultivates and generates a sense of embracing oneself with all of one's limitations, no longer striving for improvement in the future nor grousing about the past and missed opportunities.

The art of living the Shin life is thus the art of allowing oneself to be embraced by another just as one is—floundering around in the ocean of *samsara* with one's delusions laid bare. The wonder that another could care for him just as he is incites a transformation in perspective that allows the coffinman to engage in his job fully and without the additional reminder that the dead are considered polluted. It is in this way that he is humbled by the compassion of his former girlfriend. He is humbled, as well, by the capacity of the other to give so freely, leading the coffinman to the deep experience of gratitude. The life of gratitude is the life of the ego-bound being who recognizes its deep interconnection with all forms of life. This gratitude leads to another realization: that even in the darkest moments of loneliness, there can be found a light that shines, enabling the lonely being to see that it is not alone. Rather, it is embraced by a universal cosmos and web of existence of which it is an integral strand.

The coffinman's ritual duties include far more than the tasks of bathing, dressing, tying, and casketing the body; the job rests on giving due recognition to the dead for the sake of the living. Mr. Sasaki and Daigo prepare beautiful bodies for the living so that the lives of the deceased are experienced in the now rather than in the past. Through the careful preparation of the corpse, the coffinman brings family and friends into an intimate space where they can begin to really say hello and goodbye simultaneously. Each ritual ceremony includes the dressing of the body in appropriate attire—the director offers a number of scenes of corpse preparation where the *nōkanfu* painstakingly attends to each corpse through a process of beautification and making the bodies pleasing so that the moment of coming and going of the deceased can unfold in the context of the memorial.

Each *nōkanfu* receives a memorial image of the deceased while living and the *nōkanfu*'s ritual duties include painting the face of the deceased with foundation, rouge, and makeup so that the deceased's face is suddenly returned to life. I suggest that the significance of this beautifying of the corpse is to invoke a sense of nowness in the ritual moment itself. That is, the *nōkanfu* brings the dead back to life for an encounter with the mourners that allows for an opportunity to resolve old tensions with the deceased.

If, in fact, we accept Dorsky's premise that the spiritual dimensions of film are conveyed through the transcendence of the ordinary notion of time, then *Departures* can be seen as devotional in and of itself. Each ritual ceremony creates that moment of nowness whereby viewers come to appreciate the oneness that characterizes the relationship between all beings—the living and the dead. By acknowledging and accepting death, one learns how to truly live, for all the worries of the afterlife are already settled. It is in the settling into the reality of death and an embrace of death as but another moment on the continuum of time, that family members and viewers are free to live deeper lives. Over the course of the film, we observe the young apprentice come to embrace his role as *nōkanfu* who not only deals with the dead but also deals with the living by re-presenting death as a moment of hello and goodbye.

Taitetsu Unno's *Shin Buddhism: Bits of Rubble Turn into Gold* shares many narratives of deep appreciation and gratitude for those who have departed.[23] Each narrative shared in this text offers a glimpse of what it means to lose someone and yet through compassion and gratitude one has a deeper awareness of that being in one's life. There is grief and the debilitation that grieving inspires, yet there is also the experience of transformation of that grief into a deeper appreciation of all the causes and conditions that have led to the moment of that person's birth, life, and death. That being is reborn in the heart of the bereaved and I would argue that the *nōkanfu* is the one who sparks that rebirth. This rebirth into the heart of the bereaved takes place during the funeral preparation that Daigo and his master perform.

The dignity offered the dead gives rise to a deep acceptance of the departed for what he or she truly was and in that acceptance a rebirth takes place in the heart of the mourner. In the film's opening sequence, the audience observes Daigo and Mr. Sasaki driving in silence under a blanket of snow that has fallen upon a small village in Yamagata. We soon learn that Daigo has been on the job for two weeks, and during this encoffining Mr. Sasaki decides that it is time for

Daigo to take the lead on the job. In a somewhat humorous sequence, Daigo proceeds to solemnly and calmly wash the body of a woman, Tomeo, who died a "beautiful" death from carbon monoxide poisoning. We learn from Mr. Sasaki that this kind of suicide manages to preserve the body and face of the deceased. As he moves the cloth slowly and gentle down the corpse's body underneath a draped cloth, his calmness is suddenly interrupted as he realizes that the woman he is cleaning is anatomically male. Unsure of how to address this new revelation, Daigo consults Mr. Sasaki who then asks Tomeo's mother if she would like for him to use makeup for a man or for a woman on her deceased child. The mother then sighs and cries, "If I gave birth to a girl, this never would have happened." She then directs Mr. Sasaki to use makeup for a woman and in the process of beautifying Tomeo's face, the mother comes to see her transgender son for who he was. Through the work of Daigo and Mr. Sasaki, her son is restored to his true identity—a woman. And in that moment, she experiences her son's "whole lifetime in a single encounter" that attests to the fragility and gratitude for such moments that will never happen again. Takita later returns to this scene to show the transformation of the father through the ritual preparation of Tomeo's body, which concludes with laying the body into the coffin. Daigo then rests a bright red dress on top of Tomeo as a symbol of her true identity. Tomeo's father witnesses the *nōkanfu*'s preparation of his son's body and face, transforming him into the woman that Tomeo truly felt he was. In so doing, the father comes to accept his transgendered son and expresses his love for his deceased child.

In this tender scene, the father experiences a rebirth of his child in his heart. This moment of appreciation and acceptance reflects that first moment of sincere greeting where the authentic self of the departed is revealed and

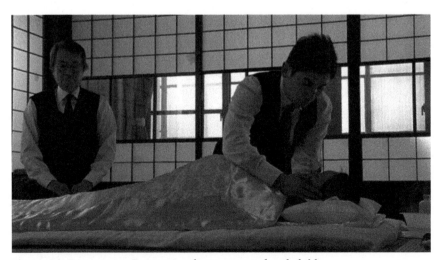

Figure 6.2 Departures. *Daigo attends to transgendered child.*

the ego attachments of the mourner dissolve. As he cries in grief and joy, the father remarks, "Once he went like he did, we did nothing but fight. After that I was not seeing him. But when I saw him smile I remembered him. He may dress as a girl, but he is still my son." The father bows in deep gratitude for the spiritual workings of the *nōkanfu* who has made such an encounter possible. The resentment, the bitterness, the regrets, and the loss of what could have been, are given a moment in time where release and true letting go can happen. Thus the ritual of the funeral preparation becomes a sacred time of healing for the bereaved.

Although Daigo faces stigmatization and criticism for his job, loses his friendship with his childhood schoolmate, Yamashita, and is temporarily abandoned by Mika who detests that he is polluted by death, Daigo recognizes the significance of each encounter between the living and the dead and refuses to find another job. Mika moves out and Daigo continues in his training and eventually experiences a makeshift family with Mr. Sasaki, the administrative assistant, and his friend's mother Tsuyako Yamashita who runs the local bathhouse. Eventually Mika returns to Yamagata and informs Daigo that she is pregnant and that he should reconsider his line of work because his child will be ostracized by his father's job. Daigo again refuses and is later called away to perform the encoffinment of Tsuyako Yamashita in the presence of his friend Yamashita, Yamashita's wife, their daughter, and Mika. Mika pays her respects to the deceased woman and observes in awe how Daigo gently treats the body with the greatest dignity, respect, honor, and poise. As he completes the task of dressing her for her coffin, Daigo thoughtfully attaches a scarf around her neck that she had received from her dear friend Sokichi Hirata, who used to come to the bathhouse every day to keep her company. It is in this ritualized space that her son Yamashita comes to truly grieve the loss of his mother and, dissolving past disputes, he embraces her as she was. It is in this quiet space of grieving that Mika, too, has a change of heart and begins to understand the depths of gratitude and appreciation that mourners have for Daigo's efforts. There is compassion and grace in his work and Mika realizes these qualities are worth risking the negative attitudes her fellow Japanese have toward the *nōkanfu*.

Departures concludes with Daigo's own spiritual transformation when he finally accepts the responsibility of preparing his long-lost father's body for encoffinment. Abandoned by his father at the age of six for another woman, Daigo carries a lifetime of resentment and bitterness at his father's sudden departure and presumes that his father has forgotten all about his son. Having had no contact with him, Daigo learns through a letter that his father has recently died in a small fishing village, alone in his seaside apartment.

At first, Daigo refuses to see his father but is later persuaded by his coworker—who had abandoned her own son in pursuit of another relationship—to do so. Having shared with Daigo the remorse that she experienced over not seeing her son again, Daigo realizes that his father's absence did not mean his father did not also grieve and regret the loss of their relationship. His heart softened, Daigo returns to the village with Mika and arrives just as the hired coffiners are about to awkwardly place the body into a coffin. Daigo intervenes and begins the process of offering the rites of purification and preparation for his own father himself. I suggest that the scene of preparing his father's body is one of resolution and the first sincere greeting where Daigo comes to realize that his father had never actually forgotten him. He learns that his father never stayed with the woman he pursued decades earlier. Instead, he worked alone, silently longing for reconciliation and reunion with his son. As Daigo attempts to move his father's stiff fingers to place the Buddhist rosary beads into his aged hands, he suddenly discovers that his father's hands are still clutching a small white pebble that the young Daigo had given to his father before he abandoned the family. It is at this moment of recognition that, for the first time since he was a young boy, Daigo is suddenly able to remember what his father's face looked like. Out of his grief over his abandonment, Daigo had suppressed his memories of his father to the point of not even recognizing him when he first came to the fishing village. However, during the ritual cleaning of the body and placement of the rosary beads in his hands, his father is suddenly born again in Daigo's heart and memory. This moment is thus the first sincere hello where Daigo can accept his father for all of his ego limitations and comes to greet his father anew.

The Shin Buddhist expression of gratitude and reverence for life which could only come by the acceptance of the inevitably of death is instructive.

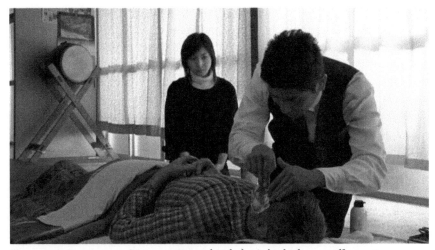

Figure 6.3 Departures. *Daigo prepares his father's body for encoffinment.*

When reading through the poems of the near-dead in Aoki's diary, as well as Taitetsu Unno's *Shin Buddhism: Bits of Rubble Turn into Gold*, one finds striking parallels between the expressions of gratitude, freedom, and the ease that the dying have experienced. They have come to a deep experiential understanding of the interrelatedness of all phenomena, phenomena that in Aoki's work are connected by a mysterious light that glows from the bodies of the maggots that infest the corpse and in the faces of the dying who have acknowledged that they are on the brink of death. What tremendous strength it takes to be free of fear in the face of death. Death is no longer the bogeyman inciting us with fear; instead, death is accepted not as a stranger but as a friend who awaits us. Such an acceptance of death is one that brings a sense of ease and gentleness in everyday living where the worry of the afterlife is already settled.

Departures uses the intimacy between the *nōkanfu*, the dead, and the bereaved, as an opportunity to illuminate what it means to live an artful life of humility, wonder, and gratitude. Daigo transforms from second-rate cellist in search of fame to a mortician lacking self-value and finally, to a ritual specialist bringing self and other together in an experience of oneness that cannot help but express itself through compassion. The Buddhism thus rendered by this film is one where the striving for the exotic, the drive for spiritual perfection, and the quest for enlightenment through spiritual betterment is turned on its head. Instead, spiritual perfection is understood to be the acceptance of imperfection and the embrace of the other as but an extension of self.

This kind of Buddhism receives little recognition in the West because it is neither exotic nor heroic. Yet as *Departures* demonstrates, acceptance of life as it is, with all of its defilements and pleasures, is, in fact, profoundly heroic. The art of living with humility, wonder at both the nowness of life and its interconnectedness, and the gratitude that comes from the realization that all things are causally conditioned, gives rise to a new way of seeing and being in the world. This is the gift of the ordinary as extraordinary that Shin Buddhism conveys. The spiritual life in *Departures* and Shin Buddhism itself is not honed by refining the self or in uprooting the passions. Rather, the spiritual life comes into play when one humbly accepts one's limitations.

In the many popular iterations of Buddhism discussed early in this book, we find the predominance of the image of the Oriental Monk and the quest for enlightenment, and the experience of nirvana as the end goal. While many a receptive audience has been swept away by the exotic sway of the Buddhist monastic life that appeals because it is so other than ordinary, the popularity of such images of difference has resulted in the tendency to overlook what might be considered a more ordinary form of Buddhism that holds this very world of suffering to be the place of enlightenment. In this context, enlightenment is not beyond the world of *samsara* but rather takes place in it.

In short, *Departures* offer a glimpse into a Buddhism that has not yet received ample attention by popular audiences seeking otherness. Yet I would argue that it conveys what comes to be the heart of Buddhism—the experience of compassion not only because one becomes the compassionate *bodhisattva* bestowing gifts upon others, but rather through the realization that one has already been held compassionately by the other. A film like *Departures* is not a mere approximation of a text about religion but rather it becomes the instantiation of Buddhism itself. It offers a potent source of Buddhist practice that has not yet gained much traction in the world of cinema.

Buddhist films have the potential to serve as analogies of religion and adaptations of literary visions of religion. But even more importantly, they can be sites for spiritual transformation and religious awakening. In this way, we might see film *as sutra* and as a potent source for re-visioning and re-embodying Buddhism as a religious tradition that sees everyday life as the *dojo* for awakening. In the following chapter, I take up a Buddhist film that is explicitly influenced by a beloved Mahayana Buddhist *sutra* known as the *Gandavyuha (Entry into the Realm of Reality)*. Like *Departures*, this film also provides an occasion for a more capacious vision of Buddhism that is based on social integration and the repositioning of those on the margins of society into the center. In so doing, the film functions to imagine Buddhism anew such that even the miscreant, the drunkard, the destitute, and the maimed, can be enlightening *bodhisattvas*.

7

Film as *Sutra*

Hwa-om-kyung raises many social and political questions, but as far as I'm concerned it centers on questions of individual completeness and the freedom of the individual. I had the idea of adapting Ko Un's novel (an imaginary biography of Sonje, the protagonist of an ancient Buddhist Sutra) because I felt dissatisfied with existing ways of evaluating the direction our society is moving in. I sensed that viewing it through the world of the Sutra would provide a new perspective.[1]

While *Departures* does not make explicit reference to its underlying Buddhist world view, Chang Sun-Woo's 1993 film, *Hwa-om-kyung* (*Passage to Buddha*) portrays a world envisioned through the lens of a Mahayana Buddhist scripture.[2] As a critique of Korean society in the early 1990s, *Hwa-om-kyung* presents a fragmented world whose socially marginalized characters are brought together through a series of intertwining karmic encounters. These encounters ultimately affirm their humanity and place in the larger cosmos of what the *Avatamsaka Sutra* calls, "The Jeweled Net of Indra." Upon this net hangs a multitude of many faceted gems, each of which reflects all the other gems within the net—this Jeweled Net of Indra represents the Mahayana revelation of interconnectedness and interdependence of all phenomena.

As I show in the following chapter, *Hwa-om-kyung* can be viewed as a meditation on the process of enlightenment and the role of *kalyānamitras* (good spiritual friends/advisors) on the pathway of the *bodhisattva*. In the opening scene we are introduced to the young protagonist Sonje who, suddenly parentless, begs to look upon the ashes of his father whose remains are unceremoniously disposed of in a crematorium at the government's expense. Because his father was a petty thief, his cremation warrants only the basic minimum in care and Sonje must fight just to have access to his father's ashes. Abandoned by his mother in his infancy, he embarks on a pilgrimage to find her, a journey undertaken at the request of his father. As the young wandering representation of the Buddhist character, Sudhana, in the *Gandavyuha ("Entry into the Realm of Reality")*, the boy now embarks on a seemingly directionless journey, propelled on the pathway to completion by the embodied *bodhisattvas* he meets in a series of interconnected and often humorous picaresque encounters.

The Buddhist vision offered in Chang's work also draws from the Mahayana teachings that all beings have the Buddha nature and that wisdom and truth can be found in all aspects of society—from beggars, wayward monks who drink and curse, prostitutes, prisoners, lovers, and other such *bodhisattvas* who appear in a myriad of forms in times of need. As such, Chang's film evokes a world where the existence and value of all beings, from the highest to the lowest, are radically affirmed as an integral part of humanity and the cosmos. In this chapter, I argue that such an image of the affirmation of the marginalized and the low as integral to the religious life offers a significant resource through which to re-vision the Buddhist tradition both in lived reality and on screen. It also creates a more horizontal picture of the Buddhist tradition and its practitioners (e.g., monks, nuns, laywomen, and laymen) that deconstructs the hierarchy and overemphasis on the widely distributed image of the meditative monk as the primary symbol of Buddhism that holds sway in popular culture.

As a filmic interpretation of a Buddhist *sutra*, *Hwa-om-kyung* borrows readily from images of the *bodhisattva* or enlightening being in Buddhist texts, who guides individuals toward their own awakening through a myriad of methods or skillful means. One of the significant forms of skillful means that Chang's film employs is that of the female *bodhisattva* who appears in a variety of forms such as an anonymous apparition of a mother, an abandoned maimed woman, a poor young girl, a courtesan, and a young lover, all for the sake of transforming an abandoned boy during his journey to find his mother.

Hwa-om-kyung is unique in its adaptation and interpretation of one of the most popular Buddhist texts (known in Sanskrit as the *Avatamsaka Sutra* and in English as the *Flower Ornament Sutra*), a text that figures centrally in the Hua-yen school of China compiled around the fifth century CE.[3] Because of the text's vast size, which includes 40 chapters of deep philosophical breadth, it is considered to be a compendium of Mahayana doctrine. As a result, its influence can be found in Zen, Pureland, Tientai, and other Mahayana schools of Buddhism. An elaborate visionary exposition on the nature and stages of development of the enlightened mind with multiple Buddha lands and countless *bodhisattvas* populating jewel-encrusted thrones emerging out of grains of sand, the *Avatamsaka Sutra* expounds upon the doctrines of Buddha nature, emptiness, and interdependence, while overturning linear constructions of time and conventional morality.

While cosmic in scope, it is the *sutra*'s thirty-ninth chapter, known separately as the *Gandavyuha*, that Chang draws upon as a model and lens through which to critique the fragmentation of the individual in contemporary Korean society precisely because the text argues for the complete interdependence of all phenomenon through its emphasis on the enlightening potential of all members of society. The *Gandavyuha* portrays the process of awakening the mind through the character of the young Sudhana (literally "good wealth"), who as a developing *bodhisattva*, embarks on the quest to attain enlightenment to emancipate all beings from suffering. The *sutra* offers in narrative form the tale of Sudhana and his remarkable meetings with 52 "good knowing advisors" or *kalyānamitras* who serve as the spiritual teachers that represent the various stages and characteristics of enlightened mind in the Mahayana tradition.[4] According to Douglas Osto, the *Gandavyuha* presents the *kalyānamitra* not only as good friends serving as spiritual guides, but also as *bodhisattvas* "who, through their skillful means (*upaya-kausalya*), assume various social roles as costumes or disguises in order to train other *bodhisattvas*."[5] He also notes that such disguises are magical creations, which may account for the illusory and often complicated hypersexualized images of women that I discuss below.

Chang's film borrows readily from the characters, plots, and themes found in the *Gandhavyuha* as well as from the narrative reimagining of the *sutra* in the novel, *Little Pilgrim*, by Korean poet and former monk, Ko Un.[6] Ko Un's tale of Sonje (Sudhana) adheres closely to the enlightening peregrinations of the *Gandhavyuha*'s very same protagonist who travels throughout India on a quest for truth. It is through relationships with various members of Indian society that Ko Un's Sonje experiences one of the central teachings of the *Avatamsaka Sutra* as a whole and the *Gandhavyuha* in particular—that of the oneness of all phenomena and the interpenetration of all things. Ko Un's novel closely follows the narrative structure of the *Gandhavyuha* which offers a variety of lessons learned from different *kalyānamitras* or "good friends," yet Chang clearly establishes *Little Pilgrim* as its main inspiration. This focus may well be due to Ko Un's own personal history as a political activist imprisoned because of his critiques of Korea's military dictatorships that the director draws upon.

Chang utilizes Ko Un's Buddhist poetic tale as the basis for his depiction of the journey of an 11-year-old orphan through Korea in search of his mother. The film takes place in the 1990s, as Sonje, guided by a diverse group of Korean society's alienated beings (e.g., the poor, the blind and abused, prostitutes), embarks on his search after the death of his father. As an orphan, Sonje is propelled along a path of self-discovery through a series of encounters with what the *Gandavyuha* would refer to as the lowest of society. In the process, he is transformed through brief, albeit profound, meetings with such *kalyānamitras*. Sonje's journey reflects Sudhana's, but with an important twist; that is, Chang employs his *kalyānamitras* in the form of beggars and drunkards not only to illustrate spiritual awakening, but also as a direct critique of the poverty found in the margins of many parts of rural and urban Korean locales. Here the Buddhist *sutra* becomes an opportunity to level a social critique against the rapid modernization that South Korea witnessed and the subsequently huge gap between the wealthy and the impoverished.

Because *Hwa-om-kyung* is a filmic adaptation of a novel that is itself a literary interpretation of a *sutra*, parts of the film are nearly inaccessible to the viewer who has no previous knowledge of Buddhist philosophy and ethics. Protagonists and main characters in the film such as Sonje, the antinomian monk Bubwon (representing *bodhisattva* Manjushri), Iryon (Sonje's best friend, lover, and mother of his unborn child), and Ina, the blind homeless singer, are all loosely based on Ko Un's characters who act as catalysts for the young pilgrim's mental and spiritual transformation. An analysis of the representation of Buddhism in this film would therefore be incomplete without reference to both the *Gandavyuha* and Ko Un's *Little Pilgrim*.

The *Avatamsaka Sutra*, with all of its illusory play on reality and the constructed nature of words encourages the practitioner to see all aspects of reality reflected in all others, an ontological and social perspective articulated in the famous vision of the Jeweled Net of Indra noted above, a vision that marks the culmination of the Mahayana view of reality. Hua-yen scholar, Francis Cook explains:

> Far away in the heavenly abode of the great god Indra, there is a wonderful net which has been hung by some cunning artificer in such a manner that it stretches out infinitely in all directions. In accordance with the extravagant tastes of deities, the artificer has hung a single glittering jewel in each 'eye' of the net, and since the net itself is infinite in dimension, the jewels are infinite in number. There hang the jewels, glittering like stars of the first magnitude, a wonderful sight to behold. If we now arbitrarily select one of these jewels for inspection and look closely at it, we will discover that in its polished surface there are reflected all the other jewels in the net, infinite in number. Not only that, but each of the jewels reflected in this one jewel is also reflecting all the other jewels, so that there is an infinite reflecting process occurring.[7]

The Jeweled Net of Indra represents a cosmos in which there is an infinitely repeated interrelationship among all the members of the cosmos. This relationship is said to be one of simultaneous mutual identity and mutual inter-causality. In his translation of the *Avatamsaka Sutra,* Thomas Cleary explains:

In seeking to understand individuals and groups, therefore, Hua-yen thought considers the manifold as an integral part of the unit and the unit as an integral part of the manifold; one individual is considered in terms of relationships to other individuals as well as to the whole nexus, while the whole nexus is considered in terms of its relation to each individual as well as to all individuals.[8]

This Hua-yen Buddhist vision that was extremely popular in China maintains a social vision in which the individual (even the social misfit) is considered to be part of the whole rather than to be separated out. Thus, it is the individual of sometimes questionable but expedient means that enables the enlightenment of Sonje. It is for this reason that he meets individuals such as an alcoholic, meat-eating monk, a foul-mouthed doctor, a poor girl who becomes his companion, and a drunken astronomer. All these individuals engage in questionable behavior, the moral judgment of which must ultimately be suspended in order to obtain a deeper understanding of the Buddhist teachings expressed in the film. For Sonje, the pursuit and search for his mother represents the search for truth, awakening, and ultimately, the experience of wholeness and oneness symbolized by the Jeweled Net of Indra.

As a metaphor for the journey to enlightenment, *Hwa-om-kyung* teaches that Buddhahood can be experienced in the midst of everyday life, for ultimately there is no distinction between *nirvana* (liberation) and *samsara* (suffering). Both are empty of inherent existence. Sonje attains this knowledge as he travels searching for what always seems just beyond his grasp—his mother or enlightened mind. As he searches for his mother, he later comes to realize that she, like enlightenment, has always been available to him and exists in all things without discrimination.

Hwa-om-kyung engages its viewers in a dream-like pilgrimage from suffering and ignorance to awakening and liberation. The liberation that is attained, however, does not take place in a far off mountain temple, but instead in the midst of complicated relationships for Sonje. Rather than existing as isolated individuals, the worldview presented by Chang is a relational one where one's identity is formed through webs of relationships among beings who are mutually defined and, therefore, responsible for the other. Although Sonje's early life experiences include abandonment by his mother, poverty, and eking out an existence with his thieving father in a shanty town, Chang shifts a marginalized character like Sonje from the outskirts of Korean society and places him in the center of a dramatic tale that affirms the humanity of the outcast and his place in that society. Chang's directorial lens probes the economic, political, and social disparities in Korean society and offers the vision of Hua-yen as a possible cure. For, as Francis Cook puts it:

In the Hua-yen universe, where everything interpenetrates in identity and interdependence, where everything needs everything else, what is there which is not valuable? To throw away even a single chopstick as worthless is to set up a hierarchy of values which in the end will kill us in a way in which no bullet can. In the Hua-yen universe, everything counts.[9]

The social fabric of Korean society is therefore intertwined in such a way that each thread in the fabric represents an individual who contributes to the totality of the fabric itself. Each is an integral and essential element of the whole; in other words, the whole cannot be defined without the sum of its parts.

Prior to his father's death, Sonje's makeshift family had consisted of squatters living in delapidated shacks on the outskirts of the modern industrialized city, a group of men that modern society has abandoned. It is amongst Korea's outcasts that Sonje begins and ends his journey of enlightenment as he follows in the footsteps of the pilgrim Sudhana who is advised by the bodhisattva Manjushri:

Good man, if one wishes to accomplish the wisdom of all wisdom, then one must decisively seek a true good knowing [spiritual] advisor. Good man, in seeking for a good knowing advisor, do not become weary or lax. And upon seeing a good knowing advisor, do not become satiated. As to a good knowing advisor and all his teachings, you must follow and accord. As to expedient devices employed by a good knowing advisor, do not find faults.[10]

Chang takes these words literally as he traces the journey of the young boy through a maze of seemingly chance encounters with characters who are amusing, mysterious, and full of wisdom.

Sonje sets out on his journey to find his mother carrying his only belongings—a backpack and tattered yellow baby blanket that serves as the only visual reminder he has of his mother. He has no idea what she looks like and clings to his blanket as a symbol of her nurturing. Since he does not remember his mother's face, he naively hopes that she will recognize him as he stands in the middle of subway stations and street corners holding up his blanket that has his name crudely written in black marker. Chang's critique of the invisibility and abandonment of the poor in Korean society is notable as no one stops to aid the young boy; rather they stare at him for a brief moment, ignore his plight, and move on. Sonje's search for his mother also reflects on his desire and attachment to the goal of enlightenment, which, as I show, has always been with him. Like Sudhana, however, he needs the help of good friends for his spiritual maturation.

Chang sets up his film as an explicitly Buddhist tale by introducing each scene with interpretive quotes from both the *Gandavyuha* and *Little Pilgrim*. Sonje's journey thus begins in the context of a religious quest with the statement that, "Everything low becomes the ocean and the sky descends on it." The Buddhist philosophy reflected in this preliminary passage indicates that high and low are of the same essence; rather than viewing the world with a distorted mind that views all phenomena dualistically, Buddhism encourages a vision of completion where all are nondual. Here Buddhist teachings come alive as they are recited by the characters themselves right before Sonje bows to them and departs. It is in this way that his story clearly parallels that of Sudhana who receives words of wisdom and advice from the *kalyānamitras* he meets on his journey.

Sonje's first encounter with a *kalyānamitra* occurs in a cramped restaurant where the boy stops for a cheap meal. As soon as he sits down, he is encouraged to have a drink by an alcoholic meat-eating monk named Bubwon who mysteriously remarks "I'll tell you how to cross the boundary of birth and death and enter nirvana." In so doing, he establishes himself as Sonje's first spiritual advisor and "good friend." The fact that the monk is a drunkard reflects the *Avatamsaka Sutra*'s admonition that practitioners must ultimately dissolve the distinctions between high and low, good and bad, and accord all beings equal value along the pathway to enlightenment

Rather unprompted, the monk seems to know the needs of the child and his future as he predicts that the young boy will live and die on the road as a wanderer. Knowing the desire of the boy, the monk explains humorously to Sonje:

> Wine and meat can be a law, truth or Buddha depending on how you think about it … Isn't this what you are looking for? If you have faith you will find her. But how can you find her, if you can't clean the eyes of the mind of wisdom?

That is, the journey to liberation and enlightenment cannot be completed without letting go of attachments to discriminations between high and low, right and wrong. And one must not critique the expedient means of the myriad *bodhisattvas*, even those that appear in our world as miscasts and miscreants. While something may seem independent and separate, this appearance is but an illusion, the play of the unawakened mind that separates reality into its seemingly component parts. Following this initial encounter, the monk then tells the boy to look to the East for a foul-mouthed doctor named Hae-Wun who will further enlighten him. This recommendation spurs Sonje back on the road in search of his mother and to further his understanding.

As Sonje's journey unfolds, Chang establishes another visual connection between his tattered yellow blanket and an apparitional figure that appears as his mother throughout the film wearing a yellow traditional Korean dress. This apparitional woman compels the young pilgrim on his search for his mother yet disappears as mysteriously as she arrives. Because she also arrives in dream-like moments carrying the iconic Buddhist lotus flower, a symbol of enlightenment, her image also makes a direct reference to the female *bodhisattva* of compassion, Kuan Yin (Kwan Um in Korean) whose very name means, "One who hears the cries of the world." While Sonje longs to find his mother, she appears to him in a variety of manifestations as all *bodhisattva* do. Yet it is only at the film's conclusion that he comes to recognize that this apparition is the mother who has always been with him, just as Mahayana Buddhism sees enlightenment and the Buddha nature as inherent in all sentient beings.

Along his travels throughout poor cities, seaside towns, and villages, Sonje encounters many other spiritual advisors such as a comical truck driver with a penchant for seeking out women who encourages the eleven-year-old to abandon his quest for his mother and take up the search for a suitable girlfriend. It is this truck driver who aids in Sonje's meeting with Hae-Wun, the compassionate yet foul-mouthed doctor who administers to the elderly and destitute in a seaside shantytown. While observing the doctor's selfless care for the marginalized, lonely, and abandoned, Sonje comes to understand the *Avatamsaka Sutra's* teachings about the vastness of the cosmos and how all things are part of it—it is here that he learns about the equality of all phenomena where the low becomes the high and the high descends upon the low. As the doctor notes him at the conclusion of this brief visit, "There is nothing in this world that is not great." Here we see the doctor's vision of goodness in all things—even the poor and broken down. The humorous contradiction between the doctor's foul mouth and compassionate heart are in line with the philosophical thinking that ultimately all are one and the same reality. The doctor then propels Sonje on his journey by sending him in search of the political prisoner, Hae Kyung, who was imprisoned for demanding social equality.

The next Buddhist teaching to emerge on the screen expounds that, "There is no bigger space than nihility." This filmic chapter introduces Sonje to a homeless blind woman whose beautiful voice sings out to the stars in the darkness of the night, and enchants the boy who soon finds her living beneath a bridge in the countryside. The woman, Ina, was purposefully blinded by her lover and continually abused. As she narrates the story of her life to the young pilgrim, we learn that the woman both loves and hates the man who blinded her in a rage, thus holding two contradictory emotions simultaneously. Almost wistfully she explains, "[t]he person I hate, I most love." After giving Sonje shelter for the night and imparting her enlightening wisdom, the young boy bows to the blind woman, and continues his journey to the prison to find Hae Kyung.

In Ko Un's novel, the blind woman represents the experiences of an old blind singer named Laritha whose eyes are gouged out with an iron skewer and whose genitals are mutilated after sleeping with a king whose castle she lived in for many years. The acts of violence committed against this woman were done in order that she would experience the deepest form of suffering, a suffering that would enable her to sing the saddest of songs. Yet, in singing the saddest of songs, she is also able to find the deepest joy for she believes it is her fate to be blessed through her singing.

Ko Un continues, "Laritha had become an artist and spoke as one. Hearing her song, Sudhana was able to rid himself of all the illusions he had been harboring as if dawn's azure darkness had come to lodge within his ears. Songs emerging out of deep sorrow can give rise to tremendous joy."[11] In other words, within the deepest *samsara*, *nirvana* can emerge just as the lotus blossoms from the mud of the swamp.

The young pilgrim continues his journey and encounters an ox in a field that he decides to steal so that he can get himself arrested in order to meet Hae Kyung, the dissident sage in prison who is none other than a representation of the poet Ko Un himself. Here is where the film takes a fascinating unreal turn as the ox wanders through an ethereal mist that begins to blur the lines between dreaming and awakening. One of the most startling aspects of this film's portrayal of Buddhism relates to these dream sequences that Sonje experiences with women who simultaneously play his mothers and his lovers. While riding atop the ox, the 11-year-old boy encounters a woman who appears to him at night in a long white flowing gown, whose draping folds echo those of the white porcelain statues of Kuan Yin.[12] Just as Chang's film depicts mist-filled cliffs, vast oceans, and warm, buttery light juxtaposed against scenes of a harsher reality where the elderly live in shacks, swamps are filled with trash, and children are abandoned, the scene that soon unfolds is equally distorting. Within her grand, softly-lit home where time seems to stand still and where there are no windows to reveal the outside world, reality as we ordinarily experience it slips away. When Sonje meets this woman, she reveals to him that she had called for him and proceeds to caress him lovingly as if he were her own son. The two fall into an easy relationship of mother and son; however, the entire scene is fraught with sexual ambiguity, for the maternal figure's caresses transform from those of a nurturing mother into sexual caresses more akin to a lover or a client. The mysterious woman treats Sonje as a grown man by offering him alcohol to further entice the boy. Chang deliberately avoids over-simplifying this mysterious scene as the viewer cannot help but question if this woman is a high-class prostitute trying to serve a client, a mother nurturing her son, or Kuan Yin attending

Figure 7.1 Hwa-Om-Kyung. *Female Bodhisattva greets Sonje.*

compassionately to those who hear her cry. When viewed through the lens of the Buddhist philosophy set forth in the *Gandavyuha*, however, we would be urged to see her as all three characters without mental discrimination.

The conflation of mother and lover in Chang's film has been called Oedipal by Francisca Cho, yet in order to more fully understand the attitude toward women and sexuality in Buddhism, our inquiry should proceed further by exploring the role of women, particularly prostitutes, in the *Gandavyuha*.[13] That is, what is the vision of Buddhism expressed in the Buddhist text that can elucidate the Buddhist vision of reality reflected in this scene? To leave the scene understudied or to reduce it to a mere instance of Oedipal love alone would be to leave it to the realm of sexual deviance on the part of the woman, which does not seem to fit the overall tone of the film.

Douglas Osto's study of the role of women in the *Gandavyuha* proves invaluable for deciphering the sexual suggestiveness and ambiguity of this scene. Within the Buddhist text itself, many *bodhisattvas* emanate in female forms such as the prostitute Vasumitrā who uses her own sexuality to entice men to a deeper understanding of nonduality. Osto notes:

> The courtesan is described as extremely beautiful, and is said to be skilled in languages, the arts and sciences and the means (upaya) of bodhisattvas. Vasumitrā tells Sudhana that she has attained a liberation known as "Ultimate dispassion ..." Through it she is able to assume the female form of any being to teach them the Dharma and lead the lustful to a state of dispassion... Those that come to her attain this state through various means: seeing her, talking to her, holding her hand, dwelling with her, embracing ... her, and kissing ... her.[14]

When he first accepts the drink of alcohol from the woman, Sonje informs her that he is looking for his mother. The woman then replies, "If you're okay, you can think of me as your mother." In this provocative scene, the meeting between the two becomes highly sexualized as the woman begins to kiss and caress the young boy as a lover. As spectators to this unexpected scene, we cannot help but struggle with our own discomfort. It is as though the director is playing with our expectations and pointing out how our own judgmental perspectives can also skew our perceptions. We are left to wonder whether what we are seeing is really happening. Can it be that this woman is having a sexual relationship with a child? Is he truly being seduced or is it that the boy is a symbolic man-boy? Is Sonje really a man with a childlike innocence or is he a being that represents the childlike mind that is so highly touted in Zen Buddhist literature? It is up to the spectator to grapple with these questions as there is no easy answer offered, but examining the role of women like Vasumitrā in the *Gandavyuha* certainly proves edifying.

In typical Mahayana rhetoric, the mind must grapple with the problem of perception. It is our own perception that is challenged here and the scene works marvelously in pointing out the problem of preconceived notions of right and wrong and, at the same time, gives the clearly Buddhist answer that reality and dreams are not so different. I suggest that the film encourages us to see this woman as a *bodhisattva* who brings the boy to a breakthrough in perception as she guides him towards his eventual destination. Enlightening wisdom can be found in all places and times—here in the film we see where "good and bad" collide into one moment of suspended judgment. As *bodhisattva,* she plays the role of lover and mother as she uses expedient means as her main methodology.

The female characters in *Hwa-om-kyung* are fascinating because of the ways in which their bodies are utilized for the formation and spiritual trans-formation of men. This explicit use of the female form for enlightenment has its precedent in early Indian Buddhist texts such as the *Gandavyuha*. In such early Indian Buddhist texts, the female form is not always envisioned as simply the negative snares of *samsara* to be avoided at all costs; instead the female form can often be envisioned as a means of liberation from a mind of attachment to the mind of enlightenment. Susanne Mrozik notes in her study of physiomoral bodies in *Virtuous Bodies: The Physical Dimensions of Morality in Buddhist Ethics* that while bodies are often negatively viewed and caught up in monastic arguments and preoccupations with celibacy, they are often valorized in Buddhist texts as a means of providing mental transfor-mation for men.[15]

Douglas Osto applies and elaborates upon Mrozik's theory of virtuous bodies to his study of the *Gandavyuha* and its particular version of women.[16] Osto argues out that while scholars of women and Buddhism such as Diana

Paul highlight several Mahayana Buddhist texts that express some of the most open and laudatory toward women, it is the *Gandavyuha's* elaboration of women of *all* types and their roles as *kalyānamitras* for Sudhana that offers one of the most positive attitudes toward female enlightenment. While texts describing female bodies in Buddhist literature have often been described as examples of ascetic misogyny, there are also counter models where the female *bodhisattva* envisions herself as an enlightening gift to men.[17]

In the case of the *Gandavyuha*, it is the sexed body of the female *bodhisattva* that serves to enlighten the men. The *Gandavyuha* posits that the prostitute Vasumitrā is one whose body brings manifest compassion and wisdom; the body also brings or gifts Sudhana with insight into the Buddha's teachings. It is worth noting that the text acknowledges the seeming paradox of a gifted student like Sudhana demonstrating any interest in a courtesan like Vasumitrā; as the text notes, it is the unwise townspeople who see Vasumitrā solely as a sex worker capturing men in the web of *samsara* with her feminine charms that are most caught up in a dualistic framework. They are seen, according to the compiler of the *Gandhavyuha*, as ones who lack the proper understanding of the truth.

Following their sexually charged evening, the next morning we find Sonje and the mysterious woman holding hands on an outing to the top of a mountain. The intimate scene offers an unusual companionship between two seeming lovers by most measures, yet lest we get too attached to this relationship, the director provides us with a shock and jolt as the mother-lover figure suddenly stumbles along the trail and plummets to her death with little explanation. Again, we are left to wonder if she was ever actually real. Did Sonje really meet this woman or was this all a dream? In congruence with the mysterious and often nonlinear time-sequencing of the film. Chang provides no easy answers or ways to anchor ourselves to a solid perspective. Instead, we are left to struggle with our sense of uneasiness, filled with disbelief as the woman begins to stroke Sonje suggestively and challenges our sense of conventional morality. In this way, Chang hits the spectator over the head with a scene that forces us to awaken from our complacency and re-evaluate the world unfolding in front of us.

After the initial shock of watching the mysterious woman of questionable moral values cascade down the cliff, Sonje seems to easily detach himself from the tragedy, although it is quite evident that he has found aspects of the mother in her tender caresses and kisses. As spectators in this unconventional relationship, we are then propelled forward through time, approximately three years later where we find the pilgrim in jail searching again for the political prisoner Hae Kyung. After Sonje descends the mountain on the very same ox that brought him up to the woman's house he is caught and jailed for stealing the ox. It is here that he meets the political dissident who has been jailed for over 40 years for fighting for political and social equality. Curiously, the film suggests that Sonje has stolen three oxen over the course of a few years in order to finally get arrested and thrown in jail so he should in fact be physically aging, yet in the film we never see this physical transformation occur. Instead, he remains in the same visual form of an 11-year-old. Much like his interactions with the mysterious woman, the boy's lack of aging serves as a critical clue to understanding the Mahayana Buddhist conception of time as a seamless whole, rather than as a linear progression.

After finally encountering the political dissident in jail, Sonje is advised by Hae Kyung, "Real equality is that all beings have no birth, nor death at all … A world is like a shadow reflecting on water or a mirror. At the point that our body and mind are mere shadows reflecting on the mirror, we are equal."

In response to this wise teaching, Sonje at first merely replies, "I'm no shadow."

In other words, his response indicates that he still sees himself as a substantively separate entity, apart from the whole interpenetrating reality that is the universe.

In reply, the prisoner says to him, "I am sorry to give you nothing but nihility but there is no bigger space than emptiness. Only enlightenment can take in everything."

Prison is like a monastery for Hae Kyung and Sonje where the encounter between the boy and man is recast as the meeting between a Zen Buddhist master and his young disciple. The *Avatamsaka Sutra*'s philosophy of an interrelated cosmos where the high and low, and the margins and center meet in the middle is brought to bear on the film to help make sense of the social injustices and economic losses that beset individuals like the prisoner and Sonje. The prisoner as monk calmly accepts all experiences with an equipoise that comes from embodying the principles of the *sutra* itself. Acknowledging the wisdom of the prisoner, Sonje soon bows to his teacher and takes his leave, although he remains disappointed because he cannot yet imagine being a mere shadow or an illusion.

Sonje then re-encounters the blind woman, Ina, on the road who exhorts him to "Follow those who flow but don't follow those who don't flow." The notion of flowing is reminiscent of the Taoist ideals of water that flow naturally in whatever direction it is compelled. Rather than being blocked by obstacles in its way, water naturally yields. The person who flows is one who does not have attachments and delusions. According to the Buddhist vision represented in this film, to flow means to move freely in the world beyond the constructs of self, time, and limited space. Rather than obstruct the mind with dualistic thinking, one must flow and remove attachments to phenomena that are essentially empty of true existence.

Thus, after a three-year stint in prison, Sonje meets Ina again selling flowers in broad daylight. She has aged considerably, yet Sonje curiously still appears as the eleven-year-old orphan that he was at the start of the film. Although he is spiritually developing, the young pilgrim is still plagued by loneliness and despair as he longs to find his mother.

Sonje's endless trajectory takes him back on the road where he re-encounters Iryon, a young girl who had tried to sell him flowers at the crematory years ago when his father died. It is Iryon who serves as another sexual partner for Sonje, yet this relationship is also fraught with ambiguity for the viewer. The first troubling issue in this scenario is simply that Iryon has grown into a young woman who is sexually attracted to Sonje. She has physically matured whereas Sonje remains ever the youngster in a boy's body. Noting the age disparity between himself and Iryon, he wonders why she would be attracted to him since he is a child. Iryon, however, knows and sees something that the audience and Sonje himself doesn't see; that is, that his mind has in fact significantly matured. She informs him quite assuredly, "Although your body is young, your mind is bigger and more beautiful than anyone else." In this scene, past, present, and future collapse upon one another to reveal the ultimate fiction of linear thinking that prevades the *Avatamsaka Sutra.*

Chang Sun-Woo's play on the youthful appearance of Sonje is to be understood as a metaphorical youth and innocence that evokes both a developing mind and an open mind. Such an illusion of time is perhaps the only logical explanation for the next sexually charged scene where Sonje again engages in sexual intimacy with an older woman. Similar to the previous scene of Oedipal proportions between Sonje and the mother-lover *kalyānamitra*, Iryon and Sonje hike up into a misty, fog-enveloped mountain where ordinary reality appears magical and illusory. The Buddhist world view in the film asserts that all life is an illusion, a perspective that the director thrusts upon his viewers who become spectators to a sexual tryst initiated by the older Iryon as the two wrestle in the grassy landscape of the mountains.

The Buddhist world view that serves as the thematic base for *Hwa-Om-Kyung* provides the illusory effect of keeping Sonje young while his friends age more naturally and allows for magical realism within the narrative. Such illusions are, of course, plays on the nature of reality as both ephemeral and a projection of the mind. The women in Sonje's life reflect an antinomian sexuality that serves to enlighten the boy. Yet, whether or not Sonje's character is bound by conventional notions of time does not affect the very real socio-political concerns that Chang brings to the screen.

The scene is undoubtedly jarring, yet I would argue that Chang does not focus so much on the troubling sexual ethics of the scene, but rather plays with the notion of the pilgrim learning and developing through a variety of different encounters with different types of *kalyānamitras*. In the case of

Iryon, she evokes the female bodhisattva of the *Gandavyuha* whose sexual enticements serve as catalysts for enlightenment. In addition, Chang provides a direct assault against our comfortable illusions about reality. The sexually charged and skewed nature of these questionable relationships is precisely meant to wake us up much in the way that a *koan* is said to induce a state of *satori* or sudden enlightenment, that sudden wake-up call to the ultimate nature of reality.

In setting up the scene between pre-adolescent boy and older, sexually aggressive woman, the director ensures that numerous questions pop into the viewers' heads, questions that force viewers to question our assumptions. Is this really happening in the present moment? Is Sonje looking back on his life and experiencing himself as a metaphorical child? Is he currently a grown man but we are meant to see him as a spiritual boy? The director offers no easy answers to these questions. He simply puts the image out there for us so that we might wake up and question our assumptions.

Here again, it is helpful to refer to a scene in Ko Un's novel where Sudhana impregnates a young woman in India, who is also named Iryon. He decides not to stay with her but to instead continue his journey toward enlightenment. What is clear in Ko Un's novel is that Iryon represents the life of attachment that Sudhana must abandon on his journey through the stages of enlightenment.

Ko Un also provides essential information for the reader that the filmmaker does not—that is, Sudhana's experiences with the women and his seeming failure to grow up are all just an illusion and a method of teaching. In the novel, the Little Pilgrim has a conversation with a *bodhisattva* disguised as an elephant who says to him:

> Little Pilgrim! You are still only a little pilgrim. Those twelve years [of wandering] were a dream I gave you. Since the moment you fell asleep outside of Vanavasin, you have been unable to distinguish between dream and reality. That first taste of passion for a dream was really only part of your dream ... Sudhana looked down at his body. He had not grown. There was no sign of his having become a young man able to make love with women ...[18]

Allowing the mystery to remain, Chang Sun-Woo purposefully forces the viewer to grapple with the illusions of time and the significance of the scenes' sexuality. Yet, as Osto and Mrozik both attest, the sexual nature of women cannot always be seen as a hindrance or as a snare of *samsara*. Like Sudhana in the *Little Pilgrim*, Sonje abandons his own Iryon after impregnating her and continues on his journey to find his next *kalyānamitra*—a widowed alcoholic professor of astronomy and his young son who impart a critical Buddhist lesson on emptiness with the professor's mysterious declaration that reality "exists but it doesn't."

Although he is but a boy, the professor's young son is a wealth of Buddhist knowledge and a keen scientist. He, like the *bodhisattvas* of the *Avatamsaka Sutra*, teaches that since the universe is born, it will die and disappear into emptiness, much the same as all sentient beings. The erudite young scientist explains, "What are the flower, tree, building, etc. all made of? ... We can't see energy so it is nothing. Energy is nothing in that it is empty. But the world isn't empty because it is filled with energy ... So it is empty but it is full."

Taking this *dharma* lesson from the young astronomer, Sonje descends the mountain and eventually rediscovers the errant Bubwon who has now taken up work as a fishmonger and reappears to teach the boy lessons of nonattachment to views and to such concepts as virtue and purity.

Despite Sonje's seemingly endless journey toward enlightenment and countless encounters with various *kalyānamitras*, the pilgrimage eventually exacts a serious toll on the young boy, who believes that his constant search has been in vain since he has yet to find his mother. In a moment of utter desperation and despair, Sonje hurls himself off the side of a dock and we watch him disappear under the surface of the ocean as his tattered yellow blanket slowly floats to the surface. While drowning, Sonje's mother reappears in a vision carrying a flower in her hand to help save him. Much like the scene from Bae Young-Kyun's 1989 Zen film, *Why Has Bodhidharma Left for the East?* where a young monk is saved from drowning in a river through a visionary apparition of the mother who abandoned him, Sonje is also saved from certain death. Interestingly, Bae Young-Kyun's film also establishes a direct connection between the figure of the mother who abandons her young son and a *bodhisattva* caregiver figure; in Bae's film, the *bodhisattva* comes in the form of an ox who serves as a dual icon of a *bodhisattva* and the representation of the mind.

"There is nothing that is alone in the world"— such is the opening text that brings us to a new chapter and locale where Sonje is nursed back to health by a compassionate and gentle lighthouse keeper. Sonje admits to this *kalyānamitra* that he has indeed lost hope, is destitute, and seemingly is of no value to society; by jumping in the ocean, Sonje believed that there would be no loss to humanity. It is here that the lighthouse keeper imparts an invaluable lesson from the *Avatamsaka Sutra* philosophy as he counters that, actually, "The ocean, fish, sky and I will be sad," and that indeed, "there is nothing in this world that is alone," for all things are interdependent and interrelated. That is, all phenomena are filled with the Buddha nature and are one and the same. Receiving this wisdom, Sonje bows to his teacher and continues on his travels.

In one of the most dramatic scenes in the film, Sonje soon wanders through a dirty, polluted swamp filled with refuse, clinging to his blanket in search of his mother. As he makes his way through this filthy, abandoned, and putrid landscape, he has another visionary experience of his mother-*bodhisattva* where she reveals herself quickly and turns away as if to leave him. As Sonje chases after his mother, he stumbles and begins to thrash around in the swamp which threatens to pull him under. The vision dressed in yellow then throws the lotus flower in the swamp, thus revealing the direct relationship between the lotus which emerges from the swamp and the mud of *samsara*. In Buddhist traditions, the lotus, a symbol of liberation and enlightenment, both transcends and remains rooted in the swamp of *samsara*. That is, the *bodhisattva* transcends yet remains rooted in the ordinary world to liberate all sentient beings. The next scene thus introduces a dream sequence where Sonje reappears dressed in fresh clothes in an empty room where the mother-*bodhisattva* feeds him and attends to him as her own child. When Sonje asks, "Why did you come now?" she reassures him that she always been present to him.

She explains, "I have always been next to you. I am the mother of every *sattva*, every *bodhisattva*, every Being ..." Here we find that the mother-*bodhisattva* figure is a manifestation of none other than the *Avatamsaka Sutra's* vision of ultimate reality. The woman in yellow represents the compassion that pervades the universe. In the text itself, Sudhana encounters his forty-first spiritual teacher, Lady Maya, also known as the mother of the Buddha. In a moment of great mental concentration, he obtains a resplendent vision of a great jeweled lotus out of which springs a tower in whose chamber he discovers a lotus throne "arrayed with rows of jewels which reflected the manifestations of buddhas and succession of births of all buddhas of past, present and future, rows of radiant jewels showing the lights of the activities in all Buddha-lands throughout space and the effecting of all miracles ..."[19] Upon the lotus throne sits Lady Maya manifesting innumerable forms that enabled her to enact her compassion.

To the pilgrim Sudhana she explains:

I have attained an enlightening liberation, 'magical manifestation of knowledge of great vows.' Imbued with this liberation, I am the mother of all the enlightening beings in their final existence in all the worlds in this world-ocean where Vairocana Buddha's miraculous manifestation of birth as an enlightening being in the final existence takes place. All those enlightening beings grow in my belly and come forth from my right side ...[20]

Through her great compassion, Lady Maya is also revealed to be the ground of enlightenment, the matrix from which the beings of great wisdom emerge. From her belly come forth all the Buddhas of the past, present, and future as she claims, "Just as I was the mother of this Buddha in this world in all his manifestations of miracles of birth as an enlightened being, so was I the mother of the buddhas Krakucchanda, Kanakamuni, and Kashyapa; and so will I be the mother of all the buddhas of this eon."[21] The *Avatamsaka Sutra's* vision of the world is one in which time and space collapse into one infinite expanse and it is in this compression that we can begin to see Sonje's mental transformation and process of awakening. As Francis Cook explains:

> The Hua-yen world is completely nonteleological. There is no theory of a beginning time, no concept of a creator, no question of purpose of it all. The universe is taken as a given, a vast fact which can be explained only in terms of its own inner dynamism, which is not at all unlike the view of twentieth-century physics ... Being is just that, a unity of existence in which numerically separate entities are interrelated in a profound manner ... The Hua-yen universe is essentially a universe of identity and total inter-causality; what affects one item in the vast inventory of the cosmos affects every other therein, whether it is death, enlightenment or sin."[22]

This view of timeless time and expansive nonending space wherein all actions have a ripple effect on all aspects of the cosmos through interrelatedness is precisely the vision that Chang Sun-Woo articulates in his film.

Following this dramatic event, Sonje reawakens to find himself back in the muddy swamp. At the loss of his visionary experience, he wails in torment, anguish, and suffering, but rather than allowing himself to die of thirst and starvation, he suddenly begins to drink and eat of the filthy polluted water that stagnates in the swamp. While visually disturbing, for Chang this moment becomes the precise point where Sonje begins to look beyond dualities and comes to see things as one taste—freedom and liberation. As Cook reminds us, "[b]oth life and death are part of the one ever-changing process we call being (which is really 'becoming') and thus both are conditions for that being. To see things in a totalistic perspective means to transcend a small, pathetic subjectivity and see all the pernicious, vexing contraries harmonized within the whole."[23] Sonje gains this new perspective while eating the mud for survival and sees that *samsara* and *nirvana* are but one experience.

Transformation and completeness are central themes of the film yet this transformation emerges through a radical, and at times fantastical, experience of relationality offered by Chang. That Sonje meets the same individuals repeatedly throughout his journey as they age and he remains the same, indicates that time is deliberately disordered to demonstrate that the world through enlightened vision is one where past, present, and future converge in one moment of existence. Thus, time and space are compressed to show that moment of awakening.

At the film's conclusion, Sonje's journey has come full circle as he returns to find Iryon in a troublesome relationship with the truck driver who had given Sonje a ride many years back. She is on the verge of leaving the driver and is pregnant again with the driver's child. At this precise moment of suffering, she miraculously sees a vision of Sonje as a young boy playing a flute at the swamp's edge. After his many encounters with a cast of *kalyānamitras*, Sonje finally becomes a teacher and a spiritual guide who echoes the words of the *Avatamsaka Sutra* as he proclaims:

> The sky becomes empty by losing the rain. The river becomes an ocean by losing the river. The flower becomes the fruit by losing the flower. I also became empty by losing my [dualistic/attached] mind. You have to lose your mind. If you don't do that you can't get away from the sea of foolish anger and pain.

That he now recites the Buddhist teachings projected on the screen indicates that he has experienced awakening. Iryon now becomes the object rather than the source of compassion in Sonje's life.

Sonje is thus liberated from his own clinging mind and we see him now as the apparitional *bodhisattva* who appears to the truck driver and Iryon, who both resolve to continue working on their troubled relationship. Sonje has finally discovered his mother and his enlightenment. By the film's conclusion the full implications of interconnectedness and interdependence come to fruition as Sonje returns to the fishing village to look for Bubwon who has apparently disappeared again. However, what Sonje soon discovers are traces of the monk and his enlightenment evidenced by the lotus petals scattered about the ground where Bubwon had once resided. The *bodhisattva* monk's disappearance serves as evidence of Sonje's own liberation since he no longer needs the guidance of the *kalyānamitra*. Spiritually matured, Sonje heads back over the bridge where he re-encounters and bids farewell to Ina the blind woman and has one final encounter with the matured Iryon outside a train station on her way back from work.

Sonje inquires about her life with her husband who has been jailed for stealing and asks about their new baby. Iryon then inquires of Sonje's search for his mother to which he wisely replies, "The world is my mother. The stars in the sky are my mother. The dullness is my mother." In other words, all things are Buddha. Toward the end of the scene Iryon asks him why he has come to see her and he then claims that he wants to accompany the tired Iryon just once more. Just as he had been nurtured and escorted by countless *bodhisattvas*, he now wants to serve others with compassion. He then offers his yellow blanket to the baby and she asks, "Shall I name the baby Sonje?" In this parting scene, interconnectedness and interdependence are re-established as central aspects of reality.

The film's conclusion highlights the collapse of time and the karmic relations between individuals according to a Buddhist scheme. Sonje's rediscovery of Iryon works as a moment when we begin to wonder if in fact Sonje is returning to visit his mother in the past. Iryon's marriage to the truck driver who turns out to be a kindhearted thief doing a stint in jail similarly replicates the story of Sonje whose loving father was a thief. The dialogue between the two also shows the karmic connection between them where Sonje gives Iryon's baby his own yellow blanket with Sonje's name written on it. As Sonje turns to take leave of Iryon, she calls out to him, "Shall I name [it] Sonje?" Such a scene evokes the final scene in *Spring, Summer, Fall, Winter... and Spring* where nonteleological time is presented as an ever-repeating continuum.

Just as the vows of the bodhisattva call for continual service in the world, in the final scene we find Sonje has befriended a young, orphaned boy and now teaches him how to scrounge for food and enjoy his present life. Sonje removes his itinerant's rucksack and places it gently on the back of the young boy. He then accompanies the orphan and teaches him how to live the life of a pilgrim and wanderer. As a *kalyānamitra* himself, Sonje finally appears to be physically maturing.

As noted throughout the text itself, time is a fictional construct imposed upon a world of experiences that cannot easily be captured sequentially. In fact, the *Avatamsaka Sutra's* view is one where past, present, and future

Figure 7.2 Hwa-Om-Kyung. *Sonje meets orphan and becomes his* bodhisattva.

collapse upon one another into a singular experience. Yet the final scenes of *Hwa-om-kyung* also introduce the Buddhist idea of the continual rebirth of all beings and the continual rebirth and working of the *bodhisattva* in *samsara*. Chang's world of depression, alienation, abandonment, and identity crisis are indicative of the Buddha's words that in life, suffering exists and that it exists because of our attachments and desires to things that are ultimately impermanent (*anitya*) and without essence (*anatman*). Sonje's attachment to a mother he does not even remember causes him great suffering, yet this suffering also propels him toward the profound realization that his mother is not someone to find in the future, but rather someone who is in all things. She exists in the past and the present as Iryon, Bubwon, the alcoholic professor and his son, the blind woman, the prostitute, the political prisoner, and the lighthouse keeper. As the symbol of compassion that is so pivotal in Mahayana thought, the mother represents the Buddha nature that is in all things and reflects all things just as the Jeweled Net of Indra.

Yet in what ways does this film provide us with a vision of how one should live? Ethically, the Hua-yen tradition envisions a being who, through understanding emptiness, impermanence, and interdependence, has cast aside the attachment to self and is therefore radically able to embrace the world as a *bodhisattva*. The *bodhisattva* is one who has cut off attachments, a process that takes him or her through a series of stages of development. For Sonje, the process of enlightenment comes through his relinquishment of the mother figure as an external being and the realization that the mother is in all things—including himself and that he is a part of all phenomenon. It is the text itself whose central teachings explicate a decentered cosmos that lacks hierarchy between individuals and offer a world of wholeness which provides Chang with the antidote to modern Korean social and political unrest that he sees in the early 1990s—political repression, social fragmentation, and alienation. As director, Chang turns to the Buddhist view of the totality of the cosmos and the individual's place within as a means of redressing the fractured social and political structures of South Korea. Seen primarily as an ethical vision of how the world can be, precisely because this is how the world actually *is*, the *Avatamsaka* offers solace as the unenlightened begin to see how the world, tainted by the three poisons of greed, hatred, and delusion, can ultimately be transformed.

The universe revealed in the *sutra* is one seen through the eyes of those who have awakened; thus it is a glorious revelation not only of the mystery of the world but its deepest reality. Rather than dwelling on isolation, the text reveals that humanity, society, and culture are tied together and defined by their intrinsic mutual relationships. Seeing the universe in terms of relationality cannot but transform the anguish and unrest brought about by individual isolation. The social vision revealed by the *Avatamsaka Sutra* is one that radically transforms one's sense of separation. Sonje's journey then is a pilgrimage of self-discovery and "individual completeness," as Chang Sun-Woo puts it. It is the gradual process of gathering together the disparate parts of the incomplete self through relationships that brings Sonje to the experience of fullness. The abandoned and fragmented self that longed for the caress of the mother has given way to the realization that she has always been alive in him and through his meetings with others. His encounters with the kalyānamitras validate and affirm his place in humanity, and in a larger perspective, the cosmos. This affirmation of his ultimate belonging echoes the Avatamsaka Sutra's view that "to exist in any sense at all means to exist in dependence on the other, which is infinite in number. Nothing exists truly in and of itself, but requires everything to be what it is."[24]

Because of the film's emphasis on enlightenment through the compassion of good spiritual friends who are the polar opposite of pristine monks engaged in asceticism and meditation, Hwa-om-kyung has much to offer for a re-visioning of Buddhism beyond the hierarchy of monks over laity. It offers a significant and much needed counterbalance to the debilitating and abstract stereotype of exotic magical monks perpetuated in popular media.

In the following chapter, I move from the world of the Avatamsaka Sutra and its valorization of the marginalized to focus specifically on lay Buddhist women. Through an explicitly feminist hermeneutic, I reread Samsara (2003), another Buddhist film by Indian director Pan Nalin that once again highlights the story of a monk troubled by sexual desire. In so doing, I argue that sexuality does not always have to be so troublesome or antithetical to the spiritual life. Instead, it can be generative and contribute to women's flourishing in the Buddhist tradition when freed from the diagnosis of pathology and degeneration perpetuated in the popular imagination.

8

Re-visioning the Role of Lay Women in Buddhism

Pan Nalin's 2001 *Samsara* takes place in the high reaches of Ladakh and immediately captivates audiences with its enticing entrée into yet another exotic world where monks can meditate in sacred caves attaining higher and higher levels of spiritual attainment. In one such cave resides a powerful monk named Tashi who, without food, drink, or even human contact, trains himself to overcome all desire in order to achieve Buddhahood. A retinue of saffron and maroon clad monks climbs high up to the mountain hermitage to bring Tashi home. Once they reach the hermitage nestled in a cave, they attempt to loosen the weather-beaten door that has not been opened for a number of years. One of the monks then turns his head and whispers to a young monastic boy that Tashi has been in meditation for "three years, three months, three weeks, and three days." Such an intensive period of practice is so miraculous and heroic that upon hearing this news, the little boy immediately dons a serious expression of reverence and bows his head in respect for all that the monastic virtuoso has accomplished.

Within the darkness of his cave, Tashi's hair has grown long and wild, his nails long, curled, and dirty, his body withered from years of semi-starvation. His teacher, Apo, gently slides a wooden mallet around the lip of a meditation bowl that reverberates with a quiet hum to awaken Tashi from his trance-like state. He has meditated for so long in the lotus position, with his hands folded one over the other with thumbs touching, that Apo must slowly pry apart his student's fingers that have not moved from this meditative *mudra* (symbolic hand gesture) for over three years. Audiences are privy to the sounds of his knuckles and joints cracking as the teacher reintroduces movement and circulation in his stiff digits and wonder if such a feat is even possible.

Tashi's eyes must be protected with a blindfold to block the bright sunlight that seeps in through the cracks in the doorway, for they have grown accustomed to the dark. Gently supported by the monks, he is unearthed from the

Figure 8.1 Samsara. *Tashi as meditating monk.*

meditation cave, placed atop a horse, and brought to a nearby river. Here Apo and his monks tend to Tashi's frail body as they cut his nails, bathe his body, and then shave his head. He emerges from the river a recognizable monk and is dressed in the Tibetan Buddhist monastic robes that his fellow monks wear. The spiritually-realized Tashi, a monk since the tender age of five, is treated with great reverence and care for, despite his mentally strong mind, he is unable to look after himself. So special is he that the monks must spoon feed him to try to nourish him back to health. Expectations are high—this monk is the virtuoso who has surpassed human desires and become the paragon of Buddhist saintliness and detachment … or so it seems.

He is welcomed back to his monastery as a hero and a spiritual victor but things change quickly, for during the first night of his stay his body betrays him with the first of a series of uncontrollable wet dreams. Having controlled his body for so long throughout his retreat, the virtuous monk transforms overnight into a lustful human being unable to control his desires; he has become a man plagued by nocturnal emissions as he sleeps and a fool besotted by the mere sight of a woman by day. He falls from his exotic beginnings only to be reborn a man whose sexual desires trap him in the continual realm of rebirth or *samsara*.

Audiences are just as disappointed by Tashi's failures as the fellow monk with whom Tashi shares a room and who must witness the returned monk's transgressions as he moans in his sleep each night. Tashi's exotic charisma that harkens back to the inhabitants of *Lost Horizon's* Shangri-La has been lost, as is the paradise that Orientalism constructs. The myth of the heightened spirituality of Buddhist monks quickly dispels once Tashi enters the ordinary world again. Despite honing his mind for over three years, Tashi fails in his pursuit of enlightenment as soon as he comes back to the world.

Lest audiences get swept away by yet another version of Shangri-La at the film's opening, Nalin offers something different to imagine—the vision of a failed monk who after three years of rigorous meditation with little food and water has yet to uproot the one thing that binds him to *samsara*—desire. Nalin's film thus gives lie to the myth of the magic and mystery of Buddhist monasticism and reverses the popular assumption that asceticism and meditation are the keys to enlightenment. In this chapter I suggest that Nalin's film engages in a monastic reversal that hinges upon the seemingly paradoxical relationship between sexuality, desire, and enlightenment. Rather than making claims for sexual purity as the defining characteristics of a successful monk, *Samsara* counters the prevailing notion that restraint gives rise to enlightenment. Instead, for monks *and* lay women, liberation comes from engaging the senses and experiencing desire in order to fully understand its fleeting nature. In so doing, Nalin's film opens up the possibility of an alternative view of Buddhism in which enlightenment can coexist in the ordinary world where lay women are not just snares of *samsara*, but mothers, wives, and lovers, whose everyday lives are viewed as potent sources for spiritual awakening.

For Nalin, Buddhist monastic life is not all that it is carved out to be, for restraint does not bring transformation. Rather, it is immersion in the everyday world that brings about the conditions for enlightenment. Such a Buddhist view of enlightenment is explicitly hinted at on a prayer stone Tashi picks up before he returns to the monastery—the stone has an inscription written in Tibetan on one side that poses the following question: "How can one prevent a drop of water from drying up?"

But neither Tashi nor audiences are privy to the answer at the film's opening, for that is the central question that he must work out for himself. Following his ascetic failure, Tashi leaves the monastery, marries, has a son, and then tries to return to the monastic life after a number of years. Throughout the film, Tashi struggles with his commitments and with the answer to this spiritual puzzle, yet his wife, Pema, intuitively understands its meaning. Her insight signifies her deep knowledge of the Buddhist teachings of interdependence, compassion, and spiritual transformation gained through her immersion into—rather than rejection of—the world. It is only at the film's conclusion, when Pema has left Tashi at the foot of the mountain leading back to his monastery, that he flips over the prayer stone and reads the answer to the question; yet, even then, he fails to intuit its meaning.

Samsara offers the rare opportunity to divest from the myths of Orientalism and extraordinary monks and to reimagine the Buddhist tradition through the everyday practices of lay Buddhist women. Yet because the film is ostensibly a man's tale recounting the spiritual maturation, decline, and re-investment in the asceticism of a monk, such a divestment and reimaging requires a heterodox reading of the film that shifts the focus from a monk's life to that of an ordinary lay woman. In this chapter, I offer an against-the-grain reading of *Samsara* that engages in what bell hooks refers to as the oppositional gaze that both critiques and re-visions the images of women that appear on screen.[1] In so doing, I reread a film that narrates the experiences of a sexually intrigued monk who leaves the monastic life. However, rather than viewing *Samsara* as a story about a monk who cannot control his own desire and falls prey to the allure of women, I flip the script by reading it as a film about a lay woman who cares for a monk, engages in sexual intimacy with him after he leaves the monastery, marries him, has a son, and then abandons her husband when she learns that he has decided to go back to the monastery after having a good dose of the woes of ordinary life.

Pema's character is significant because, in contrast to how women are presented in the other Buddhist films I've discussed, in *Samsara* her sexuality is not cast as something shameful or detrimental to men. She expresses desire for Tashi and seeks him out for a mutually enjoyable tryst and she breaks off an engagement with another man because she prefers the former monk. Her sexuality is neither pathological nor threatening. As I show in this chapter, Pema seeks pleasure for herself *and* serves as an example of an ordinary lay Buddhism based on a compassion for others that Tashi cannot seem to express. Desire and compassion are not mutually exclusive but can and do coexist in the real Buddhist world; nonetheless popular renditions of the tradition on screen simply do not find such a relationship as compelling as the magical mystery monk.

By focusing on Pema's story, it becomes clear that the ordinary lay world of Buddhism can be just as effective a place for enlightenment as a monastery and that sexual desire, the usual foe to all monastics, is not always detrimental to a spiritual life. Rather, desire can be friend or foe depending on one's level of spiritual attainment, which is not always best honed through asceticism, as many Buddhist texts and films would have us believe.

The unquestioned assumption that women are by nature hypersexual, and therefore problematic, in the Buddhist tradition is a common theme in many films that in turn make women rather hyperinvisible as agents in their own spiritual lives. In other words, their sexual desires have been so exaggerated and made so hypervisible that it has been near impossible to see desiring women as anything less than excessive to a normative ethical Buddhist world.

Celine Perreñas Shimuzu's study of race, sexuality, and images of Asian American women in film illuminates the significance of a subversive rereading of images that hinder female agency to suggest that they can in fact be productive "... sites for imagining alternative subjectivities."[2] Perreñas Shimuzu asks a significant question in her work that inspires much of my own study of *Samsara* and other Buddhist-themed films—"How can we deploy representation so as to imagine new worlds and possibilities for Asian/American women?"[3] In the chapter that follows, I extend the focus of my analysis by examining the representational possibilities for Asian and Asian American *Buddhist* women.

Perreñas Shimuzu, much like bell hooks, eludicates the power of (re)interpretation on the part of the spectator of racialized and gendered spectacles. She writes:

In the case of engaging figures of mastery on screen, independent interpretation becomes a form of work that introduces the possibility of transformation. The potential process in which actors, spectators, and critics can embark on a transformation of racial, sexual, and representational bondage is the claiming of the critical and creative work of interpretation located within the practices of authorship, spectatorship, and criticism.[4]

Even in the midst of the debilitating or calcified images of female Buddhist sexuality as Mara's legions, it is the spectator who has the power to rewrite the text associated with such images.

There is of course, as Celine Perreñas Shimuzu puts it, a kind of moral panic that can ensue when looking at and valorizing the sexuality of women in film from a feminist standpoint out of fear that one might simply be engaging in bad politics by continuing to subordinate women to the male gaze.[5] She thus reminds us that "[w]hen moral panic continues to inform our understanding of racialized sexuality in representation, informing theories that privilege ordinary normalcy, we lose the opportunity to reimagine what is missing, unaccounted for, and excluded in the normal ..."[6] An exploration of female sexuality in Buddhist films therefore refrains from dismissing women as impure and immoral and intentionally embraces their materiality and presence in the Buddhist realm.

A study of the hypersexuality of Asian and Asian American women on screen proves particularly helpful for the context of Buddhist text and film as a prompt to theorize the ways in which such excessive sexuality binding women to *samsara* can be approached productively. Otherwise, one might be tempted to simply write off such representations as yet another means to delimit the possibility of women's flourishing in the tradition.[7] To be certain, exploring the positive representations of the hypersexuality of women in

Buddhist text and films runs the risk of running afoul of "good politics" by reinscribing women as snares of *samsara*. Yet to override the possibility of agency with and through such images out of fear of moral panic means to leave unchallenged the historical and contemporary attitudes that women are excessive to proper Buddhism because of their very sexuality. As I argue below, recasting Buddhist women's sexuality in scripture and film as a politically productive site of resistance means to create alternative readings of women's sexuality that do not marginalize their subject positions but rather render their representations less scandalous, less excessive, and therefore, more real.

Because there is little to no valorization of lay female Buddhist women or acknowledgment of their full lives from the religious to the sexual in the popular imagination, this chapter draws upon bell hooks's use of the oppositional gaze, the noncanonical Buddhist biographies and poetry of the Buddha's wife, and Audre Lorde's theorization of erotic materiality to reinterpret the images of Buddhist women on screen. In so doing, I engage in a re-visioning of Buddhism where laywomen's religiosity can be seen front and center rather than as a watered down version of some alleged orthodoxy.

bell hooks: The oppositional gaze and critical spectatorship

In her essay, "The Oppositional Gaze and Black Female Spectatorship," bell hooks recounts the terror and fascination she had as a child over the act of looking and the power of the gaze.[8] Often punished for staring back at adults who read her stares as insouciance and resistance to authority, hooks recalls both the fear of looking and the rebellious desire to continue doing so anyway. For hooks, the act of looking involves not only domination by those who deny one's right to look, but also resistance in the form of an oppositional gaze deployed as a strategy of survival. She thus remarks:

> Spaces of agency exist for black people, wherein we can both interrogate the gaze of the Other but also look back, and at one another, naming what we see ... Subordinates in relations of power learn experientially that there is a critical gaze, one that "looks" to document, one that is oppositional. In resistance struggle the power of the dominated to assert agency by claiming and cultivating "awareness" politicizes "looking" relations—one learns to look a certain way in order to resist.[9]

hooks thus theorizes a critical spectatorship that can restore selfhood and "presence" where it has been negated in the mediated spaces of racialized and gendered difference. As she succinctly puts it, "We do more than resist. We create alternative texts that are not solely reactions. As critical spectators, black women participate in a broad range of looking relations, contest, resist, re-vision, interrogate, and invent on multiple levels."[10] While hooks argues specifically for a black female spectatorship, the challenge to look back at received images and reinvent them certainly has its place in the Buddhist world.

The oppositional gaze of critical spectatorship proves fruitful for looking back at images of Buddhist women who are often defined by their lack of spiritual acumen and their embodiment as mantraps whose baited bodies stand ready to lure many a hapless monk from his monastic heroism. Such stories abound in textual and filmic sources of Buddhism noted earlier in this study which, if read uncritically, will continue to subsume women's experiences and positions within the Buddhist world as simply less than. Thus, in this chapter, I outline an approach to looking relations that registers the agency of Buddhist women which has oft been neglected, misread, and simply overlooked in canonical and popular sources. By offering an oppositional reading of the film *Samsara*, this chapter engages in a project of creating alternative texts about Buddhism through re-vision. Rather than focusing on the narrative of the monk Tashi, I reread *Samsara* as a potential source for a liberatory Buddhism that takes women and lay life as the locus of serious practice. In so doing, my reading of *Samsara* resists the hegemonic tendency to see women as mere catalysts for male transformation and situates women as primary actors in the Buddhist social world. Such a resistant reading necessitates a creative intertextual approach that draws together historical texts in dialogue with film to render a more complex portrait of women in the Buddhist world.

Rather than looking for women in places where they do not yet exist, my method can be considered one of *bricolage*, a drawing together of numerous sources from canonical and popular Buddhist sources to cultural studies to read women back into the tradition. In so doing, I attempt to generate a vision of Buddhist women's agency that challenges previous cultural and textual stereotypes. Because *Samsara* follows the same patriarchal script of the monk's quest for enlightenment and the relegation of women to the impure world of desire found in Buddhist texts and films, my approach also requires a more nuanced reading of female sexuality that has been hitherto plagued by the stereotypes of women as the enticing, voracious, and damaging daughters of Mara. In lieu of pathologizing women's sexuality as antithetical to liberation as Buddhist sources have done over the centuries, my reading of *Samsara* approaches lay female sexuality anew—that is, I remove lay female sexuality from the realm of the scandalous into the realm of the normative such that the seeming hypersexuality of women in Buddhism is portrayed as ordinary and no longer an obstacle to liberation.[11]

As I argue in this chapter, reading film in a counterhegemonic manner opens up spaces for the emergence of a Buddhist female subjectivity. To do otherwise would mean to continue to view women as spectral figures in the Buddhist tradition that continue to be objects to be looked at with little opportunity to look upon themselves anew.[12] Such critical spectatorship engages in an interventionist form of looking that transgresses the normative view of women in the Buddhist tradition by moving beyond a mere lamentation of the position of women both in text and film. Instead, critical spectatorship seeks to glean the agency and desire to be looked at on one's own terms through the female character of Pema who, when viewed uncritically, appears as mere catalyst for the transformation of the monk Tashi through her sexuality. Taking a cue from hooks, I approach film as a way to re-vision Buddhism and as an opportunity to "involve ourselves in a process whereby we see our history as countermemory, using it as a way to know the present and invent the future."[13] Thus the following analysis of *Samsara* is not only an act of retrieval and rereading of women in the Buddhist textual tradition, but also an act of rendering anew a tradition that can account for the centrality of lay Buddhist women as more than mere mothers of monks and/or sources of ascetic failure.

What is missing for Buddhist women is the possibility of imaging and imagining themselves as neither scandalous nor excessive, for sometimes as hooks reminds us, women's sexual desire is often about more than sexual fulfillment—it is about the desire to be seen on one's own terms and about the eroticism of attention. Rather than avoiding the hypersexuality of women in Buddhist texts as further instantiation of their invisibility, marginalization, and excessiveness to the male Buddhist order, I approach the visuality of female sexuality as an opportunity to embrace the materiality of women. Such an approach opens up new avenues for the pursuit of the spiritual in the ordinary; such a desire is nothing short of an everyday expression of the desire to live well. To acquiesce to moral panic over women's pleasure and representations of hypersexuality means to acquiesce to the disciplining of women's flourishing and expression of alternative subjectivities.

Certainly, the Buddhist textual tradition offers numerous examples of the excoriating male gaze through the Buddha's purported views on women as well as the institutional views of women as less worthy candidates of full ordination. Thus, looking at images of sexually-engaged Buddhist women can seem like a re-inscription and reproduction of age old tropes of women as snares of *samsara* whose very bodies are visually dissected into component parts during some of the most extreme meditative practices known as *dhutanga* (outer practices).

One does not need to look far into the Buddhist canonical sources for additional negative views of women—take for example the following dialogue between the Buddha and his disciple Ananda on relations with women from the *Mahaparinirvana Sutra*:

> [Ananda:] "How are we to conduct ourselves, Lord, with regard to
>   womankind?"
> [The Buddha:] "As not seeing them, Ananda."
> [Ananda:] "But if we should see them, what are we to do?"
> [The Buddha:] "Not talking, Ananda."
> [Ananda:] "But if they are to speak to us, Lord, what are we to do?"
> [The Buddha:] "Keep Wide Awake, Ananda."[14]

Thus the Buddha exhorts his disciples to keep vigilance with regard to women who might speak to them and to act as if they did not see the women. Such textual passages highlighting the invisibility of women and the meditative object-making of their bodies surely gives rise to a deep concern that seemingly negative images of women in Buddhism today should be viewed with caution. At the same time, the Buddha's exhortation to avoid looking at women has the opposite effect of rendering women hypervisible and therefore overdetermines their negative presence in the Buddhist moral, social, and political economy.

Yet what happens when we engage in a critical spectatorship that refuses to accept the visible absence of women? What happens when women in Buddhism wish to be seen as subjects with agency rather than as objects for meditative deconstruction for male edification? Is there another way to view women's sexuality in Buddhism such that their desire and pleasure are not seen as counterproductive to the spiritual life? These are some of the central concerns that animate the remainder of this chapter on female looking, being seen, and critical spectatorship in *Samsara*.

Samsara introduces its audience to some of the same Buddhist teachings found in *Spring, Summer, Fall, Winter... and Spring*, such as the notion of rebirth through cyclical time and attitudes toward women as catalysts for male transformation through their tempting bodies. Like *Spring, Summer, Fall, Winter... and Spring*, the film commences and concludes with the same image—Nalin opens the film with the plaintive cry, "Not again!" heard from a goat herder whose goat has been struck dead by a stone dropped from the claws of a hawk circling above in the expansive turquoise sky. Covering his eyes to protect them from the sun's glare, the goat herder's frustration and despair reflect the title of the film itself—the endless round of rebirth from which one must seek an escape. Nalin later revisits the image of the hawk circling above at the closing of the film as audiences witness Tashi looking up to the same turquoise sky, weeping in shame over his abandonment of

Pema. Although we do not see the actual event, Nalin sets up the scene such that we undoubtedly expect another rock to fall from above and strike Tashi down. It seems that Tashi has a long way to go before he can experience enlightenment.

As noted earlier in this chapter, Tashi emerges from the isolation of his meditation cave and receives an honorary *khenpo* degree bestowed upon him by a visiting monk for his spiritual prowess that marks the conclusion of an intensive three-year period of meditation. Yet despite all his efforts, when Tashi re-enters the world of the monastic community that is supported by the laity, he falls from spiritual grace because he is constantly distracted by the alluring bodies of women throughout the small Ladakhi village below the monastery. Dogged by sexual desire in his sleep and brought to his knees by the mere sighting of a nursing mother's breast, Tashi cannot seem to shake the desire that has suddenly ignited in his mind and body. After witnessing Tashi's inability to withstand the allure of so many snares of *samsara* that come his way, Apo dispatches his student to another mountainside temple to learn from the master there who has taken a vow of silence.

The elderly master serves Tashi tea and begins to teach him about the follies of passion through rather graphic depictions on paper scrolls of men and women having sex. At first all Tashi can see are illustrations of Indian men and women engaged in various sexual positions, but when the master encourages him to look more closely by placing the pictures above the candle light, he suddenly sees that beneath the overlay of the figures are the skeletons of the people in the same positions. The same thing happens when Tashi takes the illustrations of Japanese men and women having sex—he sees multiple skeletons and death.

Much like the monks in the Indian hagiographical texts who meditated upon women as if they were nothing more than heaps of bones and skin in cremation grounds, these images are intended to incite loathing in Tashi, but he instead remains unmoved and unchanged in his desire for women. Returning to his own monastery, he barges in on Apo in one of the Buddha sanctuaries. Apo calmly plays a horn while Tashi demands to know why it is that he was brought to the temple at the age of five, before desire and lust ever entered his mind. Challenging his unquestioned dedication to monastic purity, he stands in front of a large golden statue of the Buddha's face and passionately asks:

Even He was allowed a worldly existence until the age of 29. But since the age of 5 I've been disciplined to live like Buddha after he renounced the world? Why? How do we know that his Enlightenment was not a direct result of His worldly existence too? Apo, where is that freedom promised to me after a strict monastic discipline? Where is the promised satisfaction from our vow of celibacy? "You should not accept my teachings as heresay [sic] unless and until you understand it from your own point of view" he said once. There are things we must unlearn in order to learn them and there are things we must own in order to renounce them.

Citing the Buddha's own words, Tashi argues that renunciation is pointless unless there is something to give up and asks how he could possibly know that the ordinary world is full of desires that cause suffering if he has never had a chance to experience them. It is at this moment that Tashi resolves to leave the monastery to experience the householder's life for the first time in order to know intimately that which he must learn to give up. He then packs up his few belongings, steals away in the middle of the night, and heads back to the village where he meets his future wife.

When they first meet, Tashi is completely mesmerized by the sight of Pema's wrists and the sound of her silver bangles clanging together as she ladles food onto his plate. In fact, as he is served a traditional meal of dumplings, the camera zooms in only on her wrists, and as his eyes make contact with her body, his passions ignite. They meet again that evening as she hurries back to her home and nearly runs into Tashi. During a long take, the camera settles on Pema's beautiful eyes as she gazes at Tashi who appears more like a deer caught in the headlights because he has yet to experience a woman like this in his entire life. Rather than look away, the camera zooms in on Pema's eyes as she stares directly at Tashi without shifting her gaze. Later, at night as he sleeps, we see Pema appear like an apparition and lie down beside him, only to disappear in an instant, leaving the audience and Tashi himself to wonder if she was in fact really there. Tashi wakes in the morning and Apo assures him that he was only dreaming. However, as soon as the young monk resolves to leave the monastic life to experience the world of desire, Apo informs him that Pema's visit was not in fact a dream. Rather, as Pema later recounts, she came to him and lay with him simply because he looked lonely and needed comfort. Thus begins Tashi's pursuit of an answer to the koan-like question posed by Apo that becomes his to practice: "Is it better to satisfy one thousand desires or conquer just one?"

As soon as Tashi leaves the monastery, he removes his monastic robes, bathes in the river, and emerges an ordinary layman who Pema's father assumes is a migrant worker. He soon finds work with Pema's father who hires him to work their grain fields. When Pema sees him, she realizes that he is the monk from the monastery and hopes that he hasn't left the monastery because of her. Tashi then challenges her to admit that she isn't attracted to him, but the young woman still desires him and comes to him as he rests in the woods. In a rather long, slow sequence that follows, audiences are privy to the sexual tryst between the two lovers, which is instigated by Pema. Later that night, when she returns home Pema is caught by her parents, leading her fiancée to learn of her betrayal. As he begins to beat Tashi, Pema's father intervenes when he discovers that the worker his daughter has been with is actually a monk. Eventually, the young lovers get married and thus begins Tashi's life as an ordinary householder who works for his father-in-law's grain business, fathers a son, and eventually indulges his lust for Sujata, a beautiful young migrant field hand whose scantily-clad body entices with every movement and every suggestive glance at the married Tashi.

Tashi thrives in the business and profits increase after he suggests that, instead of selling the grain to the local middleman, they sell it directly to villagers in town. But having been cut-out, the middleman gets revenge by setting the family's wheat fields ablaze. Tashi, devastated at the loss and offense, comes to realize that the householder life is full of stress and suffering. Throughout the narrative, Tashi gains what in Nalin's view seems like the experience necessary for renunciation—experience with the vagaries and vicissitudes of desire, attachment, lust, and folly after he has sex with Sujata. Following his secret tryst while his wife and son journey into town to sell their grain, Tashi finally decides that he has experienced the world of desire and attachment long enough and he is finally ready to re-embark on the monastic journey to enlightenment.

Tashi once again attempts to steal away in the dark of night. This time he gazes on the sleeping bodies of his wife and his son, Karma; in this scene Nalin offers a perfect parallel to Siddhartha's midnight departure from his own wife and son before renouncing his princely life and setting out to become the Buddha. Packing up his monastic robes once again, Tashi thus sets out for the monastery at first light. Heading toward the mountain and readying himself for monastic life again, Tashi immerses himself in the same river that transformed him from monk to layman early in the tale and emerges with a freshly shaved head ready for the meditative life. Seemingly untroubled by his departure since he is merely following in the footsteps of the Buddha himself, Tashi wanders happily back to his monastery until Pema suddenly appears before him as if in a dream. She stops Tashi in his tracks to deliver perhaps one of the most powerful critiques of the invisibility of women in the Buddhist tradition and one of the only feminist interventions I have seen in Buddhist films.

While Tashi believes that he can simply return to the temple life without worrying about his wife and family, Pema intervenes with the following monologue delivered as she circles Tashi. Slowly pacing, Pema asks:

Yasodhara.
Do you know that name?
Prince Siddhartha, Gautama, Shakyamuni, Buddha. Everyone knows
    those names but …Yasodhara? Yasodhara was married to Siddhartha.
    She loved him dearly.

One night Siddhartha left her and their son Rahul while they were
sleeping to seek Enlightenment to become Buddha. He did not say
even a word to her when he left.

As Pema speaks, Tashi falls to his knees in despair as he begins to cry and
call out his wife's name. Pema continues:

Yasodhara had shown compassion to the sick and ailing long before
Siddhartha ever did, long before Siddhartha was even aware of suffering!
Who can say if he owed his enlightenment to her? Perhaps Yasodhara
wanted to leave Siddhartha and Rahul. How can we ever know if Yasodhara
fell victim to anger, to loneliness … to bitterness after Siddhartha left her?

Here Pema reinserts Yasodhara into the historical landscape as the abandoned
wife of the future Buddha who demonstrated a compassion for others and
became a role model for the prince himself. Pema asserts that Yashdohara's
compassion was sufficient for enlightenment—yet it was for someone else.
She continues:

Who even thought about her? What must she have said when Rahul asked
her that eternal question, Where is my father? What must she have told
him? How could a mother leave her own child in the middle of the night? It
is only possible for a man to do. Tashi, only for a man. After that, Yasodhara
had no choice. She had to lead a life of renunciation. Oh Tashi, if your
thoughts of Dharma were of the same intensity as the love and passion
you have shown me, you would have become a Buddha in this very body.
In this very life.

Figure 8.2 Samsara. *Pema teaches Tashi about Yasodhara.*

In this monologue, Pema gets to the heart of the problem with male monasticism and its seeming disregard for the existence and experiences of women such as herself throughout history. By invoking Yasodhara's name, Pema gives powerful voice to those whom tradition seems to have forgotten. She locates Tashi's abandonment in the long historical lineage of men leaving their wives to become monks and offers a critique of the monastic institution that condones such behavior without regard for those left behind.

Her words reflect the limited choices for women in the Buddhist world but also the important point that perhaps men like the Buddha owed their enlightenment not to experience alone, but rather to women like Yasodhara who, through numerous examples of compassion and wisdom, modelled what the Buddha came to know only later after he left her in the palace. Pema's words are more than a mere criticism of monks who leave; what she also offers is a deep insight into the experiential component of Buddhism where desires must be felt and experienced but not necessarily uprooted. By inserting herself into the historical trajectory of women like Yasodhara, Pema also rightfully demands to know what choices women may have in such a world.

Pema invokes Yasodhara's name because no one else seems to remember much about the Prince Siddhartha's wife and the mother of his son, Rahula. No one seems to pay adequate attention to the burden of being left behind in the middle of the night, abandoned to tend to her son as a single mother and symbolic widow. As a support of the tradition, Yasodhara had borne their son, Rahula, so that he would one day follow in the footsteps of his father as a renunciant. In uttering the name Yasodhara, Pema invokes a long lineage of women who shared a similar fate—marriage, birth of a child, and abandonment by the husband for the sake of enlightenment. By questioning the history of Buddhism and its rights afforded to men to leave the householder life and abandon the smaller family for the larger family of humanity, Pema pushes Tashi to reconsider his act of abandonment and quickly departs, leaving Tashi to wallow in tears, rolling on the ground in despair. His wife has left him for good at the base of the mountain with a bundle of food to send him off. Although Tashi apologizes and wants to return home, Pema seemingly disappears into thin air.

After sobbing over his loss and realizing the effects of his abandonment, Tashi rediscovers the prayer stone he read at the beginning of the film. He flips the stone over and reads the answer to the question of how one keeps a drop of water from drying up: "By throwing it into the sea." It is at this moment that he looks up in the bright blue sky while we wait for the hawk to drop the stone and knock him down like it did the goat in the beginning of the film. Tashi has not yet conquered the vexing problem of desire and must therefore return to earth after death for another round in the cycle of *Samsara*.

Unlike her failed monk of a husband, Pema does not need to be engaged in prayer and meditation in order to have a meaningful religious life. In fact, throughout the narrative of Tashi's failures, Pema's Buddhism appears to be infused into her daily life instead of separated out from ordinary experiences. She has already solved the puzzle of how to keep a drop of water from drying up that Tashi cannot seem to understand by the film's conclusion. The following scene serves as an illustrative example of Pema's Buddhist wisdom earned not from heroic asceticism, but through an intuitive experiential understanding. Following an exceptionally cold snowstorm, Pema sits with her son and husband for dinner as ice forms outside their windows and the wind howls through the home. As they eat, their son Karma asks where their food comes from—in particular, he wants to know where the meat inside their dumplings comes from and if any animals were killed for their food. His parents acknowledge that the meat comes from the goats whose lives have been taken. Distraught over this discovery, Karma jumps up from the table and rushes out the door into the snowstorm. Tashi shouts for Karma to return because it is freezing outside and his son has left the house without a coat. Pema then quietly looks at Tashi and advises him that Karma will have to learn for himself that it is cold outside. Sure enough, in a few seconds, poor Karma hurries back inside and wails, "It's cold outside!" as his mother takes him into her arms and cradles him having taught him that yes, it is unbearably cold outside.

Without careful attention to Pema's character as a mother, one might overlook the nuance of her Buddhist lessons that she imparts to her son. However, upon further consideration, it becomes quite clear that what Pema teaches her son is the same thing that Tashi has struggled to understand— the Buddhist lesson that experience gives rise to wisdom. According to the Buddha, one cannot simply believe something to be true because someone else proclaims it so. Instead, one develops direct insight through individual experience. Thus, Pema knows that her son will never quite listen or believe his parents' admonitions against running out into the freezing cold. Instead, he must feel the cold for himself, for such an experience of the bitter cold gives rise to insight and knowledge that only Karma can attain on his own.

Although the example may seem too prosaic to be considered a serious Buddhist teaching, its lesson certainly reflects what the Buddha taught. The Buddhist scholar Walpola Rahula notes the significance of experience and the importance of seeing for oneself in his famous work, *What the Buddha Taught*.[15] He explains:

The question of belief arises when there is no seeing—seeing in every sense of the world. The moment you see, the question of belief disappears. If I tell you that I have a gem hidden in the folded palm of my hand, the question of belief arises because you do not see it yourself. But if I unclench my fist and show you the gem, then you see it for yourself, and the question of belief does not arise. So the phrase in ancient Budddhist texts reads: 'Realizing, as one sees a gem (or myrobalan fruit) in the palm.'[16]

Pema's lessons to her son reflect the age-old Buddhist teaching that one simply cannot believe in something one does not see. Instead, one must see for oneself and then ascertain a truth to be so. Even a lesson so basic as going out into the cold without a coat to learn the importance of proper clothing can be full of insight.

Pema also imparts an important lesson to the village children about the Buddhist teaching of interdependence and interrelatedness. As she walks with the children alongside a stream, she casually picks up a stick and asks the children what will happen to the stick if she drops it into the water. The children make various attempts at answering the question saying, "it will drown," or "it will get stuck in the rocks," and "it will rot!" Pema keeps encouraging the kids to try to figure out the stick's fate as they follow the stick down the stream. As the children observe the stick flowing down stream, she replies, "The answer is simple. The stick will reach the sea!" Her response and lesson to the children reflects that just as a drop of water will not dry up if it is dropped into the sea, the stick will also avoid getting stuck and rotting simply by joining the sea. In other words, the individual is actually part of the larger cosmos and will be sustained by the very fact that all things are in fact interrelated and interdependent. Just as the *Avatamsaka Sutra* discussed in the previous chapter affirmed, all beings are part of the intricately faceted and reflected Jeweled Net of Indra. Thus Pema imparts profound Buddhist teachings to the children through very simple methods of observation and experience. Ironically, these are the lessons that even a monk well versed in meditation cannot seem to fathom. In the context of everyday life, Pema exemplifies the Buddhist qualities of wisdom and compassion that are necessary for enlightenment.

Yasodhara's lament as source of strength

Yasodhara, an ancillary yet underacknowledged figure in the Buddha's life, received scant mention in early canonical sources and is now known mostly as the wife of the Buddha. Despite this near omission, her name appears in later canonical sources that note her ordination and life as a nun. The biographical accounts of her life appear in the *Yasodharapadana* (sacred biography of Yasodhara) in the *Khuddaka Nikaya* of the Pali Canon which recounts her spiritual attainments and later her *arhatship*.[17] Her eventual appearance in later canonical texts, commentarial literature, and narratives demonstrates the compelling arc of her life story. Married to the wealthy and handsome Prince Siddhartha, Yasodhara becomes mother of the Buddha's son and is eventually left behind in the palace as the Buddha searches for the end of suffering. Often cast aside as a necessary sacrifice for the greater good of the universe, Yasodhara's name received little attention in early Buddhist sources. Yet just as Pema recalls her name at the conclusion of Nalin's film, Yasodhara's name and role gained popular appeal for Buddhists over time because her story of grief and its resolution resonated with the experiences of lay Buddhists.

Whether women have imagined themselves as the abandoned wife and mother when their spouses entered the monastic life, or when mourners recite her story as a form of lament, Yasodhara's story resonates far beyond what the canonical texts could have envisioned. In questioning Yashodhara's pivotal role, Pema brings her out of the margins of the Buddha's life where she hitherto has appeared as "only a shadowy figure in the larger, more important story."[18] Pema's strategic response to Tashi's abandonment offers a necessary intervention in the otherwise male-centered development of the Buddhist tradition.

The memory most readers have of Yasodhara is of her sleeping as she cradles her son on the eve of the Buddha's Great Departure from the palace in pursuit of enlightenment. As a parallel to Yasodhara's story, Nalin replicates the same scene from the Buddhist *sutra* with Tashi leaving his sleeping wife and son in the middle of the night to return to the monastic life. Through the Buddha's actions, Yasodhara quickly transforms from companion, wife, and mother to an obligation that could potentially keep the Buddha from his enlightenment. Canonical depictions of the Great Departure leave little room to contemplate and imagine how it would feel to be left behind and abandoned by one's spouse or father while asleep. Yasodhara would have faded into historical obscurity were it not for the emotional connection Buddhists have felt with her experiences of loss and suffering.

Despite her absence from early canonical sources, Ranjini Obeyesekere notes that "her elusive figure has continued to fascinate Buddhists over the centuries" and has become an object of veneration through the continual retelling of her story at rituals marking loss and suffering such as funerals so that the mourners could find solace since even the Buddha's wife could manage to survive the despair that comes from the loss of a loved one.[19]

Obeyesekere highlights the continued significance of Yasodhara for Buddhists in both Sinhalese folk poems and funeral laments that gave expression to the hardships they faced as villagers and farmers, as well as the emotional appeal of her laments over the loss of her husband. Yasodhara's lament becomes a potent source for coming to terms with great suffering and, as Obeyesekere notes, such laments:

... while being expressions of grief over a loss, they also express resignation and acceptance of what Buddhists believe to be a necessary condition of samsaric existence. The core verses that form the lament in the poem *Yasodharavata* ... are sung at rural funerals in order to help mourners achieve that acceptance. The verses speak of grief and loss, but there is also an emotional progression, a slow movement toward resignation and final acceptance of a situation that cannot be changed or reversed, a loss that cannot be recovered. It is perhaps this sense of finality—such as comes from Yasodhara's knowledge that her husband Siddhatha will not, cannot, ever come back to her as her husband—that makes the verses of her lament both a powerful vehicle for grief as well as an acceptance of and resignation to loss. The Buddhist resignation, the hard but necessary acceptance of the inevitability of parting, is what enables the singing of the verses to bring solace to mourners.[20]

Certainly Pema invokes her name and seeks to restore her to common knowledge in the Buddhist tradition; however, Pema's lament is also her bold claim that the enlightenment of the Buddha has its origins in the contributions of Yasodhara.

In her translation of the thirteenth-century Sinhala work entitled the *Pujavaliya* (*Garland of Offerings*), Obeyesekere recounts the efforts Yasodhara makes to include herself with wit and intelligence as an engineer in the success of the Buddha's meritorious actions. Yasodhara goes so far as to recast her previous lives' cruelty toward the Buddha as opportunities for him to practice patience and generosity. The significance of such a story lies in its bestowal of real emotion and feeling to Yasodhara. Hence, Yasodhara reminds the Buddha:

> For a long time in *samsara* I lived united to you like your shadow. I was always faithful and supportive of you in all the different places we lived. However, women are frail and have little intellect. So you may at times find shortcomings [on my part]. But if you look with wisdom at each of these wrongs you will know that they did in fact help to strengthen your *paramitas* (perfections or virtues needed to become a Buddha). Thus even wrongs done by me were in fact a source of benefit to you.[21]

Yasodhara thus lists cruel act by cruel act committed against the future Buddha and demonstrates how each action led to the cultivation of merits and virtues required of a Buddha. Hence, as Obeyesekere reminds us:

> [the]woman who emerges from this text is not just the devoted wife and companion but a woman with razor-sharp intellect who with almost legalistic acumen transforms negative material to make a positive case for

herself. Each negative act she claims was beneficial in that it did propel the Bodhisattva Kusa to perform the actions needed to fulfill each one of the Ten Perfections or *dasa paramita*.[22]

The story of Yashodhara in its various forms provides a necessary emotional balance to the otherwise rather detached depictions of the Great Departure by the Buddha. The elation of marrying the Buddha, the mourning and grief over his departure, the sharp wit, and the lament—all of these emotions capture the hearts of the listeners who receive the stories with broken hearts, suffering, anger, and loss. Through such a meeting of narrative and listener, a resonance grows that allows the text to continue to breathe as a living resource and permits the listener to give expression to struggles in a religiously-sanctioned idiom.

The biography of Yasodhara depicts a woman in despair who eventually comes to terms with great loss, and who is given the opportunity to tell the Buddha of her laments, her devotions, her contributions to his success, and finally of her spiritual advancements as an *arhat* ("noble one" destined for enlightenment). Her story is a narration and, therefore, an inscription of a "woman of great merit and character, a powerful, almost divine being, and an example and role model to laypersons" due to the full range of emotions she displays that give a real weight to her existence.[23]

Samsara, too, provides that emotional opportunity for women like Pema to grieve the loss of their husbands and, at the same time, serves as a necessary intervention that demands due attention to the women who have been key players in the enlightenment of men. What Nalin gives us, much like the *Yasodharapadana* does, is a portrait of a woman who is capable of enlightenment as well. For Pema, her enlightenment comes through the practice of everyday life and, as such, the religious life is clearly fused with the ordinary.

Like many other biographical texts, the *Yasodharapadana* illuminates doctrinal elements of the Buddhist tradition and does so in a narrative form that resonates with the listener much like film does with the viewer. In the case of the biographies of Yasodhara, the intended audience is the layperson. Her story is also critical for this study in providing the necessary back story to Pema's lament so that we can ascertain the significance of her citing of Yasodhara's name and her direct criticism of Tashi. By invoking Yasodhara's name, Pema also lays claim to the textual development of the Buddha's wife from abandoned mother to enlightened nun destined for nirvana. As an enlightened being, Yasodhara proves her spiritual prowess through various magical acts such as transforming into a *garuda* bird whose body spans the size of the universe and proclaiming boldly, "I am the Theri Yasodhara."[24] Prior to her death, Yasodhara also publically cries, "I am none other than Yasodhara who was the Buddha's wife when he lived the life of a householder."[25]

Following this proclamation, Yasodhara recounts all of her sacrifices for the future Buddha that she had made in her previous lives and, in Pema's reminder of her actions, Yasodhara's effects on the Buddha are made clear. Thus *Samsara*, the *Yasodharapadana*, and other such commentaries, when read as a piece, reflect the desire to situate women not as mere shadow figures but as women who narrate themselves into existence. To do so is a significant act for a Buddhism that attends to and cares about women's experiences in a tradition that has held such virtues primarily for men.

Samsara thus offers an opportunity to grapple with the politics of representation of Buddhist women with regard to gender relationships, sexuality, and enlightenment whereby the man's world envisioned by Nalin becomes the discursive playing field for a different kind of seeing and what Celiñe Parreñas Shimuzu refers to as a "more productive optic."[26] This kind of seeing is directly tied to constructing new images of Buddhist women to be seen by others, as well as images through which Buddhist women might "see themselves anew."[27] As such, my analysis of Pema is a reimagining and reimaging of lay Buddhist women as politically productive sites expressing a "yearning for better representations and realities for those marginalized by race and gender."[28]

Reading *Samsara* through Audre Lorde

In highlighting the materiality of Buddhist women's experiences, I have sought to theorize a critical space for the emergence of an alternative view of women in Buddhism. That space is one carved by a multifaceted methodological tool forged out of the felicitous joining together of Indian Buddhist texts, Asian American filmmaker and cultural critic Celine Perreñas Shimuzu, and black feminists bell hooks and Audre Lorde. While at the outset such a dialogue across multiple centuries and geographical and social locations may seem curious, there is much to learn in so doing about the potentiality for a new liberatory practice of Buddhism that takes lay women's materiality and spiritual flourishing as central to the tradition rather than continuing the practice of relegating lay women to the margins of the practice and what counts as authentic religion.

Like hooks, Lorde urges us to rethink our looking relations and to move beyond a mere dismissal of female sexuality as another reminder of their less-than-spiritual bodies. It is the theorization of sites of resistance and the development of agency and subjectivity in places that have not traditionally been viewed as particularly progressive that intrigues me. When watching and observing women in Buddhist texts and films, Lorde's work inspires one to ask if there might be a way to reread and revise the representations of women in both mediums? Is there a way to look for the presence of women in places they might not otherwise be seen? With a critical and searching eye, I take up *Samsara* as a source of rethinking the materiality, location, and motivations of lay Buddhist women in the tradition. I do so out of deep concern about the need to attend to their experiences, for they have been looked at in various states of decomposition in Buddhist texts and looked over as invisible or antithetical to the religious life.

What Nalin's film offers is a provocation to imagine anew. In other words, how might we provoke new ways of understanding and identifying what constitutes Buddhism through filmic interpretations and adaptations of traditional Buddhist lessons? Why should a film that offers images of women as snares of *samsara* engaged in graphic sex be valuable for a kind of Buddhism that attends to the needs of the ordinary lay person? How can such images challenge the very understanding of what constitutes healthy Buddhism? As I demonstrate throughout this chapter, *Samsara* allows us to take account of the values of lay life without the burden of a self-negating sexual purity, and to put forward a Buddhism that neither rejects nor dismisses women's agency, desire, pleasure, and religiosity.

Audre Lorde's theorization of the erotic as political—that is, as a form of power wielded for the sake of self-edification, proves illuminating for this study of *Samsara*.[29] In her oft-cited essay, "Uses of the Erotic," Lorde refers to the erotic as "a measure between the beginnings of our sense of self and the chaos of our strongest feelings. It is an internal sense of satisfaction to which, once we have experienced it, we know we can aspire."[30] This attunement to internal satisfaction strikes me as particularly valuable for reading Pema's sexuality as an example of self-edification rather than one that is merely derivative of male pleasure. Rather than suppress the erotic and engage in a rigid kind of asceticism, Lorde encourages the cultivation and generation of deep feeling and connection between all living beings. The use of the erotic thus challenges the self-denial that many a Buddhist textual passage claims as normative and expected, particularly of laywomen like Pema.

For women in *Samsara*, knowledge of self, the experience of love with and through others, and the embrace of the female body in all of its sensory pleasures gives a nuanced understanding of what it means to be religious in a worldly life-affirming manner. The affirmation of the materiality of the female lay religion that Pema demands is held in stark relief against Tashi's asceticism, or what Lorde would refer to as self-abnegation. She explains, "[t]he severe abstinence of the ascetic becomes a ruling obsession. And it is one not of self-discipline but of self-abnegation."[31] Instead, it is the erotic—"the sensual—those physical, emotional, and psychic expressions of what is deepest and strongest and richest within each of us, being shared; the passions of love, in its deepest meanings" that leads to fulfillment of the self and others.[32] The very body that Buddhism has denied thus becomes the radical source of "all of our deepest knowledge."[33] The negation of self certainly has been a Buddhist preoccupation for over 2,500 years, yet such self-abnegation offers little succor or tonic to the kinds of suffering that the Buddhist textual, institutional, and social order has both imagined and placed upon its women.

For Lorde and Buddhist women like Pema, the denial of the self has little liberatory potential within traditions that define such women first and foremost by what they lack—in the case of Lorde, as a nonwhite, nonheterosexual non-male, and for Pema, as a nonmonastic, nonpure, non-male. In my reading of *Samsara*, the Buddhist concept of *anatman* (no self) finds its ultimate meaning in Pema's acceptance and cultivation of the erotic and the material, which confirms her very existence in a larger relational and interdependent world. Pema's Buddhist practice rests on everyday interactions as a laywoman, mother, employer, daughter, and wife whose very roles require her to administer to this world rather than reject it. Might her way of being Buddhist not be instructive for others?

While the monks at the temple sit in silent meditation seeking to uproot desire and attain *nirvana* through the disciplining of the self, Pema's Buddhism rests wholly in the realm of the ordinary, the mundane, as it is experienced in the body, and through the senses. Thus, the pleasure she derives with her body *vis-à-vis* Tashi is not to be read as an act of transgression or further proof of her incompatibility with the Buddhist order. Rather, such pleasure is best understood as self-enhancing and self-affirming and, in the words of Lorde, as an example of the power of the erotic and "a question of how acutely and fully we can feel in the doing."[34] For, "[o]nce we know the extent to which we are capable of feeling that sense of satisfaction and completion, we can then observe which of our various life endeavors bring us closest to that fullness."[35] Yet, the notion of the erotic as power and as an exercise in fulfillment is not simply about self-affirmation. Rather, I suggest that such power functions as a means of fully connecting with others such that all such encounters are mutually enhancing. For Pema, the use of the erotic in her sexual relationship with Tashi and her role as mother who teaches her son the Buddhist lessons of impermanence and interconnectedness through experience, reinforce an intersubjectivity that we might understand as the ethical manifestation of Buddhist emptiness.

The experience of interdependence, as Nalin shows, cannot be achieved through self-denial but only through radical self-acceptance and the embrace of the material self in relationship with others. Such a Buddhism opens up the possibility for developing a lay Buddhist woman's subjectivity and positive measure of selfhood—not for the self's sake alone, but rather for the sake of all beings collectively. Such is the ethical standpoint behind the teaching of no self.

My attraction to Lorde's work and to Pema as a character emerges from my own desire to reimagine women's sexuality in Buddhism not as a threatening force or impure act, but rather as one that affirms the material world and one's body in it as a life-enhancing engagement in the everyday world of *samsara* within which liberation is possible. My theorization of lay Buddhism as a technique of self-edification and enhancement might be considered heterodox for the monastic elite, but it seems an important political act to counteract an otherwise trenchant regulation and disciplining of female sexuality, materiality, and agency. There is much to relearn about Buddhism when we attend to "that which is female and self-affirming in the face of a racist, patriarchal, and anti-erotic society."[36] Such an education is in great demand.

9

Conclusion: Recreating the Buddhist World Anew

But in whose image?

In widening the field of vision that has previously limited our looking relations *vis-à-vis* Buddhism, I am reminded again of a beloved scene in Julia Kwan's *Eve and the Fire Horse* (2005) that always makes me smile and makes me wish that this kind of a film had more purchase in the American popular imagination than *The Big Lebowski*. In this film, Kuan Yin *bodhisattva* has left the Pure Land and has come to life as she dances freely in beautiful flowing white robes right smack in the middle of the night in Eve's dining room. Kuan Yin, the *bodhisattva* of compassion, whose story of her multiple manifestations that save all sentient beings is recounted in the *Lotus Sutra*, appears in Eve's Chinese Canadian immigrant home as a flesh and blood woman who speaks in colloquial, laid back, and articulate English. She speaks full sentences without an exaggerated accent and manages to seem hip and relatable even though she is an enlightening being. Kwan images Kuan Yin as a contemporary Asian and Asian American Buddhist woman who, despite the fact that she is a manifestation of compassion *and* a figure of Eve's imagi-nation, seems rather ordinary.[1] She is neither exotic nor a mysterious fount of wisdom like Mr. Lee, whose "Ancient Chinese secret" was the supposed source of getting his whites so clean in the Calgon laundry detergent commercial from my childhood in the 1970s.

Eve's houseguest Kuan Yin is pretty cool for a *bodhisattva* and lets Eve know that it is fine for the young girl to believe in Buddhism, folk traditions, *and* Christianity. When Eve worries about what will happen to her dead grandmother, since the Catholic church she now attends with her older sister Karena teaches her that "... in the Bible it says that Buddhists are going to hell," Kuan Yin gives a slight wag of her finger, a shake of her head, and mere shrug of the shoulders and claims nonchalantly, "Personally, I don't go for all that fire and brimstone." Kuan Yin's matter-of-factness and familiarity with Eve removes her from the exotic mysterious realm of the Pure Land and into a young girl's immigrant home where she tells it like it is. In other words, Kuan Yin manifests in a form most needed and understood by Eve ... and, I admit, myself.

In Kwan's semi-autobiographical independent film, set in Vancouver, BC in the 1970s, we learn that Eve, a nine-year-old daughter of Chinese immigrants, was born in the Year of the Fire Horse. According to Chinese astrology, the Year of the Horse is a rather unfortunate year that can bring about misfortune and bad luck; thus, Eve believes she is doomed to bring harm to her family. Indeed, Eve's grandmother dies, her uncle falls ill, and her mother experiences a devastating miscarriage. Yet, Eve is raised in a Chinese household, and therefore her religion takes many forms, as witnessed by the plethora of gods and goddesses displayed in the family home to help counteract the negative associations with the Fire Horse birth year. While the appearance of Kuan Yin in the living room and, later, the Buddha and Jesus, who dance hand in hand around the home, might not seem out of place in the imagination of a young Chinese Canadian girl, such images are not the norm in Eve's white Canadian suburban neighborhood.

Consider the following scene: Eve stands in front of her elementary school classroom giving an introduction to the Buddhist deities that populate her family home. Her classmates stare in rapt attention as she shows them statues of porcelain goddesses and again we see the vision of Kuan Yin come to life to dance about her living room. Eve explains, "These are the goddesses. When everyone is asleep, they come alive. And they dance with wild abandon all through the night." Eve recounts these nightly visits in a casual tone that reflects her multi-deity household that fuses Confucian, Taoist, Buddhist, Christian, and folk traditions. Not sure what to make of this "foreign" religion, Eve's prim and proper white teacher humors her, claps her hands in appreciation, and says hesitantly, "Yes, very good Eve. Very ... exotic."

Yet what's exotic for one may well be commonplace for another. *Eve and the Fire Horse* does a marvelous job demythologizing and deconstructing the image of Buddhism as an otherworldly religion of monks and celestial Buddhas shrouded in mystery. Despite the fantastical appearance of Kuan Yin, Buddha, and Jesus in her home, unlike in many of the films I analyze in this book, the Buddhism reflected through Kwan's lens leans toward the ordinary and away from the enigmatic constructions influenced by Orientalism, sexism, and racialization. In this charming coming of age story, the highly revered *bodhisattvas* and Buddhas of the *sutras* step into everyday life to keep Eve company and teach her that it's okay to practice more than one religion. If the Buddha and Jesus can appear in her home and dance as friends, then surely it is okay for this young Chinese Canadian girl to worship as a Buddhist, be baptized by her sister in the bathtub, *and* believe that her beloved grandmother has reincarnated as a goldfish in a tank.

Because I see the ordinary as extraordinary and the extraordinary as ordinary, Eve's understanding of Buddhism serves as a comfort, a tonic against the ravages of the racist and sexist images of Buddhism, a source of humor and laughter, and a prosaic and pleasurable example of a Buddhism that is of this world. Kwan thus gives us a religion that focuses more on the daily vicissitudes of a multigenerational immigrant family that happens to be Buddhist among other things. Being Buddhist in Eve's family is not defined by meditating on mountaintops or sitting *zazen* for hours, as popular interpretations of Buddhism suggest. Instead, it includes lighting incense at a temple, praying for good fortune, warding off noxious spirits through appeasing rituals, and sometimes finding another religion to add to the mix when things go awry.

Julia Kwan's independent film thus offers what many of the feature films studied in this book lack, namely, an insight into ordinary lay Buddhism where racialized images of Asians, Asian Americans, and exoticized versions of monastic heroes are simply absent. Their absence does not, however, detract from the film's appeal. Instead, their intentional absence allows for the clearly defined presence of a lay Buddhism that includes women and Asians and Asian Americans as primary actors. Yet just because the Buddhism featured is not a heroic monasticism does not mean that there can be no room for the magical, for Eve's world is filled with a magical realism that helps resolve many of the tensions and conundrums of her immigrant life. What makes *Eve and the Fire Horse* different is that its use of magical realism reflects the workings of an actual lived religion whose lines between different traditions only exist from a distant bird's eye view. In reality, the lines are blurred to reveal a *bricolage* of religious practices deployed whenever needed and aimed at living a good life.

Film as spiritual technology

One of the guiding principles of this study is that there are better ways to imagine Buddhism on screen and that the world recreated on screen can either limit or expand what religion looks like. In his book *Religion and Film: Cinema and the Re-creation of the World*, S. Brent Plate reminds us:

Through the very technology of film, a new world is assembled—the camera lens and in the editing room—and then projected onscreen.

Viewers see the world, but see it in entirely new ways because everyday perceptions of space and time are altered ... And through the re-creation of time and space, we have a world, created anew.[2]

By analyzing representations of Buddhism in and through film, I show that film provides the opportunity to reflect upon the Buddhist tradition as it has been historically received, but, more importantly, how it might continue into the future to widen and deepen the understanding of what it means to be Buddhist.

As a spiritual technology that creates our perceptions and, in turn, our worlds anew, film refines, revises, and reimagines our understandings of self and other. While it provides a creative entrée into the Buddhist tradition and practice, it also engages viewers in a state of suspended time where new visions of how to live flow into our consciousness. Most of us come to film to escape the ordinary and open ourselves to a dreamtime of illusion no matter how realistic it may seem and, in so doing, we welcome the occasion to see the world from a different vantage point. Film viewing thus becomes a meditative practice of seeing the world afresh. But, as I have cautioned throughout this study, we would do well to ask—whose world do we see and who is missing from it?

In her study of film and cultural identity, Rey Chow argues that film narrates the relationship "between absence and presence, [and] between disappearance and reappearance."[3] Problematizing the kinds of identities constructed on screen, Chow explains:

Whether what is captured is a human face, a body, an object, or a place, the illusion of presence generated is such that a new kind of realism, one that vies with life itself, aggressively asserts itself. If cultural identity is something that always finds an anchor in specific media of representation, it is easy to see why the modes of illusory presence made possible by film have become such strong contenders in the controversial negotiations for cultural identity.[4]

Chow's critique of film's ability to conjure identities is particularly instructive for this study of Buddhist films that engages in the process of people-making, gender-making, and race-making.[5] As I have shown in my analysis of racialized and gendered images of Buddhism in film, the types of Buddhism and Buddhists in Asian and Western films have favored an elite male monastic over and against an otherwise more diverse population. Such a privileging echoes the popular renderings of the tradition off-screen. Thus, while the potential for film to recreate the world and people anew is an exciting proposition, we would do better to ask: In whose image do we recreate the world?

This study is an attempt to answer such an important question and encourages viewers to take an active or oppositional gaze rather than imagine that the screen has a totalizing authoritative power that can control interpretation. But of course such a gesture toward a destabilization of debilitating yet trenchant images of Buddhism requires not only significant critique, but also a re-visioning that can account for who and what has been missing for so long. Thus, as a few of my significant interlocutors have asked: What makes for an inclusive and commendable Buddhist film? This book offers has offered some suggestions.

The films I have analyzed in this book range from the earliest introduction of Buddhism on the silver screen, beginning with D. W. Griffith's *Broken Blossoms*, which set the stage for imagining Buddhism and Buddhists as both idealized representations of peacefulness *and* icons of racialized difference. This racialized difference found its way into the Orientalist constructions of Shangri-La, Asian and Asian American mystery and otherness in Frank Capra's *Lost Horizon* up through the Western films that idealize Zen Buddhist iconoclasm in the Coen brothers' *The Big Lebowski*, Jim Jarmusch's *Ghost Dog* and Marc Rosenbush's *Zen Noir*. Julia Kwan's *Eve and the Fire Horse* offers a different understanding of Buddhism that succeeds in portraying the everyday complexities of religion in a Chinese Canadian family whose Buddhist religion blends into a religious pastiche with other traditions. While engaging in magical realism, its portrayal of Buddhism is both playful *and* realistic.

Yet, as I have argued throughout, it is not just Western directors who engage in the idealization of Buddhist otherness; rather, the appeal of Buddhist exoticism finds its way into narratives such as Kim Ki-Duk's Korean film *Spring, Summer, Fall, Winter... and Spring* about a young monk in a floating temple who learns the follies of desire through his dalliances with a young woman. In my reading of this film, I not only show the exoticization of Buddhism that takes place in some Asian-directed films, but also the absorption of age-old stereotypes of women as the snares of *samsara* that threaten monastic purity found in Buddhist texts. Such uncritical adoptions of early Indian Buddhist views of women serve to negate the possibility of imagining the healthy flourishing of an ordinary laywomen's Buddhism. The foreclosure of such possibilities has of course had damaging effects on the representations of women in Buddhism as anything other than dangerous, mute, invisible, and marginal to a tradition that favors the meditating male monk.

In some ways, this book is a reclamation project of sorts, yet I do not suggest that I can reclaim some essence of Buddhism that remains once the layers of racialization and sexism have been peeled back. Rather, the reclamation project that I engage in has far more to do with the construction of a Buddhism that can accompany those images of the religion that have been narrowly envisioned as monastic, mysterious, and exotic. As such, my analysis of Buddhist films is one that is both historical and future-oriented, one that endeavors to create as much as it seeks to restore a vision of the Buddhist imaginary that lays bare both the tradition-specific rhetoric of male dominance as well as the influences of racism that have shaped much of what we conceive Buddhism to be today.

Surely my analysis of the intersecting threads of race and gender negative imagery that have foreclosed the possibility of visualizing a more expansive Buddhism implies that there must be something more commendable out there. It is for this reason that I have sought to provide an alternative reading of films like *Aje Aje Bara Aje* that offer a different way of seeing the vexing sexuality of women that the Buddhist tradition excoriated. Rather than merely dismissing instances of female sexuality as continuations of sexist attitudes toward women, I argue that sexuality can serve as a potent metaphor for self-fulfillment and agency so long as we don't get overly hung up on the sex itself. Rather than imagining Buddhism to be merely a religion of monks and nuns isolated from ordinary society, I also highlight an *other* side of Buddhism that has made few appearances on the silver screen. Thus, my analysis of *Departures* shows that there are many different ways of being Buddhist if one knows where and how to find it. *Departures* draws our attention to the practice of gratitude and compassion that gives rise to the experience of presence and the nowness that is so crucial to the tradition.

In highlighting the significance of presence in Buddhism, I also suggest that a film like Chang Sun-Woo's *Hwa-Om-Kyung* generates a more expansive view of Buddhism that restores often invisible and marginalized actors in the Buddhist world that rarely make it onto the screen: women, the laity, and Asian Buddhists. As an explicitly Buddhist film, *Hwa-Om-Kyung* functions as a *sutra* that allows us to imagine Buddhism differently and, as I argue, more accurately. Finally, through my analysis of Pan Nalin's *Samsara*, I restore lay women to the Buddhist world on screen to show that the religion includes not only the ascetic realm of monks that has been privileged in mediated images, and in scholarly as well as popular interpretations, but also the active and powerful presence of women historically. Monks are not the only heroic actors in the world of Buddhism. As I have shown, it is often lay women and their less than exotic expressions of Buddhism that can serve as potent sources of experiencing Buddhist liberation.

Yet I hesitate in making such generalized statements about debilitating and commendable Buddhist films, particularly when progressive standpoints can still be found in what otherwise might appear to be a rather backward vision of Buddhism on screen. Therefore, I am not arguing that films about monks meditating on mountaintops or secluded from society in spiritual utopias do not have something powerful to offer spectators. Surely, *Lost Horizon*'s

Shangri-La and *Spring, Summer, Fall, Winter... and Spring* allow us to imagine what it might be like to live simply in moderation away from the poisons of greed, hatred, and delusion. Who doesn't want to escape the everyday world and float peacefully upon a temple floating on an Edenic lake? The problem, however, with such beautiful lands is that they are populated by heroic monks at the literal expense of women's lives.

As I have shown, visions of such exotic Buddhist lands are open to only a small section of the population, which makes for a rather limited spectrum of what it means to be Buddhist. If women, Asians, and Asian Americans are prohibited from entry in such Buddhist lands, cast as silent objects to deconstruct, or racialized as mysterious unintelligible others, then surely such lands are not real Buddhist lands. For in real Buddhist lands, all beings are interdependent and the ethical relations between all beings are based on horizontal relationships rather than vertical power structures. As I have argued in this analysis of Buddhism in Asian and Western films, Buddhism is a multifaceted religion comprised of many different religious actors whose daily lives include attachment to the self, sexual desire and pleasure, and other examples of the messy realm of *samsaric* life. I am therefore less interested in a disciplining of the self as Buddhism is often described, especially since women, Asians, and Asian Americans have so often been under the disciplining gaze of racialization and patriarchy. Thus, calling for a flourishing lay Buddhism means to embrace the full range of emotions—jealousy, greed, joy, sorrow—as opportunities for spiritual fulfillment. Rather than uprooting or dissolving the roots of such emotions as Buddhist texts would have the monastic heroes do, I propose a Buddhism of acceptance of our karmic limitations and reimagine them as opportunities for liberatory experiences of the self. I am far less interested in theorizing yet another Buddhism based on the rhetoric of a lack of self or the suppression of ego and desire. Instead, I find the move toward self-edification and a subjectivity that also attends to the experience of others a more appealing form of practice, and one that I often look for in Buddhist films.

Upaya: Film as skillful means

In Chapter Three of the famed Mahayana Buddhist text *The Lotus Sutra*, the Buddha preaches the parable of the burning house, a story that narrates the expedient measures and skillful means that a father (the Buddha) devises in order to lure his children out of a burning house (*samsara*). The children, engrossed in their play, do not heed the father's warnings of the dangers of this burning house so the father must utilize what is known in Buddhism as his skillful means (*upaya*) or an expedient device to wake the children up to the fires that threaten to burn them. He must speak to them directly in a manner and form that they immediately understand to avoid a painful death. Consider the following story narrated by the Buddha in verse to his disciple Śāriputra in the *Lotus Sutra*:

> At that time, the great man had this thought: 'This house is already aflame with a great fire. If we do not get out in time, the children and I shall certainly be burnt. I will now devise an expedient, whereby I shall enable the children to escape this disaster.' The father knows the children's preconceptions, whereby each child has his preferences, his feelings being specifically attached to his several precious toys and unusual playthings.

> Accordingly [the father] proclaims to them: "The things you so love to play with are rare and hard to get. If you do not get them, you are certain to regret it later. Things like these, a variety of goat-drawn carriages, deer-drawn carriages, and ox-drawn carriages, are now outside the door to play with. Come out of this burning house quickly, all of you! I will give all of you what you desire." The children hear what their father says. Since rare playthings are exactly what they desire, the heart of each is emboldened. Shoving one another aside in a mad race, all together in a rush they leave the burning house.[6]

Thus does the Buddha succeeds in offering a variety of different methods of teaching that act as the proverbial "finger pointing to the moon" in the direction of enlightenment.

The Mahayana Buddhist tradition from which the *Lotus Sutra* emerges holds that there are multiple means of reaching enlightenment and a plethora of different *sutras* that help point the way out of *samsara*. It is less important which method one chooses—what matters is that the method be effective so that one experiences liberation. If the method is expedient and efficacious, then it is the right one. The form of the Buddha's teaching is therefore based on the needs of the listener and, as I make clear, film has the potential to serve as one such expedient means. Film can thus function as a skillful means, a meditational device, and a Buddhist *sutra* that occasions deeper levels of understanding.   In this book, I have argued for a re-visioning, reimaging, and reimagining of Buddhism and film beyond its male monastic leanings through the conceptualization of film as *sutra*. My approach thus challenges received stereotypes of the religion and its practitioners on screen. The term *sutra* itself refers to the process of weaving together the teachings of the Buddha and relates to the medieval term *suture* or to stitch something up. The theorization of film as *sutra* thus finds resonance in the study of suture theory in film, which examines how spectators are "stitched" into the film itself. According to Kaja Silverman, "The concept of suture attempts to account for the means by which subjects emerge within discourse" or the film as text.[7] While an in-depth analysis of how spectators are interpellated into the filmic text is beyond the scope of this book, I find the occasion to draw together my conceptualization of film as *sutra* and film suture theory significant, for each must grapple with the vexing question of how the reader/listener/viewer of a Buddhist (filmic) text comes to identify with or resist the cinematic image. For the purpose of my study of Buddhist films, it is necessary to ask how one might disentangle from the suture's attempt to hold the spectator to the camera's gaze. Furthermore, I suggest that we consider to what extent a spectator actively rejects the act of suturing but not the promise of healing that suturing implies. After all, any suture stitched over a wound implies both the pain of the cut and its recovery. By theorizing film as *sutra*, I have been insisting on a more capacious and democratized vision of Buddhist life that finds the extraordinary and the ordinary working in concert. The potent spiritual technologies of the silver screen and its analogues all commend a more just vision of Buddhism both on and off screen.

Notes

Chapter One

1 According to the recent Pew Forum on Religion & Public Life survey of 2012 on *Asian Americans: A Mosaic of Faiths*, only 27 percent of Asian American Buddhists surveyed claimed that they meditate weekly or more. Of those surveyed, 61 percent claimed that they seldom or never meditated. Such low percentages of meditators among Asian Americans is certainly at odds with more popularized accounts of the religion that upholds meditation as the primary method of practice.

2 bell hooks, "The Oppositional Gaze: Black Female Spectators," in *Reel to Real: Race, Sex, and Class at the Movies* (New York and London: Routledge Press, 1996), pp. 197–213.

3 See H. Leedom Lefferts, Jr. "Buddhist Action: Lay Women and Thai Monks," in Ellison Banks Findly (ed.), *Women's Buddhism, Buddhism's Women: Tradition, Revision, Renewal* (Boston: Wisdom Publications, 2000) pp. 63–79. Lefferts argues persuasively that the tendency to overlook the significance of female laity in the Buddhist tradition has obscured and rendered inconsequential their devotional practices. The assumption that the salvational goal for laity rests in a better future birth serves only to perpetuate the image of monastics as an elite force aimed at transcendence and suffering. As I argue in my book, *Being Buddhist in a Christian World: Gender and Community in a Korean American Community* (Seattle: University of Washington, 2004), many laywomen do not find such arguments to be relevant and are far more interested in creating a better life for themselves in the present rather than a future rebirth or *nirvana*.

4 As a European invention that reflects a geopolitical awareness and investment in its own superiority, Said argues that Orientalism "is a style of thought based upon ontological and epistemological distinction made between the 'Orient' and (most of the time) 'the Occident,' where the Occident maintains its own hegemonic power over the other." Edward Said, *Orientalism* (New York: Vintage Books, 1978), p. 2.

5 I am grateful to David Kyuman Kim for his insights on racist ideology and white supremacy in the transmission of "real" Buddhism to the West.

6 My use of Buddhist films to rethink religion *after* illuminating their hidden transcripts of race and gender is what sets this study apart from other analyses of Buddhist films that I mention throughout the book.

7 Diana Eck notes that the Indian religious traditions from which Buddhism emerged place particular emphasis on the experience of *darshan* or "divine exchange" in religious life where the devotee sees and is seen by the deity; that is, the devotee has a direct encounter with divinity through the process of looking, gazing, and seeing. See Diana L. Eck, *Darshan: Seeing the Divine Image in India*, (Anima Books, 1985). Malcolm David Eckel also notes the significance of seeing the Buddhist tradition from both the philosophical standpoint of emptiness and its complex rendering in devotional imagery and interactions between viewer and image. Malcolm David Eckel, *To See the Buddha: A Philosopher's Quest for the Meaning of Emptiness* (Harper San Francisco, 1992).

8 I am particularly indebted to bell hooks's analysis of the intersection of gender, race, and sexuality in film as a way to re-present reality and her emphasis on what she refers to as the "oppositional gaze" that refuses racist ways of being looked at in contemporary American film. See bell hooks, "The Oppositional Gaze," in *Reel to Real: Race, Sex, and Class at the Movies* (New York and London: Routledge, 1996), pp. 197–213.

9 I use the term "silver screen" to refer specifically to the projection screens used in the early film industry, and more generally to refer to the cinema industry.

10 Eugene Wong, *Shaping the Lotus Sutra: Buddhist Visual Culture in Medieval China*, (Seattle: University of Washington Press, 2005), p. xv.

11 Margaret Miles, *Seeing is Believing*, (Boston: Beacon Press, 1996), p. 7.

12 Andrew Greeley, *God in Popular Culture* (Chicago: Thomas More, 1998), p. 250.

13 Hyangsoon Yi, "The Real, Anti-real, and Transcendental in Four Korean Buddhist Films," in Sang-Oak Lee and Gregory K. Iverson (eds), *Pathways into Korean Language and Culture: Essays in Honor of Young-Key Kim-Renaud* e (Seoul: Pagijong Press, 2002), p. 638.

14 If we are to take seriously the notion that film viewing is a ritualized activity whose potency can transform theaters into temples as has been the case with the Indian cult classic *Jai Santoshi Maa*, then approaching Buddhist films as opportune *sutra*s or texts that incite the religious imagination proves a fruitful endeavor for the study of religion in general and Buddhism in particular. See Philip A. Lutgendorf's "*Jai Santoshi Maa* Revisited: On Seeing a Hindu 'Mythological' Film," in S. Brent Plate (ed.), *Representing Religion in World Cinema: Mythmaking, Culture Making, Filmmaking* (New York: Palgrave/St Martins), pp. 19–42. The medium of film has been well explored by religion scholars in volumes on religion and film such as S. Brent Plate's edited volume *Representing Religion in World Cinema: Mythmaking, Culture Making, Filmmaking* (New York: Palgrave/St. Martins, 2003) and William L. Blizek's *Continuum Companion to Religion and Film* (London and New York: Continuum, 2009).

15 Francisca Cho's "Imagining Nothing and Imaging Otherness in Buddhist Film, (eds), in *Imag(in)ing the Other: Filmic Visions of Community* (Atlanta: Scholar's Press, 1999), pp. 169–95.

16 See Francisca Cho (1999). Cho notes elsewhere that "Buddhist seeing is marvelously realized by cinematic projections, and the art of film is substantially dignified by Buddhist perceptions," in Francisca Cho,

"Buddhism," in John Lyden (ed.), *The Routledge Companion to Religion and Film* (Hoboken: Routledge, 2009), p. 17.

17 See Francisca Cho (1999).

18 "The God of Small Films" by Susan Jakes/Chendebji, *Time Magazine*, Monday 27 January 2003. http://content.time.com/time/magazine/article/0,9171,411452,00.html (accessed November 13, 2013).

19 I am indebted to David Kyuman Kim for this felicitous phrase.

20 Kandice Chuh, *Imagine Otherwise: On Asian American Critique* (Durham and London: Duke University Press: 2003).

21 bell hooks, "The Oppositional Gaze," *Reel to Real: Race, Sex, and Class at the Movies* (London and New York: Routledge Press, 1996).

22 Francisca Cho, "Imagining Nothing and Imaging Otherness in Buddhist Film," in David Jaspers and S. Brent Plate (eds), *Imag(in)ing the Other: Filmic Visions of Community* (Atlanta: Scholar's Press, 1999).

23 George Aichele and Richard Walsh (eds), *Those Outside: Noncanonical Readings of the Canonical Gospels* (Bloomsbury Academic, 2005). I would like to thank Jeffrey Staley for bringing this work to my attention.

24 Walsh and Aichele (2005), p. x.

25 Ibid., p. x.

26 The five precepts are: to refrain from taking life, to refrain from stealing, to refrain from lying, to refrain from intoxicants, and to refrain from sexual misconduct. The Noble Eight-fold path includes: right view, right thought, right speech, right action, right livelihood, right effort, right mindfulness, and concentration.

27 hooks (1996), p. 4.

28 Janet Gyatso, "Sex" in Donald S. Lopez, Jr. (ed.), *Critical Terms for the Study of Buddhism* (Chicago: University of Chicago Press), p. 274.

29 Liz Wilson's study of women in post-Ashokan hagiographical literature offers a most extraordinary analysis of the images of women in Buddhist text and their edification as mere objects for male transformation. See Liz Wilson's *Charming Cadavers: Horrific Figurations of the Feminine in Indian Buddhist Hagiographical Literature* (Chicago: University of Chicago Press, 1996).

30 Karen Lang, "Lord Death's Snare: Gender-Related Imagery in the Theragatha and the Therigatha," *Journal of Feminist Studies in Religion*. Fall 1986, Vol. 2, No. 2, pp. 72–3.

31 Wilson also offers an insightful feminist critique of the act of gazing upon women's bodies in Buddhist texts that render women mute objects for it is "always the man who sees and the woman who is seen, the man who speaks and the woman who is spoken about." Wilson (1996), p. 4.

32 Susanne Mrozik. *Virtuous Bodies: The Physical Dimensions of Morality in Buddhist Ethics* (New York: Oxford University Press, 2007).

33 Reiko Ohnuma. *Head, Eyes, Flesh, and Blood: Giving Away the Body in Indian Buddhist Literature* (New York: Columbia University Press, 2007); John

Powers. *A Bull of a Man: Images of Masculinity, Sex, and the Body in Indian Buddhism* (Cambridge: Harvard University Press, 2009).

34 Diana Y. Paul, *Women in Buddhism: Images of the Feminine in the Mahayana* Tradition (Berkeley: University of California Press, 1985); Rita Gross, *Buddhism After Patriarchy: A Feminist History, Analysis, and Reconstruction of Buddhism* (Albany: State University of New York, 1993); Liz Wilson, *Charming Cadavers: Horrific Configurations of the Feminine in Early Indian Hagiographic Literature* (Chicago: University of Chicago Press, 1996).

35 bell hooks. *Reel to Real: Race, Sex, and Class at the Movies* (New York: Routledge, 1996), p. 3.

36 Ibid., p. 227.

37 Ibid., p. 231.

38 Ibid, p. 5.

39 I am grateful to David Kyuman Kim for this wonderful phrase.

40 Robert Lee, *Orientals: Asian Americans in Popular Culture* (Philadelphia: Temple University Press, 1999).

41 David Loy, *Money, Sex, War, Karma: Notes for a Buddhist Revolution*, (Boston: Wisdom Publications, 2008), p. 4, (my emphasis).

42 Joseph Cheah, *Race and Religion in American Buddhism: White Supremacy and Immigrant Adaptation* (Oxford University Press, 2011).

43 Cheah (2011), p. 31.

44 Cheah is careful, however, to move beyond the totalizing effects of Orientalism and the Protestantization of Buddhism by examining the intercultural mimesis that occurs between European scholar-practitioners and Buddhist monks in the development of a Modern Buddhism extracted from devotional rituals deemed irrational and superstitious. He does so by locating nationalist and modernist impulses within the Theravada Buddhist nation of Burma in response to and yet shaped by colonialism through the teachings of three renowned vipassana masters: the monks Ledi Sayadaw (1846–1923), Mahasi Sayadaw (1846–1923), and layman U Ba Khin (1904–82), who advocated a Modern Buddhism echoing a European Protestant framework that included the textual studies, the elevation of meditation, and the scientific. This key point is crucial for Cheah's subsequent theorization of a critical agency on the part of Burmese American Buddhists to resist the hegemonic effects of white supremacy.

45 Jane Iwamura, *Virtual Orientalism: Asian Religions in American Popular Culture* (Oxford University Press, 2011).

46 Ibid., p. 9.

47 See Philip Lutgendorf, "*Jai Santoshi Maa* Revisited: On Seeing a Hindu 'Mythological' Film," in S. Brent Plate (ed.), *Representing Religion in World Cinema: Mythmaking, Culture Making, Filmmaking* (New York: Palgrave/St Martins, 2003), pp. 19–42.

48 See Don S. Lopez, *Prisoners of Shangri-La* (Chicago: University of Chicago Press, 1999) and Orville Schell, *Virtual Tibet: Searching for Shangri-La from the Himalayas to Hollywood* (Owl Press, 2001). To date, there are two popular books that fully address Buddhist themes in non explicitly Buddhist films. The first book entitled, *The Dharma of Star Wars* by Matthew Bortolini (Wisdom Publications, 2005), is more of a practice oriented text that examines how the Star Wars films represent aspects of Buddhist philosophy. The other, entitled *Cinema Nirvana: Enlightenment Lessons from the Movies* by Dan Sluyter (Three Rivers Press, 2005) looks at contemporary American films that do not explicitly represent or reflect Buddhist imagery.

49 Ronald Green's recent introduction to Buddhism through film, *Buddhism Goes to the Movies* (New York and London: Routledge, 2014) examines Asian and Western films and offers a basic study of Buddhist philosophy that appears on screen, but it does not attend to the intersections of gender and race that complicate filmic renditions of the religion.

Chapter Two

1 Robert Lee, *Orientals: Asian Americans in Popular Culture* (Philadelphia: Temple University Press, 1999).

2 Erika Lee, "Enforcing the Borders: Chinese Exclusion along the U.S. Borders with Canada and Mexico, 1882–1924," in *The Journal of American History*, Vol.89, No.1 (June, 2002), pp. 54–86.

3 Robert Lee, p. 64.

4 Thomas Burke, "The Chink and the Girl," in *Limehouse Nights* (New York: Robert M. McBride & Company, 1917), p. 19.

5 Ibid., pp.18–19.

6 Jacob Riis, *How the Other Half Lives*, (Boston, MA: Bedford/St. Martin's, 1996), p. 63.

7 Julia Lesage, "Artful Racism and Artful Rape in BROKEN BLOSSOMS," from *Jump Cut: A Review of Contemporary* Media, no. 26 (December 1981), p. 4.

8 Lesage, p. 9.

9 Lesage, p. 4.

10 Susan Koshy, "American Nation as Eugenic Romance," in *Differences: a Journal of Feminist Cultural Studies* 12:1, (2001), p. 57.

11 Jane Iwamura, "The Oriental Monk in American Popular Culture," in Bruce David Forbes and Jeffrey H. Mahan, *Religion and Popular Culture in America* (Berkeley and Los Angeles: University of California Press, 2005).

12 Jane Iwamura (2005).

13 Ibid., p. 27.

14 Ibid., p. 31.

15 Robert Riskin, *Lost Horizon* Screenplay, Shooting draft (Columbia Pictures, 1937), p. 23.

16 Edward Said, *Orientalism* (New York: Vintage Books, 1978), p. 1.

17 Donald S. Lopez, *Prisoners of Shangri-La: Tibetan Buddhism and the West* (Chicago and London: The University of Chicago Press, 1998).

18 Ibid., p. 3.

19 Orville Schell, *Virtual Tibet* (Owl Press, 2001).

20 Ibid., p. 8.

21 Ibid., p. 9.

22 Robert Riskin, *Lost Horizon Screenplay*, Shooting Draft (Columbia Pictures, 1937).

23 Ronald S. Green, *Buddhism Goes to the Movies: An Introduction to Buddhist Thought and Practice* (New York and London: Routledge Press, 2014), p. 90.

Chapter Three

1 Jeff Bridges and Bernie Glassman, *The Dude and the Zen Master* (New York: Blue Rider Press, 2012), p. 61.

2 Ibid.

3 Glassman does note in their co-written book that he had studied clowning years before and that he uses a clown nose to dissipate excessive seriousness in uncomfortable situations, yet on television when Bridges used the same tactic, it fell flat. Jeff Bridges and Bernie Glassman (2012), p. 2.

4 Jeff Bridges and Bernie Glassman, *The Dude and the Zen Master*, p. 61.

5 Ibid., p. 95.

6 Ibid., p. 2.

7 Ibid., p. 3.

8 Ibid., p. 4.

9 Michael Bird, "Religion in Film," in Jolyon Mitchell and S. Brent Plate (eds), *The Religion and Film Reader* (New York and London: Routledge Press, 2007), p. 391.

10 Ibid., p. 393.

11 From Dudeism's homepage, www.dudeism.com (accessed March 3, 2014).

12 S. Brent Plate notes Jarmusch's continual play with myths and stereotypes and argues that Ghost Dog also embodies the image of Ralph Ellison's Invisible Man. See S. Brent Plate, "Film Review: Ghost Dog: The Way of the Samurai," *Journal of Religion and Film*, Vol. 4, (October 2000).

13 Ibid.

14 Paul Bowman, *Deconstructing Popular Culture* (New York: Palgrave McMillan, 2008), p. 69.

15 S. Brent Plate, "Film Review: Ghost Dog: The Way of the Samurai," *Journal of Religion and Film*, Vol. 4 (October 2000), p. 1.

16 Jane Iwamura, "The Oriental Monk in American Pop Culture" in Bruce David Forbes and Jeffrey Mahan (eds), *Religion and Popular Culture in America*, (Los Angeles and Berkeley: University of California Press, 2005), p. 32.

Chapter Four

1 "Dhammapada Verse 147 Sirimā Vatthu," http://www.tipitaka.net/tipitaka/dhp/verseload.php?verse=147 (accessed July 19, 2014).

2 Liz Wilson, *Charming Cadavers: Horrific Figurations of the Feminine in Indian Buddhist Hagiographical Literature* (Chicago: University of Chicago Press, 1996), p. 51.

3 Ibid., p. 51.

4 Ibid., p. 51.

5 Susanne Mrozik. *Virtuous Bodies: The Physical Dimensions of Morality in Buddhist Ethics* (New York: Oxford University Press, 2007).

6 Walpola Rahula, *What the Buddha Taught*, (New York: Grove Press, 1974), p. 29.

7 "Materializations of Virtue: Buddhist Discourses on Bodies," in Ellen T. Armour and Susan M. St. Ville (eds), *Bodily Citations: Religion and Judith Butler* (New York: Columbia University Press, 2006).

8 Liz Wilson (1996), p. 67.

9 Ibid., p. 67.

10 Ibid., p. 67.

11 Ibid., p. 87.

12 Ibid., p. 15.

13 Elizabeth Wilson, "The Female Body as a Source of Horror and Insight in Post-Ashokan Indian Buddhism," in Jane Marie Law (ed.), *Religious Reflections on the Human Body* (Bloomington: Indiana University Press, 1995), p. 84.

14 Ibid., p. 84.

15 Wilson (1996), p. 23.

16 bell hooks, *Reel to Real: Race, Sex, and Class at the Movies* (New York: Routledge, 1996).

17 Laura Mulvey, "Visual Pleasure and Narrative Cinema," *Screen*, Vol. 16, No. 3 (Autumn 1975), pp. 6–18.

18 Hyangsoon Yi argues that the monastic complete is replete with these traditional or "primitive" implements that represent a prelapsarian and idealized past that is automatically identified with Zen Buddhism. When two police officers come to the temple's gates seeking a former monk who fled the ascetic life to pursue a young woman, they encounter an idyllic world of mystery that renders their guns unnecessary. In fact, in a rather humorous scene where the cops fail to hit a can floating in the lake with their guns, it is the head monk and his mysterious Zen powers who manages to hit the can by throwing a pebble across his shoulder without even looking. See Hyangsoon Yi, "Buddhism, Orientalism and Zen Ethnography in Korean Cinema," delivered at American Academy of Religion, November 18, 2006.

19 Yi, p. 18.

20 Wilson (1996).

Chapter Five

1 Ranjini Obeyesekere, trans. *Jewels of the Doctrine: Stories of the Saddharma Ratnāvalya* (Albany: SUNY Press, 1991).

2 For an analysis of the exoticization of Zen or Sŏn life in Korean films, see Hyang-Soon Yi's paper, "Buddhism, Orientalism, and Zen Ethnography in Korean Cinema." The 2006 Annual Conference of the American Academy of Religion. Washington DC, November 18, 2006.

3 Donald Lopez translates one particularly lucid commentary on the mantra as follows: "Gate, gate:' gone, gone; all mindfulness has gone [to be] like illusions. Paragate: 'gone beyond;' beyond mindfulness, one goes beyond to emptiness. Parasamgate: 'gone completely beyond'; beyond the illusion-like and emptiness, one goes beyond signlessness. 'Bodhi svaha:' become enlightened; having purified the afflictions and all objects of knowledge, one transcends awareness." Donald Lopez, *Elaborations on Emptiness: Uses of the Heart Sutra* (Princeton: Princeton University Press, 1996), p. 214.

4 For a more detailed examination of the bodily sacrifice of Rūpāvatī, see Susanne Mrozik's "Materializations of Virtue: Buddhist Discourses on Bodies," in Ellen T. Armour and Susan M. St. Ville (eds), *Bodily Citations: Religion and Judith Butler* (New York: Columbia University Press, 2006)

5 Susanne Mrozik, "Cooking Living Beings: the Transformative Effects of Encounters with Bodhisattva Bodies," *Journal of Religious Ethics*, Vol. 32, No. 1 (2004), pp. 175–94.

6 Ibid., p. 176.

7 Ibid., p. 183.

8 Ibid., p. 183.

9 David James, "An Interview with Im Kwon-Taek," in Jolyon Mitchell and S. Brent Plate (eds), *The Religion and Film Reader* (New York: Routledge, 2007), p. 152.

10 See Diana Paul, *Women in Buddhism: Images of the Feminine in the Mahayana Tradition*, (Berkeley and Los Angeles: the University of California Press, 1985), and Jose Ignacio Cabezon (ed.), *Buddhism, Sexuality, and Gender* (Albany: SUNY Press, 1992) for introductory overviews of attitudes toward women and the female form.

11 David James and Kyung Hyun Kim, *Im Kwon-Taek: The Making of a Korean National Cinema* (Detroit: Wayne State University Press, 2002).

12 David James, "Im Kwon-Taek: Korean National Cinema and Buddhism," *Film Quarterly*, Vol. 54, No.3 (Spring 2001), pp.14–31, 25.

13 Ibid., p. 20.

14 Ibid., p. 15.

15 Mahayana Buddhist texts offer numerous examples of females who become high-level buddhas-to-be, although such examples are often fraught with ambiguity and tension, particularly because some of these women must change their bodies into male bodies right before enlightenment. In fact,

such sex transformation is often characterized as the requisite witness to the deep realization of the bodhisattva in question.

16 Mrozik (2007), p. 57.

17 David James, "Im Kwon-Taek: Korean National Cinema and Buddhism," *Film Quarterly*, Vol. 54, No. 3 (Spring 2001), pp.14–31, 19.

18 David James (2002), p. 75.

19 Ibid., p. 77.

20 The larger textual passage reads: "When Shakyamuni Buddha was at Mount Grdhrakuta [Vulture Peak], he held out a flower to his listeners. Everyone was silent. Only Maha-Kashayapa broke into a broad smile. The Buddha said, 'I have found the True Dharma Eye …, the Marvelous Mind of Nirvana, the True Form of the Formless, and the Subtle Dharma Gate, independent of words and transmitted beyond doctrine. This I have entrusted to Maha-Kashyapa.'" Katsuki Sekida, trans., *Two Zen Classics: the Mumonkan & Hekiganroku* (New York: Weatherhill, 1977).

21 Hui-Neng states: "At midnight the Fifth Patriarch called me into the hall and expounded the Diamond Sutra to me. Hearing it but once, I was immediately awakened, and that night I received the Dharma. None of the others knew anything about it. Then he transmitted to me the Dharma of Sudden Enlightenment and the robe, saying: 'I make you the Sixth Patriarch. The robe is the proof and is to be handed down from generation to generation. My Dharma must be transmitted from mind to mind. You must make people awaken to themselves.'" Philip Yampolsky, *Platform Sutra of the Sixth Patriarch* (New York: Columbia University Press, 1967), section 9, p. 133. For a discussion of Mahakasyapa's smile and the establishment of the silent transmission as a key feature of Zen, see Albert Walter's "Mahakasyapa's Smile: Silent Transmission and the Kung-am (Koan) Tradition," in Steven Heine and Dale S. Wright (eds), *The Koan: Texts and Contexts in Zen Buddhism* (New York: Oxford University Press, 2000), pp. 75–109.

22 Bae Yong-Kyun's *Why Has Bodhidharma Left for the East?* A Milestone Film & Video Release, p. 4.

23 Yi (2006), p. 647.

Chapter Six

1 Shinmon Aoki, *Coffinman: The Journal of a Buddhist Mortician* (Anaheim: Buddhist Education Center, 2002).

2 Ibid., p.44.

3 Jodoshinshu is commonly contracted as "Shin" Buddhism and I will use this contraction throughout this chapter.

4 Taitetsu Unno, *Shin Buddhism: Bits of Rubble Turn into Gold* (New York: Doubleday, 2001), p. 19.

5 Ibid., p. 19.

6 Ibid., p. 17.

7 Ibid., p. 5.

8 Yoshiko Okuyama, "Shinto and Buddhist Metaphors in Departures," *Journal of Religion & Film*, Vol.17, Iss.1, Article 39.

9 Unno (2001), p. 51.

10 Ibid., p. 184.

11 Mark Unno, "Comparative Theology with a Difference: A Shin Buddhist View in Pedagogical Perspective," Catherine Cornille (ed.), *In Dialogue and Discernment* (Eugene, OR: Wipf and Stock, 2009).

12 Taitetsu Unno, "The Practice of Jodoshinshu," in Alfred Bloom (ed.), *Living in Amida's Universal Vow*, (Bloomington: World Wisdom, 2004), p. 69.

13 Unno (2004), p. 65.

14 Jeff Wilson, *Buddhism of the Heart: Reflections on Shin Buddhism and Inner Togetherness*, (Boston: Wisdom Publications), p. 9.

15 Ibid., p. 9.

16 Ibid., p. 3.

17 Unno (2004), p. 65.

18 Nathan Dorsky, *Devotional Cinema* (Berkeley: Tuumba Press, 2003), p. 50.

19 Edward Conze, I. B. Horner, David Snellgrove, and Arthur Waley (eds), *Buddhist Texts through the Ages* (Boston and Shaftesbury: Shambala, 1990), p. 161.

20 Aoki (2002), p.77.

21 Unno (2001), p. 58.

22 Aoki (2002), p. 21.

23 Unno (2001).

Chapter Seven

1 Interview with Chang Sun-Woo, http://www.cinekorea.com/filmmakers/Changsunwoo.html (accessed 2 September, 2011)

2 *Hwa-Om-Kyung* is the Korean translation of the Sanskrit *Flower Ornament Sutra* and is known in English as the *Avatamsaka Sutra*. The English title of the film is called *Passage to Buddha* which does not reflect the *sutra*'s role in the film but does capture the central meaning of the journey to enlightenment.

3 According to Douglas Osto, the *Gandavyuha* was translated into Chinese over the course of the sixth, seventh, and eighth centuries CE. See Douglas Osto, *Power, Wealth and Women in Indian Mahayana Buddhism: The Gandavyuha Sutra*, (New York: Routledge Critical Studies in Buddhism, 2008), p. 4.

4 Douglas Osto, *Power, Wealth and Women in Indian Mahayana Buddhism: The Gandavyuha Sutra*, (New York: Routledge Critical Studies in Buddhism, 2008).

5 Ibid., p. 28.

6 Ko Un, *Little Pilgrim* (Berkeley: Parallax Press, 2005).

7 Francis Cook, *Hua-yen Buddhism: The Jewel Net of Indra* (University Park: Pennsylvania State University Press 1977), p. 2.

8 Thomas Cleary, *Entry Into the Inconceivable: An Introduction to Hua-yen Buddhism* (Honolulu: University of Hawaii Press, 1995) p. 2.

9 Francis Cook, *Hua-yen Buddhism: The Jewel Net of Indra* (University Park, Pennsylvania: The Pennsylvania State University Press, 1977), p. 19.

10 Excerpted from the *Flower Adornment Sutra [Flower Ornament Sutra]*, Ch. 39, Part II, pp. 1ff. (Translation by Master Hsuan Hua.) Buddhist Texts Translation Society.

11 Ko Un, *Little Pilgrim*, (Berkeley: Parallax Press, 2005), p. 55.

12 The ox here is an obvious reference to the Zen association of the mind with an ox.

13 Francisca Cho, "The Art of Presence: Buddhism and Korean Films," in S. Brent Plate (ed.), *Representing Religion in World Cinema: Filmmaking, Mythmaking, Culture Making* (Palgrave Press, 2003), pp. 107–19.

14 Douglas Osto, "Proto-Tantric" Elements in the *Gandavyuha-Sutra." Journal of Religious History*, Vol. 33, No. 2 (June 2009).

15 Susanne Mrozik (2007).

16 Osto (2008).

17 Alan Sponberg, "Attitudes Toward Women and the Feminine in Early Buddhism," in Jose Ignacio Cabezon (ed.), *Buddhism, Sexuality, and Gender* (New York: SUNY Press, 1992), pp. 3–36.

18 Ko Un, p. 71.

19 Thomas Cleary, *The Flower Ornament Scripture: A Translation of the Avatamsaka Sutra* (Boston and London: Shambala Press, 1993), p. 1433.

20 Ibid., p. 1435.

21 Ibid., p. 1437.

22 Francis Cook, *Hua-yen Buddhism: The Jewel Net of Indra* (University Park, PN: The Pennsylvania State University Press, 1977), p. 4.

23 Ibid., p. 11.

24 Ibid., p. 9.

Chapter Eight

1 bell hooks, "The Oppositional Gaze: Black Female Spectators," in bell hooks, *Reel to Real: Race, Sex, and Class at the Movies* (New York: Routledge, 1996).

2 Celine Perreñas Shimuzu, *The Hypersexuality of Race: Asian/American Women on Screen and Scene* (Durham and London: Duke University Press, 2007), p. 271.

3 Ibid., p. 20.

4 Ibid., p. 272.

5 Ibid., pp. 2–5.

6 Ibid., p. 19.

7 Ibid., p. 15.

8 bell hooks, "The Oppositional Gaze: Black Female Spectators," in bell hooks, *Reel to Real: Race, Sex, and Class at the Movies* (New York: Routledge, 1996).

9 Ibid., p. 199.

10 Ibid., p. 210.

11 Of course the transformative potential of sexuality in Buddhism has received much attention by scholars examining Tantric Buddhism in the Tibetan tradition; however, such approaches to the sacred dimensions of sexuality offer little for the lay woman since these texts are addressed to the most highly accomplished monastic practitioner. See Miranda Shaw's *Passionate Enlightenment: Women in Tantric Buddhism*, (Princeton: Princeton University Press, 1994).

12 Liz Wilson argues that when women do look upon themselves in early Indian Buddhist literature, they are always looking at themselves in various states of decay. Thus, they absorb the male gaze of the monks who engage in a deconstructive meditative practice. Hence, such textual narrations do little to create spaces for agency and subjectivity for women. See Liz Wilson, *Charming Cadavers: Horrific Figurations of the Feminine in Indian Buddhist Hagiographical Literature* (Chicago: University of Chicago Press, 1996).

13 hooks, *Reel to Real*, p. 213.

14 Quoted from Diana Y. Paul, *Women in Buddhism: Images of the Feminine in the Mahayana Tradition* (Berkeley and Los Angeles: University of California Press, 1985), pp. 7–8.

15 Walpola Rahula, *What the Buddha Taught* (New York: Grove Press, 1959).

16 Ibid., p. 9.

17 Rajini Obeyesekere, *Yasodhara: The Wife of the Bodhisattva* (New York: SUNY Press, 2009).

18 Ibid., p. 1.

19 Ibid., p. 2.

20 Ibid., p. 19.

21 Ibid., p. 14.

22 Ibid., p. 14.

23 Ibid., p. 62.

24 Ibid., p. 67.

25 Ibid., p. 68.

26 Parreñas Shimizu, p. 1.

27 Ibid., p. 1.

28 Ibid., p. 5.

29 Audre Lorde, "Uses of the Erotic," in *Sister Outsider*, p. 53.

30 Ibid., p. 54.

31 Ibid., p. 56

32 Ibid., p. 56.

33 Ibid., p. 56.

34 Ibid., p. 55.

35 Ibid., p. 55.

36 Ibid., p. 59.

Chapter Nine

1 I use the term "Asian and Asian American" to also include Canadians by referencing the larger context of North America.

2 S. Brent Plate, *Religion and Film: Cinema and the Re-Creation of the World* (London and New York: Wallflower Press, 2008), p. 11.

3 Rey Chow, in Paul Bowman (ed.), *The Rey Chow Reader* (New York: Columbia University Press, 2010), p. 85.

4 Ibid., p. 85.

5 I am grateful to David Kyuman Kim for this particular formulation of the processes of race, gender, and identity formation.

6 Leon Hurvitz, trans. *Scripture of the Lotus Blossom of the Fine Dharma* (New York: Columbia University Press, 1976), p. 59.

7 Kaja Silverman excerpted in Paul Du Gay, Jessica Evans, and Peter Redman (eds), *Identity: A Reader* (London: Sage Publications, 2000), p. 76.

Bibliography

Aichele, George and Walsh, Richard (eds), *Those Outside: Noncanonical Readings of the Canonical Gospels*. Bloomsbury Academic, 2005.

Aoki, Shinmon, *Coffinman: The Journal of a Buddhist Mortician*. Anaheim: Buddhist Education Center, 2001.

Armour, Ellen T. and St. Ville, Susan M. (eds), *Bodily Citations: Religion and Judith Butler*. New York: Columbia University Press, 2006.

Benshoff, Harry M. and Griffin, Sean (eds), *America on Film: Representing Race, Class, Gender, and Sexuality at the Movies*. Malden, MA: Blackwell Publishing, 2004.

Bird, Michael, "Religion in Film," in Jolyon Mitchell and S. Brent Plate (eds), *The Religion and Film Reader*. New York and London: Routledge Press, 2007.

Blizek, William L. (ed), *Continuum Companion to Religion and Film*. London and New York: Continuum, 2009.

Bloom, Alfred (ed.), *Living in Amida's Universal Vow: Essays in Shin Buddhism*. Bloomington: World Wisdom, Inc., 2004.

Bortolini, Matthew, *The Dharma of Star Wars*. Boston: Wisdom Publications, 2005.

Bowman, Paul (ed.), *The Rey Chow Reader*. New York: Columbia University Press, 2010.

—*Deconstructing Popular Culture*. New York: Palgrave McMillan, 2008.

Bridges, Jeff and Glassman, Bernie, *The Dude and the Zen Master*. New York: Blue Rider Press, 2012.

Burke, Thomas, "The Chink and the Girl," in *Limehouse Nights*. New York: Robert M. McBride & Company, 1917.

Buswell, Robert, *The Zen Monastic Experience*. Princeton: Princeton University Press, 1992.

Cabezon, Jose Ignacio (ed.), *Buddhism, Sexuality, and Gender*. New York: SUNY Press, 1992.

Cheah, Joseph, *Race and Religion in American Buddhism: White Supremacy and Immigrant Adaptation*. Oxford: Oxford University Press, 2011.

Cho, Francisca, "Imagining Nothing and Imaging Otherness in Buddhist Film," in David Jaspers and S. Brent Plate (eds), *Imag(in)ing the Other: Filmic Visions of Community*. Atlanta: Scholar's Press, 1999.

—"Buddhism," in John Lyden (ed.), *The Routledge Companion to Religion and Film*. Hoboken: Routledge, 2009.

Chow, Rey, *Primitive Passions: Visuality, Sexuality, Ethnography, and Contemporary Chinese Cinema*. New York: Columbia University Press, 1995.

Chuh, Kandice, *Imagine Otherwise: On Asian American Critique*. Durham and London: Duke University Press, 2003.

Cleary, Thomas, *Entry Into the Inconceivable: An Introduction to Hua-yen Buddhism*. Honolulu: University of Hawaii Press, 1995.

—*The Flower Ornament Scripture: A Translation of the Avatamsaka Sutra*. Boston and London: Shambala Press, 1993.

Cook, Francis, *Hua-yen Buddhism: The Jewel Net of Indra*. University Park: Pennsylvania State University Press, 1977.

Dodin, Thierry and Räther, Heinz (eds), *Imaginging Tibet: Perceptions, Projections, and Fantasies*. Boston: Wisdom Publications, 2001.

Dorsky, Nathaniel, *Devotional Cinema*. Tuumba Press, 2003.

Eck, Diana L, *Darshan: Seeing the Divine Image in India*, Anima Books, 1985.

Eckel, Malcolm David, *To See the Buddha: A Philosopher's Quest for the Meaning of Emptiness*. New York: Harper San Francisco, 1992.

Faure, Bernard, *The Power of Denial: Buddhism, Purity, and Gender*. Princeton and Oxford: Princeton University Press, 2003.

—*The Red Thread: Buddhist Approaches to Sexuality*. Princeton: Princeton University Press, 1998.

Feng, Peter X. (ed.), *Screening Asian Americans*. New Brunswick and London: Rutgers University Press, 2002.

Greeley, Andrew, *God in Popular Culture*. Chicago: Thomas More 1998.

Green, Ronald, *Buddhism Goes to the Movies*. New York and London: Routledge Press, 2014.

Gregory, Peter N., and Mrozik, Susanne (eds), *Women Practicing Buddhism: American Experiences*. Boston: Wisdom Publications, 2008.

Gross, Rita, *Buddhism After Patriarchy: A Feminist History, Analysis, and Reconstruction of Buddhism*. Albany: State University of New York, 1993.

Gyatso, Janet, "Sex," in Donald S. Lopez, Jr. (ed.), *Critical Terms for the Study of Buddhism*. Chicago and London: University of Chicago Press, 2005.

Heine, Steven, and Wright, Dale S. (eds), *The Koan: Texts and Contexts in Zen Buddhism*. New York: Oxford University Press, 2000.

hooks, bell, *Reel to Real: Race, Sex, and Class at the Movies*. New York and London: Routledge, 1996.

—"The Oppositional Gaze," in *Reel to Real: Race, Sex, and Class at the Movies*. New York and London: Routledge, 1996.

Horner, I. B., *Women Under Primitive Buddhism*. Delhi: Motilal Banarsidass, 1989.

Hua, Hsuan, trans, *Flower Adornment Sutra*. Buddhist Texts Translation Society.

Hurvitz, Leon, trans, *Scripture of the Lotus Blossom of the Fine Dharma*. New York: Columbia University Press, 1976.

Iwamura, Jane, *Virtual Orientalism: Asian Religions in American Popular Culture*, Oxford University Press, 2011.

—"The Oriental Monk in American Pop Culture," in Bruce David Forbes and Jeffrey Mahan, *Religion and Popular Culture in America*. Berkeley and Los Angeles: University of California Press, 2005.

Susan Jakes/Chendebji, "The God of Small Films." *Time Magazine,* Monday 27 January, 2003.

James, David, "An Interview with Im Kwon-Taek," in Jolyn Mitchell and S. Brent Plate (eds), *The Religion and Film Reader*. New York: Routledge, 2007.

—"Im Kwon-Taek: Korean National Cinema and Buddhism," in *Film Quarterly*, Vol. 54, No.3 (Spring 2001), pp. 14–31.

Jaspers, David and Plate, S. Brent (eds), *Imag(in)ing the Other: Filmic Visions of Community*. Atlanta: Scholar's Press, 1999.

Ko, Un, *Little Pilgrim.* Berkeley: Parallax Press, 2005.

Koshy, Susan, "American Nation as Eugenic Romance," in *Differences: a Journal of Feminist Cultural Studies* 12:1 (2001).

Lang, Karen, "Lord Death's Snare: Gender-Related Imagery in the Theragatha and the Therigatha," *Journal of Feminist Studies in Religion.* Vol. 2, No. 2 (Fall 1986), pp. 64–79.

Lee, Erika, "Enforcing the Borders: Chinese Exclusion along the U.S. Borders with Canada and Mexico, 1882–1924," *The Journal of American History,* Vol. 89, No. 1 (June 2002), pp. 54–86.

Lee, Robert, *Orientals: Asian Americans in Popular Culture.* Philadelphia: Temple University Press, 1999.

Lefferts, Jr., H. Leedom, "Buddhist Action: Lay Women and Thai Monks," in Ellison Banks Findley (ed.), *Women's Buddhism, Buddhism's Women: Tradition, Revision, Renewal.* Boston: Wisdom Publications, 2000.

Lesage, Julia, "Artful Racism and Artful Rape in BROKEN BLOSSOMS," *Jump Cut: A Review of Contemporary Media,* No. 26 (December 1981).

Lopez, Jr., Donald S., *Elaborations on Emptiness: Uses of the Heart Sutra.* Princeton: Princeton University Press, 1996.

—*Prisoners of Shangri-La: Tibetan Buddhism and the West.* Chicago and London: The University of Chicago Press, 1998.

Lorde, Audre, "Uses of the Erotic," in *Sister Outsider: Essays and Speeches.* Freedom, CA: The Crossing Press, 1984.

Loy, David, *Money, Sex, War, Karma: Notes for a Buddhist Revolution,* Boston: Wisdom Publications, 2008.

Lyden, John (ed.), *The Routledge Companion to Religion and Film.* Hoboken: Routledge, 2009.

Lutgendorf, Philip A., "*Jai Santoshi Maa* Revisited: On Seeing a Hindu 'Mythological' Film" in S. Brent Plate (ed.), *Representing Religion in World Cinema: Mythmaking, Culture Making, Filmmaking* . New York: Palgrave/St Martins, 2003.

Ma, Sheng-Mei, *East-West Montage: Reflections on Asian Bodies in Diaspora.* Honolulu: University of Hawaii Press, 2007.

Miles, Margaret, *Seeing is Believing.* Boston: Beacon Press, 1996.

Mrozik, Susanne, "Cooking Living Beings: the Transformative Effects of Encounters with Bodhisattva Bodies," *Journal of Religious Ethics,* Vol. 32, No. 1 (2004), pp. 175–94.

—"Materializations of Virtue: Buddhist Discourses on Bodies," in Ellen T. Armour and Susan M. St. Ville (eds), *Bodily Citations: Religion and Judith Butler.* New York: Columbia University Press, 2006.

—*Virtuous Bodies: The Physical Dimensions of Morality in Buddhist Ethics.* New York: Oxford University Press, 2007.

Mulvey, Laura, "Visual Pleasure and Narrative Cinema," *Screen,* Vol. 16, No. 3 (Autumn 1975), pp. 6–18.

Murcott, Susan, *The First Buddhist Women: Translation and Commentary on the Therigatha.* Berkeley: Parallax Press, 1991.

Ohnuma, Reiko, *Head, Eyes, Flesh, and Blood: Giving Away the Body in Indian Buddhist Literature.* New York: Columbia University Press, 2007.

Okuyama, Yoshiko, "Shinto and Buddhist Metaphors in Departures," *Journal of Religion & Film,* Vol. 17, No. 1, Article 39.

Osto, Douglas, *Power, Wealth and Women in Indian Mahayana Buddhism: The Gandavyuha Sutra.* New York: Routledge Critical Studies in Buddhism, 2008.

—"Proto-Tantric Elements in the *Gandavyuha-Sutra*," *Journal of Religious History*, Vol. 33, No. 2 (June 2009).

Paul, Diana Y, *Women in Buddhism: Images of the Feminine in the Mahayana Tradition.* Berkeley: University of California Press, 1985.

Pew Research Center, *Asian Americans: A Mosaic of Faiths.* Washington DC: Pew Research Center 2012.

Plate, S. Brent, *Religion and Film: Cinema and the Re-Creation of the World.* London and New York: Wallflower Press, 2008.

—(ed.), *Representing Religion in World Cinema: Mythmaking, Culture Making, Filmmaking.* New York: Palgrave/St. Martins 2003.

—"Film Review: Ghost Dog: The Way of the Samurai," *Journal of Religion and Film.* Vol. 4, No. 2 (2000).

Powers, John, *A Bull of a Man: Images of Masculinity, Sex, and the body in Indian Buddhism.* Cambridge: Harvard University Press, 2009.

Rahula, Walpola, *What the Buddha Taught.* New York: Grove Press, 1974.

Riis, Jacob, *How the Other Half Lives.* Boston, MA: Bedford/St. Martin's, 1996.

Riskin, Robert, *Lost Horizon* Screenplay. Shooting draft 1937.

Said, Edward, *Orientalism.* New York: Vintage Books, 1978.

Scharf, Robert, "The Zen of Japanese Nationalism," in Donald S. Lopez, Jr (ed.), *Curators of the Buddha: The Study of Buddhism under Colonialism.* Chicago: University of Chicago Press, 1995.

Schell, Orville, *Virtual Tibet: Searching for Shangri-La from the Himalayas to Hollywood.* Owl Press,2001.

Sekida, Katsuki, trans., *Two Zen Classics: the Mumonkan & Hekiganroku.* New York: Weatherhill, 1977.

Shaw, Miranda, *Passionate Enlightenment: Women in Tantric Buddhism.* Princeton: Princeton University Press, 1994.

Sluyter, Dan, *Cinema Nirvana: Enlightenment Lessons from the Movies.* Three Rivers Press, 2005.

Sponberg, Alan, "Attitudes Toward Women and the Feminine in Early Buddhism," in *Buddhism, Sexuality, and Gender.* New York: SUNY Press, 1992.

Suh, Sharon, *Being Buddhist in a Christian World: Gender and Community in a Korean American Community.* Seattle: University of Washington, 2004.

Suzuki, Shunryu, *Zen Mind, Beginner's Mind.* New York and Tokyo: Weatherhill Press, 2003.

Unno, Mark, "Comparative Theology with a Difference: A Shin Buddhist View in Pedagogical Perspective," in Catherien Cornille (ed.), *Dialogue and Discernment.* Eugene, OR: Wipf and Stock, 2009.

Unno, Taitetsu, *River of Fire, River of Water: An Introduction to The Pure Land Tradition of Shin Buddhism.* New York: Doubleday, 1998.

—. *Shin Buddhism: Bits of Rubble Turn into Gold*, New York: Doubleday 2001.

Wilson, Jeff, *Buddhism of the Heart: Reflections on Shin Buddhism and Inner Togetherness.* Boston: Wisdom Publications, 2009.

Wilson, Elizabeth, "The Female Body as a Source of Horror and Insight in Post-Ashokan Indian Buddhism," in Jane Marie Law (ed.), *Religious Reflections on the Human Body.* Indiana University Press, 1995.

Wilson, Liz, *Charming Cadavers: Horrific Figurations of the Feminine in Indian Buddhist Hagiographical Literature*. Chicago: University of Chicago Press, 1996.

Wong, Eugene, *Shaping the Lotus Sutra: Buddhist Visual Culture in Medieval China*. Seattle: University of Washington Press, 2005.

Yampolsky, Philip, *Platform Sutra of the Sixth Patriarch*. New York: Columbia University Press, 1967.

Yi, Hyangsoon, "The Real, Anti-real, and Transcendental in Four Korean Buddhist Films," in Sang-Oak Lee and Gregory K. Iverson (eds), *Pathways into Korean Language and Culture: Essays in Honor of Young-Key Kim-Renaud*. Seoul: Pagijong Press, 2002.

Index